GOODY TWO SHOES

Goody Two Shoes

Alex Higgins, 1982

How the Hurricane won the greatest World Championship ever staged

John Skilbeck

First published in the UK in 2023 by On The Black

Cover picture: Mirror Pix

Title font: Engebrechtre
Back cover blurb font: Tilt Neon
Interior font: Lusitana

A CIP record for this book is available from the British Library

ISBN 978-1-916838-48-2

Chapters

SPOILER ALERT
1982 World Snooker Championship

First round

Tony Knowles beat Steve Davis 10-1

Graham Miles beat Dave Martin 10-5

Bill Werbeniuk beat John Bear 10-7

Eddie Charlton beat Cliff Wilson 10-5

Silvino Francisco beat Dennis Taylor 10-7

Dean Reynolds beat Fred Davis 10-7

John Virgo beat Mike Hallett 10-4

Ray Reardon beat Jim Donnelly 10-5

Willie Thorne beat Terry Griffiths 10-6

John Spencer beat John Dunning 10-4

Alex Higgins beat Jim Meadowcroft 10-5

Doug Mountjoy beat Rex Williams 10-3

Patsy Fagan beat David Taylor 10-9

Kirk Stevens beat Jack Fitzmaurice 10-4

Perrie Mans beat Tony Meo 10-8

Jimmy White beat Cliff Thorburn 10-4

Second round

Knowles beat Miles 13-7, Charlton beat Werbeniuk 13-5, Francisco beat
Reynolds 13-8, Reardon beat Virgo 13-8, Thorne beat Spencer 13-5, Higgins
beat Mountjoy 13-12, Stevens beat Fagan 13-7, White beat Mans 13-6

Quarter-finals

Charlton beat Knowles 13-11, Reardon beat Francisco 13-8, Higgins beat
Thorne 13-10, White beat Stevens 13-9

Semi-finals

Reardon beat Charlton 16-11, Higgins beat White 16-15

Final

Higgins beat Reardon 18-15

PROLOGUE

New Romantics and old rascals.

Jack Charlton at Hillsborough and Eddie Charlton at the Crucible.

The Blades are going up, the Owls are staying down.

Synth-pop at the Friday night bop.

Spring 1982: Sheffield's sense of self, the ferrous integrity of its individuality, faces a bombardment of bad tidings.

Kohl-eyed creatures revel after dark, but cold-eyed reality stalks this city by day.

Mines are closing, steelworks pivoting from manpower to machine. Fatha's out of work; the dole queue's a sight longer this week than last.

Computers crowd out the craftsmen. A gleaming dagger pierces the heart of the cutlery workforce in the Steel City. Blood spills.

An overdose of bitter pills.

The Human League and the human toll, and never the twain shall meet.

A brittle burg lacerated by socio-economic shrapnel, now slap bang in a Hurricane's path.

Alex Higgins is coming to town.

Here comes trouble.

'Quiet please, ladies and gentlemen.'

'Keep your traps shut.'

* *

Snooker's dream palace awaits. The stage door is creaking open. But this decade's dawn years call first for a little scrutiny.

Every drawing of lots has its losers, and the UK postcode lottery in the 1980s proves it. Industrial Sheffield is booted to the misery boondocks, a sitting duck as recession, inflation and overseas competition trigger the inevitable. Presumed jobs for life vanish as a northern powerhouse fears it has been sold down the river.

Traumas invade daily lives across the UK, serious and spurious.

Cold War fears linger on a global scale. Toyah Willcox lingers... much too often for my liking in the pages of Look-In magazine.

Big beasts are boarding the ark of our cognisance two by two: Thatcher and Reagan, Charles and Diana, Aykroyd and Belushi, George Michael and Andrew Ridgeley, Adrian Mole and Pandora Braithwaite.

The chichi pop pairings of Pet Shop Boys, Soft Cell and Yazoo will soon deliver sweet treats from their haute culture kitchens.

Cannon and Ball won't save us all, and nor will Wee Jimmy and Ian Krankie, but this is undoubtedly a fandabidozi time for duos.

And within the decade's eccentric mix lurk Alex Higgins and Steve Davis, snooker's odd couple, its Yin and Yang.

The economy might be in turmoil, but Higgins and Davis are newly rich men in a sport frothing with unimagined prosperity. Overnight success has been a long time coming for snooker, a sport devised in 1875 by a British Indian Army officer in Jabalpur.

The excruciatingly slow burn has given way to a raging blaze.

With the seismicity of the sport's impact comes toxicity in tow. This is chiefly down to Higgins, a devil-may-care Northern Irishman liable to set flames licking at every door of opportunity.

While the larrikin raises hell, straight man Davis banks the big cheques. A crankier double act you would struggle to find.

* *

Tonight, though, it's May 2, 2022, day two of the World Snooker Championship final, the match racing towards a climax.

The Crucible press room is at its most broiling, every seat at every desk taken, with Ronnie O'Sullivan about to wrap up a record-equalling seventh title. He'll be through here soon for a press conference, and so too runner-up Judd Trump to reflect on defeat and the curiously long hug he receives from an emotional O'Sullivan. I am surrounded by great friends and colleagues, tapping away at keyboards, searching for the perfect top line. This is the 12th World final I've covered in such company. As a rough estimate, I've spent six months of my life in this room.

Reports are being rushed to newspapers, blogs, websites and agencies across the world, and we are a curious bunch, as ever at the end of the tournament. There are the hardy few whose World Championship begins not here but at the qualifiers. I've ticked that box often enough. Then there are the late arrivals, checking in just in time to see the champion crowned. Levels of expertise vary, but nobody's yet asked what the yellow ball's worth.

We have the Press Association's Olympics correspondent Mark Staniforth, the Guardian's rugby league man Aaron Bower, Daily Mail all-rounder David Coverdale and the Sun's man for all seasons Rob Maul. The Times has sent Elgan Alderman. Now there's a name so pleasingly antediluvian it might have come from the snooker annals, perhaps an old foe of Fred Davis.

There is tension in the air here, adrenaline levels are soaring.

Then Jimmy White walks in with a 60th birthday cake and sprinkles a little levity on the room.

It's the Whirlwind's big day, and someone put in a double order. The press vultures tuck in. This great snooker night is always special, though the icing on the cake is usually proverbial, rarely fondant. I am having the time of my life. It's a night to treasure.

When the news emerged on July 24, 2010, that White's great mate Higgins had died, I was holidaying at a music festival deep in the Derbyshire countryside, having another time of my life.

Beep beep. An answerphone message from my sports desk. With next to no mobile signal on my knackered old Nokia, the best I could do was scramble for some reception, point to a handful of contact numbers and send my very best wishes. There was a real ale stand doing a roaring trade, so I'd raise a glass instead. This liquid tribute was what Higgins would surely have wanted... ideally complemented by a chaser and a Racing Post. And hold the real ale, make it a Guinness.

I had been the Press Association's snooker reporter for just over a year. This was an out-of-office, often out-of-hours privilege that ran alongside my main gig, sub-editing on the sports desk.

Writing about snooker was really a labour of love, and lovers don't go wishing death on others. Which is a roundabout way of saying I hadn't got around to preparing a set of obituaries.

Higgins was 61, but death had been on his doorstep for a while. Hindsight suggests a little foresight had probably been in order.

**

As a boy in the mid-1980s, I was first dizzied by the scale of snooker at, of all places, Goole's Boothferry Leisure Centre, where a 12ft by 6ft slate bed table was curiously stationed inside a squash court. The clack-clack-clack of the colliding balls echoing around the smoothly plastered walls instantly took my breath away. It hardly mattered that I could barely pot a ball.

Here on Humberside, I had found my Shangri-La.

**

It's well documented that Alex Higgins left home at 15, abandoning Belfast for Berkshire to become a stable boy.

I left home at eight. Well, sort of.

Dispatched to a Nottinghamshire boarding school in September 1986, I could only follow midweek sport via the pages of the Daily Telegraph, the inevitable newspaper of choice.

The life of Monday to Saturday term-time family separation ended in tears in September 1989. Homesick, school-sick, I leapt off the private education carousel, ditching dorm life forever. Goodbye matins. Goodbye speech day. Goodbye Oxbridge future? Hello to the world I'd missed. A classroom crush packed her trunk and said goodbye to this scholastic circus after summer term, so why would I grin and bear it any longer at Ranby House?

This was a prep school where boarders jovially sang about being taken prisoner, with HMP Ranby barely a cricket ball throw away. Yet bear in mind such dark humour came at a time corporal punishment was banned in prisons but not in public schools.

One saving grace was the games room. I close my eyes now and picture it: the busy table tennis and snooker tables; the shabby wardrobe in the corner where cues with splintered tips and bats long divorced of their rubber went to die; the heavy door leading to the chaplain's office; the wooden benches; the bulletin boards.

Once, I played pool for the school team here and won my match with a simply outrageous cut black. Pure pool from the gods.

I may have digressed.

Reporting on a World Snooker Championship was the stuff of this boy's dreams. Thrillingly, I lived that dream and got to witness and document many immortal sporting moments. But journalism is transient, and I soon had another mission in mind.

Churning out reports and player interviews had fulfilled a solid enough purpose, filling page space in regional newspapers and every so often a national. I loved the role, broke a few stories in my time and stirred up the odd hornet's nest, but was there really much to show beyond more newspaper clippings for the pile?

Great friendships were formed, of course, and from those came myriad episodes of after-hours mirth and mayhem.

One ended with yours truly stumbling off a dance floor and on to my backside in a London nightclub, to which the snooker crowd had decamped after an awards bash at the Dorchester. It was somewhere around 3am, I was supremely sozzled and had lost my dinner jacket as well as most of my mind.

Jimmy White was there, that much I do remember. He remained upright, possibly regarding the sorry scene with a little empathy.

Was this pathetic plunge into fleeting humiliation my Alex Higgins moment? Let me put it this way: it was lower than I ever intended to fall, but hold off on the Hurricane comparisons. I'm teetotal now and have been for almost three years.

Not long after the London hangover eased, I set off on a Higgins journey of discovery, and I had questions.

How does the snooker industry justify its reverence of Higgins, given the snaking trail of damage he left in his wake?

Was Alex a true black heart, or are there shades of grey at play?

How did the powder-keg Higgins summon a wind behind him at all in May 1982, when his flag that year had barely fluttered?

Higgins' ravishing Crucible triumph was an ascent from the gutter to glory; that much I knew. But what was the fuel that really propelled his improbable tour de force in Sheffield?

If Higgins was the star of the show, what of the supporting cast?

Who in all of God's potting Earth was John Bear? Is Silvino Francisco still working in a Chesterfield fish and chip shop?

Was this the World Championship that changed the face of snooker? Was it indeed the ultimate World Championship?

Might there even... be a book in it?

It was time to make some calls, knock on some doors, tease out a few secrets, and now it's time to share a tale or two.

1: A WISHFUL DRINKER

CLIFF THORBURN is sitting across the table, with a mug of coffee, a glass of water, a memory bank full of stories and an afternoon to kill. It's late April 2022 and Thorburn is in Sheffield for the last few days of the World Championship, and to give the approaching World Seniors a gentle publicity push.

We're in Starbucks on Tudor Square, between the Crucible and the Winter Gardens, and the 1980 world champion is as accommodating an interviewee as you might expect. But he is wistful too, lamenting snooker friends and former foes whose numbers are dwindling, whose company he misses on his trips from Toronto to South Yorkshire. Thorburn can wander into the tournament hotel bar and everyone will clock 'the Grinder' immediately and be cheered by his presence, but the faces he recognises are becoming increasingly a select bunch.

Willie Thorne died in June 2020 and Terry Griffiths stopped coming three years ago, stepping back from mentoring a cluster of successful professionals to quietly coach at his club in Llanelli.

This is not the first time Thorburn and I have met, and yes, the previous time was in the hotel bar, some years ago.

Thorburn is going strong here at the age of 74. I remember Thorburn the player, at the age of around 40, struggling to keep up with a new brigade led by Stephen Hendry. Yet Thorburn is also famously the player who in 1983 made the first 147 at the Crucible, and the man who took down Higgins in that 1980 final.

We chat about the opportunities snooker has opened up for Thorburn since the days he was hustling for five dollars here, five dollars there, club to club.

This is one of those meetings where I buy the coffees and he generously hands over the interview gold. My type of transaction.

Via one tangent or another, there comes a morsel of unbidden tourist advice: I must one day pay a visit to the New York Athletic Club. You've guessed where it is, and athleticism doesn't seem a prerequisite, so this only heightens the appeal.

'They've got possibly the nicest snooker room in the world. It overlooks Central Park and I would highly recommend having a Sunday brunch there in the fall, as the leaves are changing,' Thorburn says.

'The park's right there and you look down on it. With your breakfast you get a Bloody Mary for starters, and it's just a fabulous place.'

OK, I'm salivating. Should I apologise for our Starbucks setting?

Later in the day, I inevitably check out the club online. Wise to do that first, book the flight second. It's members-only. Of course it is. The snooker room looks glorious. Surely the closest I'll come to tasting those breakfasts, sniffing the pancakes, bagels and smoked salmon of 180 Central Park South is through a hefty serving of Instagram snapshots. And I feast my eyes for longer than might be considered healthy.

You can imagine Thorburn there, holding court, mixing with the noble and the wealthy, divulging the secrets of life on the snooker tour. Those tales of snooker Babylon, the stories that perhaps don't make it to books and don't quite come out over coffee with a journalist, even if it's not for the want of trying.

I've booked this appointment with Crucible royalty to go over Thorburn's prickly relationship with Alex Higgins.

I am struck by the fact Higgins was Thorburn's junior by 14 months yet has been gone almost 12 years. Higgins was struck by Thorburn in a pugilistic sense: a hefty haymaker for the Hurricane.

One fisty encounter happened in 1983, around the time of the Irish Open. According to several accounts, Higgins invited trouble by snarling – mother, clutch thy pearls: 'Thorburn, you're a Canadian cunt, and you can't fucking play either.'

It was the latest in a line of insults that ran round the block, and Thorburn resisted snapping at the others, but this one brought on the red mist. Almost four decades later, he wishes he had kept an even temper that night, saying: 'Yes, of course I regret it.'

The first time it turned tetchy between Thorburn and Higgins had been as far back as 1973, so the dust-up had been long in coming.

'We were at a card game one time, and he went to hit me,' Thorburn recalls.

Whether it was cards or snooker, Thorburn and Higgins always fought frostily for the win. 'The first day I met him we had an altercation; I beat him for some money. I took a substantial handicap off him,' Thorburn adds.

'He didn't like that outcome, and later we had the card game – probably the last game of cards I've had too because, gee whizz, I'm not a card player, but boy oh boy he really got aggressive.

'I was sat beside a girl that he was taking out and he lost some money in the card game, and he lolled towards me and said something I didn't like, and then he said it again.

'Listen, if he was six foot I would have let it go, but we had a thing that was a long thing.'

The obvious common ground Higgins and Thorburn shared was their brilliance on the green baize. They respected one another's game and could usually tolerate being in the same space, and they went to war often enough on the snooker table for it to be usually left at that.

By 1982, Thorburn had a fair appreciation of what lifting the Joe Davis trophy at the Crucible would mean to Higgins.

When doling out defeat to Higgins in snooker's biggest match two years earlier, he got to witness the disappointment in his opponent's eyes at close quarters.

Thorburn observed in Higgins a man with animal magnetism, to whom crowds would flock, often recognising a little of themselves in his tortured self, knowing that an Alex Higgins match was a guaranteed spectacle, one way or another.

A famously fearless brand of snooker was the big come-on, the guarantee of a busy box office.

'People were fascinated by Alex because he never disappointed them,' says Thorburn.

'When Alex played, he either played great, or he had a bad day – and that was a good day for the spectators.

'He had a chip on his shoulder, and I never met anybody who had to win as badly as he did. It really, truly was everything to him.'

By 1982, Higgins was thoroughly fed up with losing, dispirited by how the young Steve Davis was hogging the spotlight and the press acclaim. Snooker had reached its boom years, and Higgins' game was all bust up. Davis, despite being portrayed by critics as a robotic charisma void, was laughing all the way to the bank.

Ten years had passed since Higgins was crowned world

champion at the Selly Park Royal British Legion Club in Birmingham – a stretch in which snooker had undergone transformative change. It was high time, Higgins reasoned, that he should reign again; yet to any discerning observer this idea was fanciful, a non-starter.

While Higgins' 1981-82 season had not been a total write-off, results manifestly did not point to him conquering the Crucible, the playhouse which since 1977 had been the championship's home.

He could still pull off eye-catching match wins, and nobody doubted that. But stringing them together was happening increasingly rarely. Higgins could not resist lighting bonfires in his life, habitually leaving behind smouldering ash piles of rancour and regret.

Far from blind to his faults, but slow to address them, Higgins decided his Sheffield sojourn in 1982 would flip the now well-worn narrative; it was time for this unruly son of Belfast to be king of the cuemen and put the rest in their place.

Reining in the boozy binges, putting in the practice hours, cutting out the claptrap; that should do it. The snooker landscape had transformed since the debutant Higgins scooped its most prized trophy for the first time, and now, long overdue, the sport's best-renowned firebrand would change with it.

He would change for Lauren. Yes, this one would be for his toddler daughter, the 17-and-a-half-month-old fidgety centre of his fast-spinning world.

It's a nice theory, Alex, one that really tugs on the heartstrings.

For all the pretty patter, those who were there remember Higgins' rhetoric carrying an implausible ring: the latest case of wishful thinking by a perennially wishful drinker.

2: 'I DON'T KNOW WHY I'M HERE'

BEFORE ALEX HIGGINS threatened to have Dennis Taylor shot, before Higgins head-butted one tournament official and callously threw a punch at another, before he blamed 'a gust of wind' for a broken ankle after tumbling from a first-floor Manchester flat window, before he lurched from one last doomed love affair and onwards to sickness and semi-seclusion, and before he left his closest snooker friends distraught by resisting efforts to steer him back to health, the maverick from Sandy Row won the greatest World Championship ever played at the Crucible. On the evening of May 16, 1982, Higgins said he would 'probably die happy'.

He delivered that statement in those special, fevered minutes that followed him overcoming Ray Reardon 18-15 in the Sheffield final, tying up a long-awaited second world triumph.

'Ladies and gentlemen, as you can see, I'm very, very elated,' Higgins told the audience, moments after cradling Lauren in his arms, tears streaming from his eyes.

'It has been 10 years, and I don't know why I'm here because I've been playing so badly.'

Higgins never did dominate snooker as he had anticipated when a young man. The appeal of knuckling down to practise in the 1970s and early 1980s frequently paled against tawdry temptations, and his marriage to Lauren's mother Lynn fell apart; however, he stamped his mark on the game for evermore over a remarkable 17 days in South Yorkshire.

Has there been a more poignant moment in snooker history than Higgins imploring his wife to bring young Lauren down to the theatre floor?

'My baby... give me my baby,' he begged Lynn, the moment instantly transcending sport and becoming one of relatable family drama. Would Lynn bring Lauren down to share the spotlight? She surely would and soon did, a tear-jerker bolted on to the end of a sporting spectacle.

Did Higgins die happy, as he imagined back then? Who among us ever will sign off with absolute fulfilment? But perhaps solacing memories of his finest hour floated across that pin-sharp mind when the Hurricane became physically all blown out, tragically wasted away.

Joe Swail, Northern Ireland's 2000 and 2001 Crucible semi-finalist, says: 'It's tough to say what snooker would look like if Alex Higgins hadn't been around. I'll be brutally honest and say I don't think there would be any snooker.

'He brought the character to the game. Higgins just stood out and I think we'd be struggling, so we've got to be grateful to him, to have put the game where it is now.'

Swail is a lifelong Higgins disciple but is being sincere, and so is Steve Davis when he explains his admiration for how Higgins every so often managed to leave his demons at the stage door.

'When he won the 1982 World Championship, it was total justification of the talent that he had,' says Davis.

'For a certain amount of time he got his act together, which was a brave thing to do, because it must be hard being someone who used alcohol as a crutch.

'I don't think people understand how amazing it was for him to get himself ready for an event where it would be so easy for him to slip back into old habits.'

On the day Higgins lifted the trophy in Sheffield, Adam Ant's Goody Two Shoes landed in the UK charts at number five, and three weeks later it jumped above Madness' House Of Fun to reach the top spot.

Higgins was acting as close to a goody two shoes as he ever would in the public eye, reining in the excesses and resisting the devil on his shoulder.

Don't drink, don't choke, here's what you can do.

David Hendon, an admired commentator for Eurosport, Matchroom and ITV, and a long-time Snooker Scene journalist, concurs it was a remarkable feat pulled off by Higgins.

'His whole world came together on that night,' says Hendon.

'I think everyone realised it wouldn't last, because it never did with him. You look at that night and he's almost frozen in time. In this moment, everything is good, and a lot of the other time it wasn't.'

Nick Metcalfe, the Talking Snooker podcast generalissimo and sports writer, sees a transcendent moment in snooker history.

'At that stage it was undoubtedly the most iconic Crucible image, and I would say it still probably is,' says Metcalfe.

'The only thing that rivals the 'baby, baby', and all that, would be Dennis Taylor wagging his finger three years later. That might compare, but the Higgins moment tied in everything: family, that great humanity, the fact he'd just won a big snooker match, so the great sporting achievement.

'Snooker was getting big then, it was getting huge, but it was still something that needed those special moments to push it further forward and that gave the BBC and the watching audience an image for the ages. Shaun Murphy speaks about "that room". The Higgins moment would have put "that room" even more into the public eye.'

* *

Judd Trump, days away from winning his first Crucible title at the 2019 World Championship, is wondering how he might celebrate such a life-changing achievement. There is no baby in Trump's life just yet, but there's someone else he has in mind.

Trump jokes: 'I'd pick my brother up, but I think he's a bit too heavy for me!'

Brother Jack – Trump's practice table whip-cracker – spends much of the year on the road with the snooker set. Svelte and perhaps a couple of inches taller than his brother, Jack is not in on this conversation, oblivious to being cast in the role of Lauren in Judd's surreal reimagining of the Higgins hoopla.

Trump gushes about Higgins' 1982 triumph, finding it hard to believe the belligerent Belfast boy could hold it together for such a slog in Sheffield. The unspoken message here is that if the highly strung Higgins could go all the way, then surely the level-headed Trump could too.

On May 6, 2019, Trump experiences the joyful pandemonium that greets the winner at the end of a world final: the first-time champion's magical realisation that a lifetime's ambition has been accomplished, the hugs from Jack, dad Steve and manager Django, the flashbulbs, the crowd's giddy roar and ovation, the inevitable torrent of ticker-tape and camera bulbs flashing.

Then there is the trophy that means everything, polished and shining, having been waiting for Trump all these years.

Judd doesn't pick up Jack. There is no 'Lauren moment'; perhaps that's somewhere down the line in Trump's life.

'Everyone's just fighting to get that one Crucible title,' Trump had said. And now his breakthrough has arrived.

Where Higgins stood in 1982, so stands Trump now as I watch on from the press benches. There is a new 'People's Champion'. I stand by and marvel, taking in the multi-sensory experience. It's a love-in. Even John Higgins, the runner-up and often a grouch in defeat, marvels at how Trump played to earn his 18-9 victory.

This room is steeped in snooker history. It is where an immortal parade of champions came and conquered. Trump is comfortably the most thrilling, audaciously attacking player to jump aboard snooker's roving tour wagon of eccentrics and assiduous go-getters since the leaders of the Class of '92: Ronnie O'Sullivan, John Higgins and Mark Williams.

He plays the game with a natural verve, always moving forward and finding ways to improve, flashy yet increasingly formidable in all aspects. Video clips of his wildest shots, often evocative of Alex Higgins in his prime, are chopped up, packaged and rush-released by the World Snooker Tour media team, knowing they will quickly run viral on social channels. He combines show-stopping style with trophy-winning substance, and few have ever done that.

Snooker has taken a quantum jump since its early days at the Crucible, when a clutch of middle-aged men, alongside a handful of youthful interlopers, would play a relatively plodding game, ciggies and pints as fundamental as chalk.

'It's hard to compare eras. You're limited with the conditions, and the standard only raises when you've got other people to compete with,' Trump tells me.

'At that time, in the early 1980s, Alex, Jimmy White and Steve

Davis were pushing the game to new levels. You've got to appreciate what they've done for snooker.'

Trump at this point is both snooker's present and its likely dominant character for the next 10 years, heading the cast impatiently waiting for the sport's golden generation to leave the stage. He has studied the game's history and plotted out its future, demanding more attention for the likes of himself, Kyren Wilson, Anthony McGill and Jack Lisowski.

When O'Sullivan, John Higgins and Williams were embarking on their professional careers, Alex Higgins was still clinging to the last vestiges of his own, one that made him a snooker immortal.

The longevity of the Rocket, the Wizard of Wishaw and the Welsh Potting Machine has been staggering. Indeed, the 32-year-old Trump would go on to be crushed by a 46-year-old O'Sullivan in the 2022 Crucible final.

But it was hard not to imagine Trump soon lifting the World Championship trophy for a second time, at the very least.

* *

On the night in 2019 when Trump becomes world champion, Barry Hearn is whooping it up and glad-handing backstage at the Crucible, still one of his favourite stomping grounds.

For Hearn, who spent a decade as a giddily autocratic World Snooker Tour chairman, this is an evening that has been a long time coming.

He has long considered Trump as O'Sullivan's natural successor, a burgeoning playboy of the game who, thrillingly, really could play as well as party. Few snooker players since the mid-1980s have boasted both a cue action to coo over and tabloid appeal to die for, but Trump belongs to that select group.

This is the Hurricane Higgins lineage, albeit the rough edges have been smoothed down and cleaned up in the new model of showman.

Hearn recognised the potential some years back, with Trump's unexpected run to the 2011 Crucible final bringing it into sharp focus for the public at large.

Trump spoke of 'sexy snooker', 'naughty snooker', and, egged on by an eager press pack, he played up to the flashy image that made him a new darling of the tabloids. He soon bought the fast cars and partied hard, becoming a social media star with an unashamedly 'look at me' attitude. But this was still somewhat vanilla when stacked up against antics of cuemen of the past.

Hearn, harking back to when snooker could count on its top stars falling out among themselves, falling out of nightclubs or falling into bed with models, wanted a bankable champion with a sparkle in his eye. Failing that, a knave in the Alex Higgins mould might also be good for business.

For a while, Hearn wasn't absolutely sure he had either, much as though he was excited by Trump's patter as much as his potting.

Hearn memorably once told reporters: 'Judd, what a nice young man. All I want now is for him to smack someone in the face, have a fight, and give you blokes some tabloid inches so you can make him into a sensation.

'We'd sponsor his disciplinary process. Unfortunately, he's a nice lad who doesn't do that sort of thing.'

There was tongue firmly pressed into Hearn's cheek on that day. The entrepreneur who always resisted the chance to bring Alex Higgins into his Matchroom stable relished the prospect of a modern-day hell-raiser in the tour's ranks, but only if there was somebody else cleaning up the mess.

At the same time, the chairman's quip felt like a gentle reminder to Trump that Hearn considered him a headline-maker, and it was time for him to come good. But the veteran puppeteer of the sporting world was correct with his initial assessment. Trump is unquestionably 'a nice young man'. We'll surely be a long time waiting for that first punch to be thrown.

With 'Hurricane' Higgins, you never quite knew.

Trump is a charming guy and a magnificent snooker player. Higgins could be both of those things, but he could also be vindictive, violent, venomous.

'I had to negotiate a no-go area close to Steve Davis,' says Hearn, 'because Davis thought, "He's mad enough to whack me."

'Steve wasn't the bravest out there, but Alex would whack anybody.'

Davis acknowledges his manager's recollection as being accurate. But Davis also rushes to knock on the head any suggestion he and Higgins ever seriously clashed.

'I didn't really have any run-ins with Alex, ever,' says Davis.

'I never had a problem in the sense of any confrontations or anything like that, but I just knew to keep out of his way. That way, there was never a chance of a run-in.

'I used to turn up to play him in matches, and then get as far away as possible. Not really even because I disliked him.

'In fact, I didn't dislike him; I thought he was an amazing player, but I just knew that sometimes he could turn when he had a drink.

'He was a turner. Some people are, some people aren't, and I didn't want to be there when he turned because I'd seen the carnage, so I kept away.'

3: A PUNCH-UP FOR POSTERITY'S SAKE

THE RAPTUROUS MOMENT of Alex and the dazed little Lauren sharing the Crucible spotlight was almost never shown on television.

A tug of war between on-site production and BBC Two presentation bosses, eager to move on to the next programme, was taking place behind the scenes as a family drama played out inside the Sheffield theatre.

Tense off-camera discussions were taking place as Lynn Higgins, in a savoy blue sequinned dress, slowly made her way past row after row of spectators whose collective attire for the biggest night of the snooker year could be charitably described as history teacher chic.

Amid this convention of quaint conformity – almost every man in a tie; suits that ran the full beige spectrum – Lynn stood out as a vivid beacon.

She was carrying the wriggling Lauren, the trophy that Alex wanted to clasp more than any silverware, and Lynn greeted her husband with a fond kiss of congratulations.

Higgins had finished off Ray Reardon with a scorching break of

135 and was savouring his championship-clinching victory. He was collecting the trophy in an ocean of tears, even before his family joined him, and to certain BBC staff away from Sheffield this was considered a sufficiently fitting ending.

A repeat of the final episode of drama serial The Woman In White had been on the evening schedule, along with the Orson Welles docudrama F Is For Fake, and the snooker had already massively overrun its slim slot, with the closing session of the final initially allocated a meagre hour and 45 minutes, from 7.15pm to 9pm.

Presenter David Vine was a master of keeping his words concise when the occasion called for brevity, but he had no control over how long the match action would last. As 10pm approached, and the contest ended, the BBC crew in Sheffield had to fight their corner with colleagues in London for a priceless few extra seconds on air.

'This was another punch-up I had with presentation,' remembers Nick Hunter, who was the BBC's snooker executive producer at the time.

One more 'punch-up' came in 1983, when Hunter remembers he successfully wrestled for extra time as Cliff Thorburn approached the first 147 maximum break at the World Championship.

'I said, "How many people are unemployed in the country?"' Hunter recalls. 'They weren't too sure, and I said, "Well, if you fade me, it'll be one more."'

Hunter had at least been prepared for that Thorburn moment, having issued similar exhortations as the Higgins show of happy families gave the 1982 tournament its climactic shots.

By reluctantly resorting to warnings over job security, Hunter wangled those important extra moments on air.

'I swore after this I would never agree to an off-air time if I was going to be held to one, if things changed in front of the cameras,' Hunter says.

'I'd agreed an 'out' time because we all knew Higgins was going to win and it was just a question of when, and as the final frame approached I warned presentation and said, "Will you give me two minutes after the final black falls and everybody starts celebrating? Just two minutes after that?"

'They were in a rush to get out for some reason. I agreed that – I shouldn't have done – and we got to within one minute and 45 seconds.

'As Higgins came out, my assistant was counting us down, and we got down to 45 seconds when this commotion started in the hall, with Alex looking towards the crowd.

'And I realised that was his wife, so I said, "Presentation, I can't come out in 45 seconds, I'll give you an out time when I can – we've got babies in view."

'And presentation said, "Sorry, we've agreed this time." I can't remember what I said next, but it was along the lines of "… employed…" and they threatened to fade me.

'In the end I said, "There will be more coverage of what's about to happen than there was of the action on the snooker table," and sure enough… what pictures they were.'

Speaking in summer 2021, Hunter expressed a tinge of regret over how he handled the Higgins episode, but his professional pride at ensuring such a famous sporting moment was aired live to millions of viewers knocks that feeling of self-criticism out of the park.

'Looking back on what I said to presentation, I'm embarrassed by it really,' Hunter says.

'But it was the only way I could get this lady's attention, that if they did fade us, there was going to be a bloody riot. Nobody complained afterwards, by the way. I was expecting a note from the presentation editor, asking how dare I talk to his staff in that way, but I never got any comeback at all.'

The pinnacle of the most dramatic World Championship of them all had been saved. Hunter's work was done.

'That was maybe a turning point for them, in terms of how the BBC covered the sport,' says David Hendon. 'Maybe they realised then that it was about the people as much as the game, and they had to show these moments and invest in their personal stories.

'With Alex, he obviously had the on-off relationship with his wife, so you were never quite sure if they were together. In that moment they were, which was what made it all the more special.'

Hazel Irvine, the face of BBC snooker coverage in the 21st century, is grateful any such time constraints have been consigned to history.

'Those moments on the air at the end are seen as very precious now,' says Irvine.

'We've been very lucky in my era of presenting with John Parrott and Steve Davis where we haven't had that "You're coming off air in two minutes" thing.

'They allow you as the presenter to judge what is appropriate, when you think the guys are ready to stop, and that judgement has been left to me and others who've done it over the past few years.

'We've been lucky we haven't had that time pressure, because I don't think it warrants time pressure in those moments. You have to allow what is a hugely, hugely emotional journey that these guys have been on to play out.

'People want to hear it. We don't have that pressure that was perhaps there in '82 to get off the air. We're more happy in television now to see those precious moments for what they are. Those are the things that people remember; those are the things that people will talk about the next day.

'Seeing Sofia, Mark Selby's daughter, run on and be chucked up in the air! All of these guys, since Alex did this, it's something where they don't just want the trophy, they want to share that with their families. They want to have that in the family album.

'I think it's become a driving ambition for them as well – not just to win it but to have that moment that their family can remember and they will be proud of forever, and that they will be a part of.

'Alex set a hell of a precedent. We've had Ronnie junior, and some of the kids dancing on the tables, and we love it all, it's great.

'We're lucky in snooker that the guys are willing to share that with us. Not all sports do it or have the stage to allow them to do it, but it's become part of it at the Crucible, and it's become part of Alex's legacy.'

4: Not a dry eye in the house

RONNIE O'SULLIVAN is honking the horn for Higgins on a bright Wednesday afternoon in Llandudno, two days after what would have been Alex's 70th birthday.

'He was a great. He made snooker,' O'Sullivan says.

'He made snooker sexy. Steve Davis made it boring and Alex made it sexy. He had a great following.'

O'Sullivan is in a hospitable mood. Almost as formidable a force in his fruitful forties as he was in his troubled twenties, this Peter Pan of potting has enjoyed the kind of career that Higgins might have experienced, if it were not for the distractions and the pigheadedness that meant serious longevity and sustained success were never realistic prospects.

O'Sullivan has estimated he wasted nine years of his own career through a combination of wanton rebellion and caving in to his urges, but his best game proved retrievable. Higgins rode to snooker's summit but kept on pedalling once he hit a downward slope, neglecting the brakes. Those who gave chase, in the hope of guiding him at least halfway back to those great peaks, were witness to his sad final years.

Higgins should have been enjoying himself on the golf course in his mid-sixties and into his seventies, or at least chasing winners at the racecourse, rather than long gone.

At Higgins' funeral, Jimmy White said that amid the grief and the love, he also felt anger towards his great friend who 'never listened to anyone, close friends or family'. White, Ken Doherty, O'Sullivan and countless others extended a hand of support, but Higgins was not one to dance to anyone's tune but his own.

In Llandudno, O'Sullivan is rhapsodising on request.

'He brought the crowds; he brought the excitement. He was our George Best. Every sport needs a character, and snooker was lucky to have Alex Higgins.'

Generous words. However, it is worthwhile remembering that O'Sullivan's original snooker idol was Davis.

O'Sullivan, the five-minute maximum man, was perhaps not quite such an all-in adherent to the Higgins doctrine as has often been made out.

There have certainly been times when O'Sullivan looked to be following a similarly treacherous path, chasing down the scree-strewn trail that Higgins would dice with on a daily basis. A hepcat who made full use of his nine lives, Higgins eventually tripped down an abyss one day and never quite clambered back to solid ground.

When it comes to areas of addiction, self-abuse or over-indulgence, O'Sullivan has been there and owns the T-shirt collection. Drink and drugs have tormented him, even food. Today he is a survivor who has found an equilibrium, harmony and happiness, a structure to his life, genuine purpose.

Like the rest of us, he is imperfect, but O'Sullivan has usually responded when others have offered help, and he has learned to help himself. There was a time when he used to drain a Guinness or eight without a second thought, just like Alex Higgins. And, like Higgins, he loved a spliff.

Today, O'Sullivan's great indulgence is running.

Higgins, though once an aspiring teenage jockey, would have recoiled at the thought of a muddy morning 10k, but O'Sullivan often dashes and splashes enthusiastically through Epping Forest, the running shoes, shorts and vest joining the waistcoats in his luggage wherever the snooker tour takes him.

There was no player other than O'Sullivan who regularly mixed the theatrical and the anarchic with a winning game during the first two decades of this century. Higgins once wanted to coach 'Rocket' Ronnie, but O'Sullivan cannily declined that proposal.

O'Sullivan, for all that he has cleaned up his game off the table, is no puritan. Nobody needs him to become a model professional either. That would be like tilting Pisa's Leaning Tower back to a perpendicular poise. Nobody wants to see it. Thirty years after joining the professional ranks, he has remained a harbinger of potential mischief, but whereas the arrival of Higgins at a venue would often have staff and players scrambling to stay out of his way, O'Sullivan can typically be counted on to toe the line more or less with his behaviour.

By the early 2020s, setting aside the pandemic, the box-office appeal of O'Sullivan was only growing. He has long transcended snooker, just as Higgins did around the time O'Sullivan was first picking up a cue. With no surfeit of showmen, it appeared snooker would be considerably hurt if O'Sullivan were to lay down his cue. His pulling power far exceeds that of any of his top-16 rivals, Judd Trump included – and it was a similar story with Higgins too, in his day.

'All I know is that Alex is remembered just as George Best is still remembered,' O'Sullivan says.

'Some people might win the World Championship two or three times and you ask most people on the street their names and they'll go, "Who?" But Alex was different, he was special, and he'll never be forgotten.'

Looking out from Venue Cymru on to the glistening Llandudno promenade, O'Sullivan probably has a point. The slow strollers, dog walkers and joggers might well recognise pictures of the Hurricane above the bulk of the field competing here by the coast. But why the enduring appeal of a man his detractors look upon as a scoundrel, an obnoxious drunk, and worse?

**

'Steve Davis was my hero. I always wanted Alex to get beat,' four-time Crucible champion John Higgins once told me.

'He's not a player I would look up to myself and I don't think young players should look up to people like that, but at the end of the day you can't dispute the fact he was a trailblazer definitely for the sport of snooker.'

Not the most prolific trophy winner of his day, and certainly far from the most dedicated to his trade, Alex Higgins was besotted by snooker, even if at times he felt the game hated him in return. He was besotted in many areas; he loved many women too, and many women loved him back. Until some truly came to hate him.

Alex also loved the booze; the booze and the bookies being constants in his adult life, yet such devils on each shoulder never did make for a healthy balance.

He felt he could rely on the Guinness and the whiskey chasers; he felt he could pick a champion chaser from a field of contenders. In the end, drink and gambling were but two of the innumerable weaknesses that accelerated his premature demise.

Alex Higgins careered through his life in a manner to which many would find it challenging to relate, becoming a swashbuckling, uncompromising, trouble-inviting, rock and roll cliche of the snooker zoo. A lovely fella at times, who could charm a corpse, but on other days a contemptible loser.

Yeats in the morning, Yates's Wine Lodge by night. Henry Jekyll and Edward Hyde had nothing on Higgins, whose fierce intelligence was betrayed by a self-immolating streak that scorched through his career and perhaps drew others to prematurely burn out with him.

The best player of his day? No, he was sloshed too often for that. The George Best of the baize? For sure. Those two sons of Belfast passed through life all too briefly. In his 1986 autobiography, Alex Through the Looking Glass, Higgins noted he and Best shared 'a shining talent that made people jealous and turned them against us', albeit acknowledging 'a basic weakness of character there as well'.

In 1982, Higgins sensationally conquered all before him in Sheffield, taking down Jim Meadowcroft, Doug Mountjoy, Willie Thorne, White and, finally, Ray Reardon, the strait-laced former police officer who had trounced a well-lit Hurricane in the 1976 world final at Manchester's Wythenshawe Forum.

'Well, 1982 was the year,' Barry Hearn says, grinning.

'It had everything: the semi-final with Jimmy, the final, "Bring me my baby". You couldn't buy that and you couldn't script it. If you scripted it, everyone would go, "Nah, that's naff." There wasn't a dry eye in the house.'

This is Hearn the great survivor, the Warren Buffett-obsessed Essex accountant who both guided and piggy-backed Davis' success on the way to becoming a sporting tycoon. He was always most comfortable when observing the Higgins show from afar. The responsibility of rescuing the perennially persecuted from his latest purported persecutor held little appeal as Hearn constructed an empire around a stable of players he knew would kowtow to his rules.

They almost came to blows, did Hearn and Higgins, but an enduring respect, intensely grudging at times, underscored their relationship. At least that's how Hearn remembers it.

It was why Hearn found plenty to enjoy in Higgins' run to the 1982 World Championship title. Although, it must be said, his suggestion that this was 'the year' is an example of Hearn playing to the gallery, given he savoured Davis' glory run a year earlier a sight more readily.

With scorching hot favourite Davis wiped out in the 1982 Crucible first round by Bolton's overnight heart-throb Tony Knowles, Hearn recognised a Higgins triumph could be the saving grace for snooker from those 17 days, a result to rocket the sport on to the front pages. Hearn understood his burgeoning empire might not scoop any immediate dividend from Higgins lifting the trophy, and Davis might become queasy at the sight of his nemesis taking top honours, but the residual rewards would be enormous. It was time to stomach short-term pain for a lifetime of gain.

Matchroom Sport's annual turnover for the year to 30 June 2019 – the last full year prior to the pandemic – stood at £192.8million. What began with snooker and Davis had ostensibly become Hearn Inc, a staggering multi-national, multi-sport business.

Taking on Higgins might have derailed it all, or he could have made the empire greater. Hearn, who passed the Matchroom reins to son Eddie in 2021, remains a Higgins admirer but is relaxed about his decision to freeze out the great renegade. There were countless times that Higgins courted Hearn's management, each time being batted away, told to go home.

'I had my players, but also, in a sort of strange way, although he drove me up the wall, I couldn't help having a soft spot for Alex Higgins,' Hearn says.

'It's like being a West Ham supporter but still you love George Best.'

Best again. Higgins and Best. Those great, yet tragically intractable sons of Northern Ireland. Entertainers of their ilk are terrific to watch, but less so to manage.

Manchester United sacred cow Best may have been pushed to keep up with the lifestyles of Higgins and the snooker set during the 1980s, such was the order of the day.

Whether it was at the hotel bar, or out in the wild at The Roxy or Josephine's, a parade of potters turned from sinking balls to sinking pints when play stopped for the night at the World Championship.

* *

The Roxy – or Roxy's as many knew it – was the nightclub directly across the road from the Crucible. Come the late 1980s and into the nineties, it would be recognisable as one of the sweat boxes where Pete Waterman and Michaela Strachan filmed The Hitman and Her, their middle-of-the-night club-culture ITV weekend show where acid house and Stock, Aitken and Waterman chart pop might rub up together in an eccentric alliance, the Higgins and Davis of their strange world. Australian pop newcomer Kylie Minogue appeared on one of the show's Roxy nights, as did many energised young locals, cavorting for the benefit of an at-home audience largely consisting of insomniacs, students, the drunk, the desperate and the exceedingly late home.

Roxy's was therefore convenient and well patronised by the Crucible coterie, but it was Josephine's that invariably pulled in the biggest names in snooker. With the offer of what passed for

VIP treatment, Josephine's, with its glitter ball and neon fittings, was found at nearby Barker's Pool in the city centre, with hotels within easy stumbling range for the players.

Higgins was restrained in 1982 by his standards, but during a typical World Championship it would be easy enough to clock his whereabouts at such a spot at Josephine's.

'People like Alex would be absolutely smashed out of his head at the bar, wanting to fight everybody,' Hearn says, 'or the next minute he'd want to buy everyone a drink.'

White, Hurricane Higgins and the Canadian Kirk Stevens were among notable players who would eventually find a way to hard drugs when away from tournaments, but during Crucible time it was time-honoured after-hours activity that prevailed.

The players would have an inkling of what the night might hold before leaving the venue.

'In those days, in the dressing rooms, if you opened the window and looked outside you'd see 40 or 50 girls,' Hearn says.

'They'd be like, "Steve, give us a wave" – and it was groupie time in those days.

'The players were heroes of the day. I said to Davis the other day, "I don't think you've got a fan left with their own teeth," but they were fun times.

'I don't think anyone got hurt over it, but it was relentless because we were living the dream.

'Today it's a proper business and a proper sport and I've got responsibilities of contracts and whatever, but in those days it was like, "Fill your boots, enjoy yourselves," which we did in abundance.'

5: 'What? Somebody beat Steve Davis?'

IT'S NOT THERE any more, the Grosvenor House Hotel.

A modernist mid-sixties high-rise designed to bring affordable, chic lodging to Sheffield, the Grosvenor's cachet diminished until some considered it an ugly welt on the Steel City's cut torso.

The pulverisers and concrete crushers came in January 2017, razing to the ground the one-time flophouse of choice for South Yorkshire's baby boomers and business travellers with their entertainment expenses accounts.

It had been the sort of place that left an impression on its guests, and in April and May each year many of those customers were snooker players and fans.

'The Grosvenor was quite plush in its day,' remembers John Airey, a veteran of the front row at the World Championship.

'There were huge open plan lounges where everyone mingled. The one thing I found strange was that Yorkshire Television's Sheffield branch used to be based in the bottom of that building. There was a lady called Sheila Mercier who played Annie Sugden, the matriarch of the Sugden family in Emmerdale Farm, and I can remember walking into the Grosvenor once and there was Annie Sugden, who'd obviously been on a visit to Yorkshire TV, standing next to Bill Werbeniuk, who must have been between matches down the road.

'And all these little kids ran up to Annie Sugden for an autograph and Werbeniuk doesn't know what the hell's going on.

'He assumes they're all coming to him, and his face said, "Who the hell's this old dear?" To his mind, it was the snooker players who were meant to be the stars.'

As it happened, some snooker players were starrier than others.

In late April of 1982, Barry Hearn and his most bankable cue master Steve Davis booked out three Grosvenor suites, and eight rooms in all, for the World Snooker Championship, expecting to need most if not all of that accommodation for the 17-day run. There were minders in tow, staff to put up. Hearn himself would require the best accommodation money could buy in South Yorkshire. Tony Meo needed a bed too.

Journalist Terry Smith playfully wrote in the Daily Mirror that it was a 'Muhammad Ali style takeover'.

The Worlds was such a daunting test, it was thought wise to have the best command post money could buy.

Never mind the 'Thrilla in Manila', here the challenge was irreducible at the Crucible.

Over the years, Davis would enjoy his stays at the Grosvenor, settling into a familiar routine and wanting for nothing, with snooker's coliseum a mere 10-minute stroll away.

'The Grosvenor was the only place in town,' Davis says. 'If the fans wanted to bump into somebody, they'd go to that place. There were a couple of places outside the centre, but within walking distance it was the one that I preferred and most of the players did as well.

'I liked to just be able to walk through what is now the Peace

Gardens, past the council offices, past the Brown Bear pub and down to the stage door, and that was the route. For many years that was always the route, and even if that route didn't work, it was still the route.'

By April 1982, Davis was a heavyweight figure in British sport, reputed to have earned around £600,000 since his maiden Crucible triumph a year earlier. Yet his challenge would crumble on an extraordinary return to the Worlds, just as the Grosvenor itself would be reduced to dust decades later.

Bulldozed, grounded, the towering presence of Davis was swiftly removed from the tournament's skyline.

When Davis surrendered his title on the second morning, it was the first domino to fall in a chain that would lead to snooker's dissident at large, Alex Higgins, roaring to glory.

* *

Tony Knowles and Stephen Hendry are immersed in jovial conversation across the table from an off-duty crew of journalists, downstairs at the Mercure St Paul's hotel in Sheffield.

A mere five minutes ago, I'd been sounding out colleagues for the best way to get hold of Knowles for an interview, and lo and behold he has practically leapt into my lap.

Knowles and the snooker tour went their separate ways many years ago, but this is a private party after the 2019 World Championship final, and the one-time pin-up of the game always did love a party.

The drinks are flowing tonight; this shindig will end at around dawn. So I hear.

Plenty of water has passed under the bridge since Knowles was a household name and a favourite of the red-top national newspapers. In this company he is full of cheer.

Knowles, who battled throat cancer some years ago, obviously has plenty to catch up on with Hendry, this famous pair of potters battling to make themselves heard to one another, just a few steps away from a lively dance floor.

Soon Knowles is doing the rounds, catching up with old friends, being cornered for photographs and snatched conversations by long-time admirers, women mainly. It's a throwback moment.

He looks healthy, dapper, still instantly recognisable as the man who stunned the snooker world when he destroyed defending champion Davis 10-1 all those years ago, utterly upending the expected plot of the 1982 championship and leaving millions of viewers flabbergasted.

Davis took a bruising, one that has informed his opinion of the World Championship to this day.

'I've had moments in there when it's been the most wonderful place,' says Davis. 'And there were other times when I wanted the whole place to swallow me up because it was the worst place ever. It is the best and worst arena you can possibly have, depending on how it's going.'

The 1982 tournament began on the evening of Friday, April 30, having bulked out from 24 players in 1981 to boast a 32-strong field, while also expanding from 14 to 17 days. This was the year when everything changed for professional snooker, its showpiece event adopting the format that became its hallmark, quintessentially remaining the same four decades later, albeit shuffling slightly on the calendar.

Davis, at 24 years old, was portrayed on the cover of the 75 pence souvenir programme: a study in concentration, stooping with one eye half closed, considering his options on a table where the blue blocked the cue ball's path to a full connection with a red in shot.

It captured the essence of Davis, the most meticulous of sportsmen, inferring there would be nobody better prepared for the 17-day exercise in deep focus that is required in Sheffield.

The reigning Masters and UK champion, Davis had in January become the first player to achieve the potting perfection of a 147 maximum break in professional competition. For that effort at the Lada Classic, Davis won himself one of the sponsor's cars.

BBC Two showed the very start of the Knowles match, with David Vine going live to a UK television audience at 7.30pm, the presenter telling viewers this was 'the richest, the biggest and the most important' tournament on the calendar. Friday night snooker was beamed to millions of households in an era where British audiences had the choice of just three channels: BBC One, BBC Two and ITV.

'And of course, the question that everyone is asking: can anybody take the title away from the man who has become one of the biggest names, not just in snooker but in all sport, Steve Davis?' Vine said.

'He came here, he won the title last year. Since then, he's done everything right and the bookmakers are now so confident that they've made him 2/5 favourite to retain the title, and nobody has ever retained the World Professional Snooker Championship title here in the Crucible.

'Well, Davis is on first match. We're just waiting now for it all to start. He's down there in the wings waiting to come out, with his manager Barry Hearn.'

Knowles was waiting there too, 'twitching around just a little bit' by Vine's reckoning.

'Because it's a big test for Tony Knowles to take on the biggest name in sport – certainly the biggest name in snooker sport,' Vine said.

A headmasterly and assured presence who would continue to be the BBC's main snooker host for years to come, Vine was picking up his pace.

'Tony Knowles from Bolton. He's played in United Kingdom Championships. He's beaten Fred Davis and Doug Mountjoy and now plays Steve Davis, and they're just about to be announced,' Vine declared.

The presenter's sure-footed work was almost done, and as master of ceremonies David Harrison introduced Davis, Vine told the millions at home: 'And in he comes. His entourage are in the hallway. We saw Barry Hearn. The bodyguards are there, he really has taken over.'

The message was blunt: this was the Davis show. Buckle up, there could be 17 days of this.

Then, as the first shots of the championship were played, the implausible narrative began to unfold.

Ronnie Harper for the Belfast Telegraph wrote in Friday morning's newspaper that the match 'should be a foregone conclusion'.

Yet Davis froze. Froze like he never had before as a pro. Hearn had gone into business with a timid teenager and made Davis a warrior at the table, soon to be a millionaire, but as the eyes of the UK turned to this compact South Yorkshire arts centre, they were witnessing a startling regression.

This particular spotlight was too glaring for young Romford Slim, the pressure overwhelming. The Crucible was recast from the venue where a snooker dream came true a year previously to the stage for a living nightmare.

Some call it the 'Crucible curse', when a world champion returns and makes a pained exit, unable to rack up first and second titles in consecutive years. Davis, defending the trophy, performed as though he had been cast under a paralysing spell.

Davis had privately feared he was undercooked. He had been on the wrong end of a thrashing by Ray Reardon at the Highland Masters just a fortnight earlier and was unusually apprehensive about his trophy defence in Sheffield, albeit keeping a poker face.

'I'd started to feel the pressure a bit after Christmas. There was a tournament where I remember thinking my game had crumbled, when Ray Reardon beat me 6-0 in Scotland, and all of a sudden I started to get myself under pressure,' Davis says.

'I prepared as well as I could for the World Championship, and I practised as well as I could, but I went out there and lost a close first frame, even though I'd potted some decent balls, and just collapsed.

'I felt as though everybody wanted me to lose. That happens every time at the Crucible, where the tournament favourite goes out to face an underdog; everybody roots for the underdog. You understand that, but there was just a feeling in the room and I couldn't cope with it that time round.

'It was a build-up of how maybe you knew how exciting it had been the previous year, or you just didn't dare lose in the first round because you wanted to have a run again. Whatever it was, I just wasn't capable of coping with it, and I was easy meat, totally easy meat when I look back. I wouldn't like to revisit those frames because it was just rabbit-in-the-headlights stuff, but it happens every now and again, and it was a learning curve.

'Everybody struggles, nobody's ever won it back-to-back to start with.'

Davis says he 'felt totally out of it' as he flimsily folded, slumping 8-1 behind on Friday before Knowles completed the walloping the next morning.

Although he harboured apprehension about his title chances,

Davis had not foreseen a first-round mauling of this nature.

Hearn suspects Davis thought another waltz through the early rounds was a given, form or no form, and that the enormity of the occasion only hit him when he set eyes on the arena, some 11 and a half months after taking down Mountjoy in the 1981 final.

'And that's probably why he got beat 10-1,' Hearn says.

'There's no line between complacency and panic. Once the complacency kicks in, the next port of call is panic, and Davis has turned up, and he would never admit this himself, but I believe he turned up thinking "stroll in the park mate, stroll in the park".

'And when it got to three-nil, as early as that, you suddenly thought, "Fucking hell, what's going on here?" And then the pockets got smaller and the balls got bigger.'

Knowles had next to no public profile before taking down Davis. He went on to win ranking titles and reached the Crucible semi-finals three times later in his career, but none of that was any help in softening the immediate cudgel blow to Davis' pride.

Prised away from the bustling Judd Trump title party all these years later, Knowles turns his mind back to 1982 and bashing the champ, and it's all still there for him, perhaps in an increasingly glorious technicolour.

'It was the first match on. We started on the Friday night and finished on the Saturday morning,' Knowles says.

'He wasn't unbeatable in my eyes. The wider public had only seen him that year when he was winning, but I'd played him as an amateur so I'd already had good results against him. I knew his style of play and I knew how he'd come out.

'You do come under pressure defending the actual title and I know that he thrives on people's mistakes, and if you don't make mistakes you can get on top of his game.

'I was possibly the worst opponent for him, and I was a good tactical player. It had taken me a long while to get to that point because I was playing better in 1979 when I wasn't allowed to turn professional.'

Knowles had long petitioned to be allowed on to the professional tour, twice seeing applications pushed aside before, in 1980, he was waved through by the World Professional Billiards and Snooker Association to compete against the likes of Davis, Terry Griffiths and Higgins on a regular basis.

'I was an unknown as far as TV was concerned but not in the eyes of Davis,' Knowles says.

'Davis knew I was a solid opponent and probably a risk. He was a young gun tackling the old brigade: John Spencer, Ray Reardon, John Pulman, Graham Miles, Cliff Thorburn, Dennis Taylor, Bill Werbeniuk.

'It wasn't so much that I had nothing to lose, and more that I knew exactly what I was going to do. He probably realised I was a danger.'

Knowles remembers playing Davis at the pro-am Pontins Spring Open in 1978, at the eponymous holiday park in Prestatyn, and claims his opponent was 'dead in the water' at one point in that match.

'But he turned it around and, anyway, he went on to win the title,' Knowles recalls.

The throwaway 'anyway' is doing a lot of work there. Knowles is describing Davis at his most ruthless – a predator, poised to pounce even when the odds are loaded against him.

'Around about the same time,' Knowles says, 'Barry Hearn had sent him and Geoff Foulds around the country playing different players. He came to play me and Stan Haslam on my table in Bolton and they got beat 8-0. So we already had a bit of the measure of him.'

Puffing out one's chest after the event is quintessentially the form of a triumphant underdog. Dethroned Davis swallowed the desperate disappointment and moved on to the next season.

**

Hearn was still building his snooker empire in 1982 and was far from the only power broker in the sport.

Later in life Hearn would playfully anoint himself 'Bertie Big Bollocks', as head honcho of the Matchroom empire and chairman of World Snooker, yet he essentially had his cue sport eggs in a Davis-shaped basket in 1982, with all apologies to Tony Meo.

Had Davis not delivered on his early promise, snooker and Hearn could have followed very different paths.

Knowles, meanwhile, was managed by Henry West, whose stable of professionals for a while numbered seven, some of them very good players indeed. Not all were world-beaters, but that did not prevent the most inevitable of nicknames being bestowed on that septet.

'I was part of the "Magnificent Seven", basically,' Knowles remembers.

Meo had been a part of that West roster for a while, along with Knowles, Jimmy White, Patsy Fagan, John Virgo, Joe Johnson and teenager Terry Whitthread.

'That was a quality group of players,' Knowles says.

'Snooker was already a major TV sport and by '82 it had gained momentum. It was immediately front-page news when I beat Steve, even that afternoon.'

This stacks up. The Sheffield Star emerged in the afternoon that Saturday, and its front page led with the screamer headline 'BRITAIN ATTACKS', pointing to an RAF assault on an Argentina-occupied Port Stanley airstrip in the Falkland Islands.

But beneath that report was a write-up headlined 'Shock defeat for Steve', while the back-page splash was 'IT'S ALL OVER FOR DAVIS', describing how the 'snooker king' had been 'sensationally deposed'.

Knowles, the 150-1 tournament outsider, had caused a sporting earthquake.

The swarthy potter from across the Pennines had taken Davis down in brutal fashion, the 'Nugget' melted down and mercilessly subjected to a grim Crucible fate.

Just as in the modern era, there were two matches running concurrently in the tight arena as the tournament began, rival players having to sit awkwardly side by side between frames. Knowles and Davis were not exactly chatty. Knowles was so close he could almost feel Davis' heart thumping.

'I wasn't really worried about how he was coping with it. I was just playing my own game,' Knowles says. 'I think he knew the writing was on the wall.'

Davis had a top break of 32 in the match. Knowles only had two runs that went beyond 50, peaking with a 67 to lead 5-1 as the BBC Two television audience returned for a second tranche of the Friday evening action at 9.35pm.

Knowles recalls the highest break in the match being a mere 39, but the memory can play tricks; he had Davis squirming by reeling off runs of 67, 55 and 43 before Friday's close of business.

If his memory is clouded, that is forgivable, given Knowles had cause to be distracted.

'At that time I had a £150 even-money bet on the Davis match with a pal of mine who ran a nightclub in Manchester. If I'd have took the same bet at the bookies, I'd have probably got 10 to one. I took that bet before I even went to play Davis.'

What looked to be a fool's punt paid off, and Knowles was in a celebratory mood long before he crossed the finish line.

There was no holding back Knowles once that monster first-session lead was banked. He could justify a nightclub nightcap.

'I went to Josephine's on the Friday night, between sessions,' he says. 'We were on again at 10.30am the next day. All the players used to go there at night.

'We'd congregate in the dining room where we were well looked after. We just had a few drinks, and I was up until about four o'clock in the morning and we were back in the Crucible at 10.'

Knowles had faith both in his alarm clock and his capacity to get the job done, irrespective of how he might be feeling when the sun came up. It hardly mattered whether Davis was fresh. The match had been lost in that first session, barring the most miraculous fightback.

Knowles could safely head out on the town, enjoy a long Friday night of Sheffield hospitality, and scrape himself together to finish off the job come morning.

While he could safely count on the presence of some of his rival cue stars at Josephine's, there was no danger of running into Davis.

'He went back to his room playing his video games,' Knowles says. 'Barry Hearn had installed some video games in his bedroom so he could never get out.'

That's Tony Knowles. Still aiming little digs, delivered with a cheeky grin, at the man who would win six Crucible titles.

Hearn had selected the Grosvenor for its easy access to the Crucible, and he had indeed rented a pretty panoply of arcade machines to keep Davis amused, not to mention 40 video tapes to keep all and sundry in his party out of trouble.

Steve Acteson was the Press Association's newly installed snooker reporter in 1982, his words zipping through the wires and into newspaper offices across the country. Acteson interviewed Hearn before the tournament got under way.

'Barry was telling me how they've taken over an entire floor for Matchroom personnel,' Acteson says. 'The only two players he had there were Steve Davis and Tony Meo, and for one of the rooms he said, "We're going to turn it into a video-game room, so Steve can play, because he's mad about Space Invaders."'

Hearn's mission was to keep Davis as comfortable as possible, pampered and primed to bring another world title back to Essex. Neither man was used to such heavy bumps in the road as this.

Davis and Hearn are said to have still enjoyed champagne on that Friday night, disregarding the hopeless position in the Knowles match. They had plenty to celebrate at the end of the 1981-82 season regardless, so the lack of Crucible success was not about to stop Hearn ordering the best bubbly in Sheffield.

April turned to May at midnight as day two of the 1982 championship arrived, and on that first Saturday, before Grandstand even began on BBC One, Davis was checking out of the Crucible.

If there was a sense of outrageousness to the scoreline, Davis had added a touch of the absurd to proceedings too, going in-off from his break with the first shot on that Saturday morning. It was as though it had been he, and not Knowles, on the razz.

This scenario was less Space Invaders, more Invasion of the Body Snatchers. Davis was evidently not himself. It was approaching lunchtime when Knowles bustled his way across the winning line, roughly eight hours after he went to bed.

Knowles became an immediate hit with the British sporting public, who had been inculcated to expect a Davis procession through the early rounds.

'My pride is not hurt,' Davis told newspaper reporters. 'I will go on improving for a long time yet and this defeat will make me a harder player. I enjoyed it in a masochistic way.'

Witness Davis here at his most judicious, helicoptering above the drama on the ground to reach a verdict he could tolerate, and settling for what amounted to 'bad day at the office'.

'It was my most famous win,' Knowles points out now, but he doesn't need to.

Acteson remembers the giant-killing unfolding.

'On the Saturday morning, of course we were all down there and agog to know what was going to happen. And it didn't last very long,' Acteson says. 'I would say Matchroom's grandiose plans all backfired on them a little bit.

'There was no sense in the press room of any gloating. Nobody was pleased that Davis went out. We were all in a state of shock really. But not in as big a shock as Davis.

'A lot of the players were extremely pleased because Davis was absolutely dangerous. Nobody really fancied their chances against him, but Knowles went into that match with the attitude he had absolutely nothing to lose. And an awful lot to gain. And gain it he did.

'We didn't even have formal press conferences those days. The players used to come in to the press room, the green room, and we'd gather round and have a chat.

'But I remember Knowles coming in, and I said to him, "Were you nervous about the prospect of beating him today? I mean, did you get a good night's sleep?"

He looked at me as if I was mad and goes, "No, I went out clubbing."

Josephine's was a place where we all used to go, and he'd have loved soaking up the attention, particularly from any pretty girls that might have caught his eye. At the time, he was a very, very good looking lad from Bolton.

'Nobody expected this result, this was a bomb gone off at the World Championship.

'Steve was very subdued, very brief. All that would have done was make Davis more determined.'

Given the expansion of the tournament in 1982, a host of new faces were still finding their way around the labyrinthine backstage areas of the Crucible as Davis tumbled to defeat.

One of these was Jim Donnelly, the first Scotsman to play in the World Championship at Sheffield.

Donnelly recalls the demise of the reigning champion as an occurrence that drew gasps of astonishment from rivals.

'We were sitting in the players' lounge watching it, and nobody could believe what was happening. The players just couldn't believe it,' Donnelly says. 'Knowles played unbelievable snooker. He looked like he was playing in a knockabout match.

'When you played Steve Davis, or players like him, if you missed an easy ball, or played a bad safety shot, you went and sat down because you didn't expect to get back to the table, because that's how good they were.

'But big Tony, it was as if he was just having a day out playing snooker, and Davis couldn't put him under pressure at all. It was just frame after frame after frame. There was silence in the players' lounge.

'Most of the players were sitting and watching. There's nothing to do, nowhere else for them really to go other than to walk about the centre of Sheffield, all the shops, while waiting for a practice table.

'Everybody was gobsmacked, nobody could believe what was happening and I think Steve couldn't believe it either.'

Davis was floored, as were his supporters across the country.

'It's funny, it was so unexpected,' recalls Jason Ferguson.

In 1982, Ferguson was a 12-year-old snooker nut, living for the game in Mansfield, destined for a journeyman professional's career in the sport. It was one that would lead to bigger things.

In 2020, Ferguson completed a decade as chairman of the World Professional Billiards and Snooker Association, sitting on the board alongside Davis for much of that time. He is a practised baby-kisser with an infectious passion for promoting cue sports.

He has become an impartial observer, but on the cusp of his teens Ferguson was firmly in the Davis fan club.

'I remember hearing the score in '82 and it was like, "What? Somebody beat Steve Davis?" I was stunned. But it was a great moment for Tony Knowles and he went on to become a real star,' Ferguson says.

'I was a Davis fan because I remember Steve winning that first world title a year earlier. I had this little book that's still on my shelf. It's called Steve Davis: Snooker Champion, and it's the first book that Steve wrote. I read Steve's life story shortly after that 1981 final and I became a big fan. He was the robot; he was the winner.'

Davis was certainly a serial winner, which meant the defeats were increasingly attention-grabbing.

Donnelly recalls Hearn being skilled at easing Davis out of the line of fire.

'What Barry Hearn did with him was he kept him away. He didn't want him mixing with the other players,' Donnelly said.

While Donnelly talks of 'unbelievable snooker' from Knowles, those supposed high watermarks bear closer examination. This was a match that might forever be remembered, its highlights replayed, but the suggestion that Knowles blew away Davis with break after break can be efficiently debunked.

'One thing you have to say, and I think it's important,' says the journalist and commentator Phil Yates, 'is that although the Davis-Knowles first-round match was an extraordinary story and it remains arguably the greatest shock of all time – not so much the result but the scoreline – you have to bear in mind that the match was very, very poor.

'If you watch it back now, the standard of the match was just awful. People will say that Knowlesy played brilliantly, but he had two breaks over 50 and that was it.

'Davis had a high break of 32. So that's a myth that's got to be put to bed, that Knowles played out of his skin.'

All these years on, David Hendon charitably describes it as 'not a classic'.

'It was a terrible match,' adds Hendon, hacking the varnish from his initial verdict. 'Steve was completely flat and couldn't play, Knowles didn't play great. Great win for him, but the standard was not good.'

Fellow journalist Nick Metcalfe wonders whether the standard of the potting really mattered given the seismic nature of the outcome.

'It makes me think hard about the nature of sport that such a result can happen,' Metcalfe says. 'It was a really bad match, not great quality, but it was a great story. So that must have boosted all of them, including Alex Higgins, enormously.'

* *

Acteson admired the performance of Knowles that day but over time would conclude this new star of the Crucible had an inflated opinion of his talent.

The long-time snooker scribe harked back to a clash at Newcastle's Eldon Square, the venue where Davis meted out a 9-2 slapping to Knowles in the 1984 Jameson International Open final.

'I remember Knowles broke off in one frame, and he broke them up from the back and scattered them everywhere as if to say, "Go on then, see what you can do with that."'

What Davis soon did, Acteson says, was win the frame with the sort of clinical break that had proved beyond him when he hopelessly flatlined at the Crucible.

'Because Tony knew,' said Acteson, 'despite that first win, he was never, ever in Steve Davis' class.

'He was a decent player but not as good as he thought he was.'

**

Davis and Knowles have spoken often about their 1982 match in the years since, but rarely while in the same room. There was one instance, however, when they dissected the result mano a mano.

That came in 2000, on Sky Sports' Steve Davis & Friends chat show, a curio on the schedule.

While Knowles Cheshire-catted his way through the conversation, Davis told him: 'I remember the first frame being very scrappy. All of a sudden, I lost the first frame and then you looked like a god on the table. You never missed a ball.

'I remember the whole match as a nightmare. I remember thinking I was being outplayed but also that it was out of my control.'

They reflected on Knowles reaching the quarter-finals, where 'Steady' Eddie Charlton stunned the Crucible's new pin-up by recovering from 11-6 behind to snatch a 13-11 win, but Davis stressed he could not remember any of that.

'For the next week and a half my life was an alcoholic blur. My life fell apart,' Davis said.

In conversation for this book in May 2022, Davis explained how he had simply not been ready to leave Sheffield after the Knowles mauling, having arrived with the intention of going the distance.

'I remember going on a bender up there,' Davis said. 'It felt like I didn't want to go home. I was a bit lost for a while, not knowing what to do, because the tournament was still going on. I hung around up there and had a laugh.

'I had nothing else planned, obviously, so I used the time unwisely.'

By the time Davis and Hearn had returned to the drawing board and begun the process of plotting a more failsafe dominance of the seasons to come, the overnight success story of Knowles was being feted.

Inevitably, thoughts in the Knowles camp on that famous Saturday in Crucible history turned to how such an unexpected success should be celebrated.

The new crown prince of potting would not be back in action until the following Wednesday. The doors of Josephine's would be swinging open again in a matter of hours.

6: 'Oh Georgie, Georgie Best, what a waste!'

KEN DOHERTY draws you in with his perky, brisk storytelling and that reassuringly cheerful nature.

The 1997 world champion is always good for a lively soundbite, a snappy anecdote or a smart quip. It makes him a terrific pundit and commentator, a man who understands the pace of the game, its nuances and, most crucially for his BBC work, its audience. A popular and punchy potter in his peak playing days, 'Crafty Ken' offers knowledge few can match alongside an all-important light touch.

He's a friend of the press, welcome in our midst, never one to give it the big 'I am'.

By contrast, Phil Yates can remember hiding in toilets at a Blackpool hotel to avoid Alex Higgins, as the big bad Belfast wolf snarled outside: 'Come out, come out, wherever you are.'

Sometimes, a Higgins exclusive just wasn't worth the trouble.

But Yates, like many others, would never pass up an opportunity to talk to Doherty.

It was a wonder that Higgins and Doherty forged such a friendship as they did, given their strikingly disparate characters.

Doherty had high levels of tolerance when it came to Higgins though, not least because at the age of 12 he watched from afar with wide-eyed wonder at his fellow Irishman carrying off the 1982 World Championship title.

From the family living room in Ranelagh, a Dublin suburb, Doherty was immediately smitten with Higgins. The renegade who had conquered the snooker world once before was doing so again a decade down the line, and this time it meant more.

Volatile as Higgins was, Doherty adored him, not only in 1982 but until the end.

Doherty played many exhibitions with Higgins, including one shortly after his own World Championship triumph, a testimonial of sorts for the Hurricane at the Waterfront Hall in Belfast. Doherty may have been the champion of the day, but Higgins was still a monumental draw. For a while, though his ranking was forever slipping, Higgins remained tenuously competitive. Later, it was his presence rather than his potting that brought in the crowds.

'I once brought him down to play – or I got the sponsors to invite him down to play – at the Irish Professional Championships down in Dublin,' Doherty recalls.

It was the mid-2000s, with a sick Higgins still clinging to the pipe dream of a tour comeback.

'I knew he was struggling for money, so I told them, "Give him a few bob, he'll come down if I ring him up,"' Doherty said.

'So I called Alex and said, "Look Alex, come down, I've got a few bob for you. You'll pick up fifteen hundred quid, you're going to play the Irish Professional Championships, just come down on the train and practise with me. I'll take you up to play in the evening and whether you win or lose they're going to give you fifteen hundred quid."'

Higgins made many enemies over his career, but none would have wished on him the dreadful throat cancer that ravaged him from his late forties and for most of the rest of his life.

Doherty, like many others in snooker, Jimmy White notable among them, never gave up on Higgins.

So, not only was he inviting Higgins to earn a shilling, but Doherty was beckoning him to spend time with a community that cared for his wellbeing. By asking Higgins to practise with him, at Doherty's own basement snooker room in a city centre hotel, it amounted to an arm around the shoulder for a friend in need. There was an element of trust too: Doherty needed Higgins to make good on his pledge to show up.

'He was recovering from his cancer; he was very unwell, very skinny having lost a lot of weight,' Doherty says.

'And he came down on the train and came through to the practice room at the Radisson Hotel at ten o'clock in the morning, and he's got the Racing Post in his pocket, he's got the fedora hat on, and I said to Alex, "D'you want something to eat?" And he said, "No, just get me a pint of Guinness, babes."

'I told him, "Alex, it's ten o'clock in the morning," and he said, "There's enough iron in that to see me through the day, keep me going."

'He gets that pint, he pulls the Racing Post out of his pocket and picks his four horses for his Lucky 15, and he goes around the room, smoking his cigarette, and honestly he looked only seven or eight stone.

'He's smoking and drinking and looking at the photographs on the wall, and his photograph was on the wall more than any other snooker player's. I bring him over to a photograph of when I played George Best in Dublin. I knew Alex knew him, and he used to play him when George played for Manchester United, because Higgins lived in Manchester at the time.'

Doherty is a big United supporter.

'I said to Alex, "Here's an old friend of yours, you might recognise him."

'And he's got the glasses on the bridge of his nose, he takes a drag of his cigarette, a sup at his Guinness, and he looks at the picture and goes, "Oh Georgie, Georgie Best, what a waste!"

'Alex cracked me up, he absolutely cracked me up.'

Tuesday, March 9, 2021.

The Darling of Dublin has spent the afternoon with perhaps snooker's greatest survivor of them all: Jimmy White. The encounter is purely for practice's sake this time, but put yourself in a room with two of snooker's colossal characters and imagine the to-ing and fro-ing, the storytelling, the streetwise wit of White trading off against the wisdom, the sharp one-liners and the belly laughs from Doherty. Also, imagine the unrelenting competitiveness between them.

And now Doherty is at the wheel, breezing through lockdown traffic, cue in the boot. A day's work complete, snooker still the game that gets him out of bed in the morning, brings in the work, preys on the mind.

With a combined age falling roughly a clearance of the colours short of 147, Doherty and White have been beneficiaries of the benevolence of Barry Hearn, tour wild cards being gift-wrapped to these venerable veterans whose appetite for the game remains an example to the younger generation.

These two baize grandmasters went head to head in a magnificent Grand Prix final all the way back in 1992, White snatching a 10-9 victory at Reading's Hexagon Theatre.

The never-ending pursuit of perfection goes on for both, though their best days are surely long gone. They met in the 1994 World Championship quarter-finals too, the tournament where Doherty toppled Alex Higgins in round one, ending the Crucible career of the Hurricane.

<u>Monday, April 18, 1994</u>

Doherty versus Higgins was a clash not only of generations but of extremes in temperament, the mild-mannered Dubliner versus the volatile son of Belfast. And yet it served too as a meeting of men who held plenty in common, and who would forge a powerful friendship that would continue through to Doherty being a pallbearer at Higgins' funeral.

Back in 1994, to the 24-year-old Doherty this Sheffield first-round battle was a match where he had to take the win and run. Move on to the next. There could be no glory in beating a ramshackle Higgins, in sending his idol home with a pocketful of loser's money.

'I beat Alex in that match, but I tell you, it was a hollow victory,' Doherty says. 'It was the last time Alex played in the World Championship at the Crucible and he was my hero, the reason I was playing snooker.'

Over the course of morning and evening sessions, Doherty earned a 10-6 result over his boyhood favourite, but tackling Higgins was far from a giddy experience for the player who three years later would lift the World Championship trophy himself.

There are moments Doherty remembers fondly. There was an early start and that meant Higgins started sober, or certainly not well-oiled.

But Doherty found it a painful task as he went through the

motions against a player long past his prime. In the morning, Doherty built a 6-3 lead, making four breaks over 50 including an 83, the best of the session, against an opponent who peaked with a 49 in the penultimate frame before lunch.

'Alex was arguing with John Williams, the referee, and it was quite funny. He was trying to get John Williams to stand on his left when John was standing behind him,' Doherty says.

'Alex couldn't see him, even though it gets quite tight around the Crucible when the division is down.

'John said to him, "Alex, I'm not in your line of sight, I've been standing here all day." And Alex comes out with the perfect line – "John, you're not in my line of sight, you're in my line of thought."

'Alex had me in stitches in my chair, laughing at that one.'

Doherty creases with laughter again as he recalls the moment. Higgins has been credited with using that line on a previous occasion too. It belongs to his greatest hits. Some recall the incident in the Doherty match slightly differently and point to Higgins being more chippy than quippy.

Whatever was said in that flashpoint, Williams was big enough to take any verbal jousting from Higgins. The no-nonsense Welshman would win a war of words with Higgins any night of the week. Higgins might have been an agitator, but he was also well schooled in picking the right time to duck out of a fight, and he reluctantly acceded to authority once Williams stood his ground.

Doherty got the job done, disappointing Higgins' legion of followers in the Crucible that night, nudging his hero a foot further down that slippery slope.

'I was as nervous as a kitten playing him, because he was getting more drunk as the match went on,' Doherty says.

'He was twitching, he was having arguments with Williams, but I eventually got over the line. But I do regard that as a very hollow victory and I never got any pleasure out of it to be honest with you.'

As Doherty drew breath that night, Higgins spat repudiations.

The 45-year-old took his ire towards Williams to the press and told reporters, according to a report in The Independent the following day: 'Some referees don't know how to walk backwards. I still know how to walk backwards even with six Guinnesses down me... and sideways as well – and I can still pot balls.'

Sunday, May 16, 1982

On day two of the 1982 Embassy World Championship final, everyone had a favourite. The death-or-glory Higgins, an arch provocateur, or the 49-year-old Ray Reardon, the Welsh Dracula with the winning grin and charm to match.

'I was at home. My father was a big Ray Reardon fan, you know, and I was an Alex Higgins fan,' Doherty remembers.

'In 1982 we shared the moment of that match. It makes it more poignant for me because we sat down and we watched that World Championship together.

'He was cheering for Ray Reardon and of course I was cheering on Alex.'

Doherty's father, Anthony – Tony to many – would sadly die in June 1983, gone much too soon at the age of 58.

He went 'quite suddenly', Doherty remembers, Anthony suffering the heart attack that meant he would be denied seeing the family grow up; denied, too, a front-row seat for the moments that have seen his son become one of Ireland's great sporting heroes.

In that 1982 moment, however, it was father's favourite versus son's superman, a family occasion that Doherty will always carry with him.

'My dad used to let me watch Pot Black when I was eight or nine,' Doherty says.

'It used to come on quite late, at around nine o'clock, and I should have been in bed really by that time, but he knew I loved the game and he let me watch it, but I remember distinctly watching that 1982 World Championship with him and particularly the final, because we were on different sides of the fence.

'Because I'd seen Alex Higgins on Pot Black by then, I was already fascinated by snooker. When I was little, I got a little snooker table from Santa, it was at the end of my bunk bed on Christmas morning, you know.

'And I followed Higgins, he was my favourite, although I loved Jimmy White as well. That year, that World Championship, really did it for me, in wanting to become a player.

'I was about 12, just going on 13 that year. I was 12 when Higgins won it and it sort of convinced me that this was what I wanted to do.'

Dad dutifully bought young Ken a 6ft x 3ft snooker table that following Christmas, a step-up from Santa's starter table. It was one of a number of crucial nudges towards that dream career for Doherty.

Few of the watching millions would have been unresponsive to Higgins' snap reaction to toppling Reardon: wiping back tears of joy, embracing Lauren, particularly, and Lynn.

Doherty was so touched by the entirety of that tournament, and his snooker progress would be so rapid, that his practice became more consequential, his study of the game's subtleties running alongside his school studies, often to the dismay of mum Rose.

The snooker club Jason's, a stone's throw from the family home, was by now a regular pit-stop on the way back from Westland Row Christian Brothers school, and Doherty was Irish Under-16 champion within 18 months.

'When I saw Alex beating Jimmy White in the semi-final and then winning it a few days later, crying, and then the baby coming on, it was such an iconic moment for Irish sport and for me personally,' Doherty says.

'That was a real inspiration for me to want to play snooker seriously. I was just starting to get pretty good at it and it was only in August 1983, the year later, when I won my first national title.

'But Higgins and that World Championship was huge for me and I'm sure it was the same for the likes of Stephen Hendry, Peter Ebdon, Alan McManus, all players from that sort of era who became stars of the nineties.

'He was so charismatic, he was so unpredictable, and he was such a character, the way he smiled, the way he twitched, and of course the shots that he would play, the more adventurous shots. He was a real entertainer and he drew so many people to the game. So many people would watch snooker purely because of Alex Higgins and that's what happened with me: he drew me to the game. I have a lot to thank Higgins for.'

There has perhaps been no figure in snooker's history who splits opinion quite like Higgins. In 1982, however, he was a unifier in a sense.

'Without a shadow of a doubt he was loved all across Ireland at that time,' Doherty says.

'I think that was the one great thing about sport, and in our case snooker, that it sort of crossed the divide between the Catholics and the Protestants.

'Even though Higgins was a Protestant, coming from the Shankill Road, which was a predominantly Protestant area – Sandy Row he was from – both Catholics and Protestants revered him, and there was no distinction in that sense between whatever side of the fence you were on.

'People just loved him, north and south of the border. I remember going to school the next day, after the World Championship, and everyone had been watching it. It was a huge moment, iconic for us.'

7: 'PROPER SNOOKER GROUPIES'

JOSEPHINE'S MARKETED itself as 'the north's most exciting and celebrated niteclub', attracting the wealthy, the brassy and the beautiful. This meant footballers, the newly minted, the aspirational on their way to becoming South Yorkshire's yuppie set, and anybody chasing a slice of such action. They all flocked there on a weekend. This was Sheffield's discotheque du jour for those who considered their high-end taste discerning, for those who felt no guilt in flaunting their affluence in a city where many were struggling to make ends meet.

And for those who were dancing the night away on shoestring funds, Josie's would provide relief from the grief of reality.

Here was a slinky saloon, trading in pop-picker glamour, and along with its regular club nights it was the host venue for a regional leg of the 'Miss Lovely Legs of Great Britain' contest. A bumper first-prize bundle at that event in 1981 included a weekend's stay at Butlins in Margate for the Miss Lovely Legs national semi-finals, a £150 holiday voucher, a year's worth of make-up and six pairs of Pretty Polly tights.

For Tony Knowles, Cliff Thorburn, Alex Higgins and the cue-toting crew, it was the place to unwind after a long day in the Crucible.

'I think I was probably in there with them most of the time,' says Barry Hearn. 'Today you couldn't go in a place like that because of social media, but it was a different world then and we used to party strong, all of us.'

Thorburn, a fashion-conscious disco lover, could pull on his glad rags and hit the dance floor.

'One thing's for sure: if we went there, we weren't playing the next day,' says Thorburn.

'If Alex was over there, at one side of the club, I'd go over there, away from him. But we all had fun there. I'd love to see somebody I was due to play, if I went out dancing, and if that guy was pissed in the nightclub, beautiful.'

There must have been some memorably great nights in Josie's. Why not ask a club connoisseur.

'Probably, somewhere down the line,' Knowles says, with a smile. 'I like the vibe in Sheffield now, but even though snooker's on the up, the vibe's nowhere near how it was in the eighties.

'In the eighties the vibe was so much different. You'd get the girls outside the dressing rooms, everywhere. They'd line up outside the Grosvenor Hotel. It was the main place for the snooker.

'You got proper snooker groupies in those days.'

It was not Knowles' safety game that was drawing in the late-night admirers.

Debonair and handsome, he was thought of as snooker's answer to Shakin' Stevens, the comely Welsh Elvis whose rockabilly floor-shakers were regular chart-cloggers.

Green baize rather than Green Door, it would be getting the green light from a string of women that blew up Knowles' fame.

Knowles went on to become a tabloid figure, headlines of "What a break! Three birds in my bed" and "Tony you're a lousy lover" serving as examples of a particular transcendent appeal, the sort that drew frowns and fines from snooker's blazer brigade.

By May 1984, a send-up in the pages of Viz pilloried Knowles, a parody in which the 'Lancashire Hot Pot' was credited with taking 'so many girls back to my room with me the floor collapsed', the magazine's pseudo Tony reasoning that sexiness was affecting his cue action.

Knowles was ripe for being lampooned, but he was hardly alone in enjoying himself.

**

The authorities could control the players inside the Crucible, but once those men spilled out on to Norfolk Street, Sheffield was theirs to explore.

Rumours abound locally about what went down when the snooker set descended on Josephine's, and Knowles' recollection of 'proper snooker groupies' suggests he was not lacking for female interest when out and about.

From Thorburn's perspective, the club's music was always the draw.

'You couldn't be stupid,' Thorburn says. 'I've been stupid enough in my life, but at that time in my life, I was entering my thirties. I loved music and dancing and I guess Josephine's was the best Sheffield had to offer.'

By 1982, Mike Ganley, son of the popular referee Len Ganley, was about the age at which he would be allowed to discover what the extra-curricular fuss was all about.

'There were places where all the players used to go,' recalls Ganley, a spectator during the 1982 tournament as his father called the shots inside the arena, keeping players in line.

'They used to eat at certain restaurants after matches, rather than going back to their hotel rooms and being good boys and getting up and going to the gym.

'They might have been out at certain nightclubs – Roxy's or Josephine's, wherever it happened to be – and it was a slightly different environment. It's like when you look at the footballers, and instead of going back on the bus and going to bed, they used to go out and have a few beers and have a chat.

'Josephine's was the main place in Sheffield for a long, long time, and I think it suited both elements, even the older players, because you had a nice restaurant upstairs where people could go and have a nice meal and look down on the dance floor without needing to get involved in it. It was a friendly environment and the players were a lot more social, in the fact that it wasn't as serious as it is now.'

John Airey, a great friend of 2005 Crucible semi-finalist Ian McCulloch, has been a regular World Championship attendee since 1981, after a Christmas wish bore fruit with semi-final and final tickets.

At the age of 14, he visited for the first time with dad John – 'Doc' – and mum Val. Over the next four decades, Sheffield became the Penrith-based family's home for 17 days in April and May, the Airey clan becoming front-row mainstays.

The young John had to wait for a first real glimpse of Sheffield's nightlife, and Josephine's failed to reach the heights of the hype.

'It was an old brown building that looked like an office block from the outside. There were lots of mirrors. It was quite a low-ceilinged place with glitter balls and all that razzle-dazzle,' Airey says. 'It was the height of cheese. Knowles was a habitual visitor and considered quite the Lothario.'

Steve Davis would get the VIP treatment and, as such, he

counters the notion it was a tacky spot.

'I don't think it was cheesy,' says Davis. 'Josephine's was a decent nightclub with a restaurant, far from seedy.

'During the tournaments it felt like I reined everything in, but we'd go there maybe if you had enough days to recover. And there was another place called Napoleon's, which was a casino up Eccleshall Road. One of the good things about both places was you could get late-night food.'

** **

Everyone who made it to the 32-man draw in 1982 was assured of £1,250, a handy pay day, with the champion collecting £25,000, the biggest prize pot in snooker.

In tennis, Jimmy Connors pocketed almost £42,000 later that year for winning Wimbledon, while runner-up John McEnroe collected £20,833. Tom Watson picked up £32,000 for triumphing in The Open at Royal Troon.

Snooker was riding high and keeping good company in the money league, but prize pots in professional sport were about to soar as money flooded in from television and sponsors.

By 2022, the World Championship rewards had shot up to £20,000 for a first-round main-draw loser, with a cool £500,000 for the last man standing. The Wimbledon singles winners, however, earned £2million, and the Open champion took home close to £2.1million.

Yet taking inflation into account, snooker's purse had shot up to four times its 1982 value, and the level of dedication has surged accordingly. If a player is seen blind drunk during the championship now – and this occasionally does happen – you can usually be assured he was knocked out earlier in the day.

Comparing the early 1980s to the modern day, Mike Ganley says: 'The money difference is massive. I think they tended to enjoy themselves a bit more and go out more, and I wouldn't say they misbehaved but they enjoyed themselves a lot more.'

Ganley has been a World Snooker tournament director for 20 years at the time of writing. He'll never be a star of the show, but he efficiently keeps it running, going to admirable extremes when needed. It was his 'stinky old shoes' Ronnie O'Sullivan borrowed when his own began to rub during a 2015 first-round match and he was refused permission to play in socks.

* *

In 1982, the 10-year-old Sheffield schoolboy Brendan Moore was more likely to be playing football games on his Spectrum home computer than following the snooker with a keen eye.

And it was not until the decade was almost over that Moore, a future three-time Crucible final referee, had his first taste of Sheffield's nightlife.

'Roxy's is where we used to go as 16 or 17-year-olds, and that was just across the road from the Crucible,' Moore says. 'You get eighties reunions there now. It's a big concert venue, too.

'There was another club in Sheffield that used to be called Cairo Jax, and we used to go to Roxy's on a Friday, Cairo Jax on a Saturday and Josephine's on a Monday. At Roxy's, your feet would stick to the floor. Josephine's was more upmarket.

'Josephine's attracted the footballers a lot. All the snooker players used to go, and the refs would go there too if they had a night off.'

Roxy's was a 2,500-capacity cavern of a club and lacked the allure of Josephine's to the moneyed classes, but it was accessible to the masses. This meant it was usually a spot to avoid for the prominent potters.

As many a nouveau riche cueman would come to discover, the rush of fame and fortune was the sunny side of snooker becoming Britain's favourite new television sport. The darker side was the media's clamour for information about the private lives of players. Most players could take that in their stride and were squeaky clean; others whirled through day after day of unabashed chaos.

Among the snooker writers, some would have been hypocritical had they scandalised the after-hours conduct of the players, seeing as they were hardly monastery material themselves, but a growing number of news journalists began to descend on Sheffield, knowing the burgeoning sport had characters that could provide gold for the front pages of a morning paper as well as the back.

Steve Acteson has great memories of his time within the snooker press pack. These were the journalists all the players knew, respected and socialised with out of hours.

The news reporters were the ones that had the stars looking over their shoulders.

As long as it was the snooker writers mixing with the players, everyone concerned would have a roaring time away from the venue.

'Josephine's at that time was a preeminent night spot in Sheffield. It doesn't sound a lot, but it was, it was a good club,' Acteson says.

'We were lucky because for years, if you had an Embassy pass with you for the Crucible, that got you into Josephine's. You could pass the line and they'd let you in – players, press, whoever you were, pretty much. If you were one of the press or a player, you'd get in there and you'd get in for nothing.

'You had the dance floor down the bottom, then there was a great big bar and some steps up to a sort of VIP area where we would all mingle together, including us "reptiles" of the press.

'And it was great fun. There was a big dining area there as well that served pretty good food – steak and chips and stuff like that.

'We could go up in that VIP area, but not for the purpose of interviewing. We'd be there having a good time as well. This was all off duty when you went to Josie's. You'd go down there for a drink, for the craic, have a good time. The work had been done.

'And then, as you were leaving, I always used to notice things on the way back to the hotel. Outside there would be two or three burger vans. And because the tournament always started in April, the weather would not always be particularly warm. But in Sheffield the girls would be out with sleeveless dresses and skimpy dresses. The lads would be out in trousers and a smart shirt, but no jacket.

'It doesn't matter what the weather was, this was how they dressed, because they were out clubbing and having a good time. It was quite strange to look at, but it was all part of the Sheffield culture.'

* *

Higgins had been close to John Virgo for over a decade before the 1982 World Championship. Virgo has told of the time he visited Higgins soon after the Hurricane landed his first world title, in 1972, and found his great mate living almost in squalor.

Both men came to suffer from calamitous gambling problems, and Virgo liked a tipple, but not in the same way that Higgins would drink a bar dry, given the chance.

Virgo knew his friend had a target on his back whenever he went out on the tiles, whether in Sheffield or any city.

This concerned Virgo, just as it worried him that the snooker set did not only have to watch out for an eager public, but for a voracious tabloid press too.

'It is a different world now,' Virgo said, nostalgic for the time when players could roam free of those twin buzz-killers: press intrusion and social media.

Any newspaper reporter surreptitiously trailing a snooker player around Sheffield today would likely have to explain away a wasted day to their editor.

The professionals largely live up to their billing in the modern era. With so much money on the line, to take any risk while competing in the final event of the season would be considered an outlandishly cavalier move.

'You look at Alex, and Ronnie and Jimmy White as well,' says Mark Selby, whose world titles in 2014, 2016, 2017 and 2021 were founded on hard graft.

'I know Jimmy's not won it, but for those guys, their lifestyles, and just the way they are as people, for them to go on and reach the final or win the tournament is remarkable. You know that Alex was probably not going to go back to his room between sessions and think, "Right, I'm just going to chill out for a few hours."

'He was probably still going out drinking, he'll be smoking, and going to clubs and stuff like this.

'To win it is hard enough, but to win it with that lifestyle is probably doubly as hard and it's even more of an achievement.'

Higgins was no saint during his 1982 Sheffield stay, but largely he kept within personal parameters of moderation and gave the elbow to excess. The exact nature of those parameters went with Higgins to his grave. He was doing his best to kick a destructive vodka habit, but a local milk stout remained a favourite.

The modern-day potter might sound an anodyne breed by comparison, but with the great pleasure seeker O'Sullivan having thrived on a health food diet and exercise plan, the benefits have been clear for the rest to see.

It means, much to the disappointment of the romantics and nostalgists, today's players are more likely to be working out in the gym or catching up on television series when not competing, rather than creating a soap opera of their own.

Shaun Murphy is another who is unlikely to be keeping the bar staff company until closing time.

'I've tried all sorts,' says Murphy, as we meet in the Crucible foyer. 'Between games I've been around the venue, spent time in players' lounges, and that doesn't really work for me.

'I won't be here unless I'm playing or practising. A good box set, a bit of Netflix, a bit of iPlayer, all that stuff can be massive because you do need a distraction.'

He has also found working as a BBC commentator a soothing diversion from the stress of competition, balancing that with the benefits of switching off completely.

'It's quite nice to get into your room sometimes, slap the iPad on and watch something completely different,' Murphy says.

Perhaps this 'quite nice' out-of-office lifestyle won't cut it for those that pine for cue chaos and baize brawlers, but Murphy's low-key approach served him well as he reached the 2021 Crucible final.

* *

Scotland's Jim Donnelly, who drew Ray Reardon in round one back in 1982, recalls his solo mission to the Crucible with fondness.

'When I went down to Sheffield, I was on my own,' Donnelly said. 'That was because of the venue and where it was. When I went to Preston for the UK Championship, I had about half a dozen of the boys with me – it's only two hours or so down the road from Glasgow. But Sheffield was a different situation and it was a bit more expensive for them to get there. Fortunately, my expenses were covered with the guaranteed prize money.

'We had a few good nights in Josephine's. We'd go to Mike Watterson's snooker club too, practising up there when we couldn't get on the table at the Crucible.'

Watterson was the man who brought snooker to the Crucible in 1977, and it was Michael Watterson Ltd that staged the 1982 World Championship. He had a club on nearby West Street that provided top-notch tables for the professionals, should they be inclined to venture from the Crucible. Watterson was an accomplished player himself.

'We'd get a bite to eat up there and then all ended up in Josephine's late at night, and that was a place, so it was,' Donnelly says.

A left-hander, Donnelly has worked both as a snooker coach and fitness instructor since retiring as a player.

The 1982 visit was his lone Crucible appearance, but Donnelly maintained a top-100 ranking for almost a decade. There are countless stories to tell, and Donnelly is drawn to an encounter with Higgins at the 1983 International Open, played in Newcastle.

Donnelly battled past David Taylor in round one and was on a high, while Higgins was sent scuttling out of the tournament by the north east's own Dave Martin.

Higgins was at a low ebb, life fast unravelling off the table as his marriage crumbled, results providing scant succour. But amid his troubles he retained a magnetic presence.

'For this one, I had a couple of my mates come down with me. And once the match was played, we all decided to go up towards this nightclub, and there was myself, my two or three mates, and a couple of other players, Eugene Hughes and Dessie Sheehan,' Donnelly says.

'When we got in, there were two bars, one at one side and one at the other. And one of the bars was full up and you couldn't see any guys up there; it was all women. I thought, "We're going over there."

'When we got over to this bar, we suddenly found out why there were so many women there, and it was because the barmen were all bodybuilders with skimpy shorts and no tops on, and muscles coming out of their ears.

'I don't drink but we all got something from the bar, and all of a sudden everything changed, and all the women moved across to the other bar. And we were like, "Where are they going?"

'It turned out that the Hurricane and one of the other top players had walked in, and word got about that Hurricane Higgins was at the other bar, so all the women left us for dead.'

Higgins would have company, invited or not, wherever he roamed in the early 1980s. Trouble and temptation were usually close at hand, and it was obvious by now he would spend the rest of his life under the public glare.

8: Losing really is the pits for Ray

Ray Reardon had won six world titles by the time he rolled up in Sheffield for another shot at the big one in 1982.

He would leave as runner-up, the nearly man of the 17 days.

Reardon drove home having clinched the number one ranking for the 1982-83 season, which is hardly bad going for a man just months away from his 50th birthday.

Yet the trouble with consolation prizes such as this is they rarely provide any meaningful solace.

Finishing second at any World Championship – snooker, swimming, worm charming – is a sure-fire signifier of high achievement, but the moment of falling just short typically brings about nothing but overwhelming deflation and anguish.

Losing to anybody in a Crucible final would have brought misery for Reardon; it made it all the more unpalatable for it to have been Higgins, a career caner and anti-establishment figure, who lifted the trophy and banked the big cheque.

Forty years on, and Reardon's annoyance at how the spotlight has continued to shine on Higgins lingers.

This is a shame, because for those who know the game,

Reardon's feat of longevity has not diminished with the passing of time.

As much as the young Ken Doherty was siding with Higgins in the 1982 final, so too he marvelled at Reardon being the player standing in the way of the pride of Belfast.

'It was incredible that he reached the final. Ray was such an iconic figure within the sport,' Doherty says.

'They called him Dracula and he had that persona. He looked like Bela Lugosi, but he was a gentleman. He was always immaculately dressed and played the game beautifully. He was already a legend of the game, but to continue to play up to that standard as he did at the age of 49 was quite incredible.

'He was a very classy player and had won the World Championship six times of course. He was wonderfully gifted and had so much class that I enjoyed watching him play, even if it was against Alex.'

Patsy Fagan, in his rookie season, played Reardon on the first morning of the first Crucible World Championship, in 1977. He grew to be awestruck by veteran Reardon's unstinting devotion to his craft.

Fagan recalls Sheffield nights with affection, occasionally going 'out with the lads', as he puts it. In that respect, he remembers Reardon would play it straight both on and off the table, preferring a quiet night away from the bustle.

'Ray wasn't the person I'd be going out with,' Fagan said. 'He'd be having a gin and tonic with Rex Williams. If we went back to the hotel, that's what we'd see at the bar.'

Williams, who became a long-serving chair of the WPBSA, was an instigator of the World Championship being revived in 1964 after it was not staged for six years. A world title-winning billiards player, his snooker peak had passed by the time of the

Crucible era, and he never won a match in the famous theatre, losing eight times in the first round.

He was 48 in 1982, a year younger than Reardon, and was brushed away 10-3 by Doug Mountjoy on the first Tuesday of the World Championship.

Reardon could ham it up with the best of the new breed of entertainers, having done his time on the holiday camp circuit, but ostensibly he was a serious man. He looked rather an old 49, having packed more into almost half a century than most would settle for over a lifetime.

He declined to be interviewed for this book, unwilling to have any part in a Higgins-centred project, sticking to his guns at the invitation to simply recount his own story of that tournament.

Our short conversation was cordial enough, but it was obvious Reardon remained aggrieved at the attention afforded the man whose career trophy haul paled against his own. It was telling that Reardon did not even wish to brief the BBC any further about the Higgins match when interviewed later for Louis Theroux's Gods of Snooker series.

'There's something wrong here, something wrong,' Reardon said in front of the cameras on that show. 'You're pushing the wrong guy. They don't even mention me these days. They go back as far as he [Higgins] does but they don't go back any further than that. I won it six times; he won it twice.'

I admire Reardon, to a point, for pushing away my interest and also not kowtowing to the TV cameras on that occasion. All being well, when I reach my late 80s, reliving the most painful days of my own career will probably not be high on the priority list. The Welshman's achievements stand up to any scrutiny, whereas Higgins lacked the dedication and discipline that was a hallmark of Reardon's game and his results often suffered accordingly. Of course Reardon was going to give me short shrift; 1982 still hurts.

Reardon's snooker life, a famous journey from colliery club to the Crucible, made for a wonderful career, and reaching the 1982 final of the Worlds remains a phenomenal achievement. It would have been a pleasure to hear the great son of Tredegar recount his run through the draw, taking down Jim Donnelly, then John Virgo, Silvino Francisco and Eddie Charlton – each by a five-frame cushion – before tackling Higgins. I'd have loved to hear his memories of this Sheffield sojourn, but the message was loud and clear.

Just when it appeared Reardon had maybe spoken his final word on Higgins, up he cropped in a short docufilm for BBC Wales in early 2022, and what he said this time spoke volumes about how a two-day snooker contest four decades earlier remained a jarring memory.

He began by describing the 1982 final as 'a really good game of snooker', and stated he was convinced victory was coming his way once he plotted a route back from 15-12 adrift to 15-all.

Memories fail the best of us, and Reardon misremembered when the interval came in the final session, suggesting it fell once he had pulled all square rather than at 15-14 as was actually the case.

Reardon speculated in the BBC Wales interview that Higgins was a substance-emboldened opponent by the time the players returned to the table. He asserted that Higgins left for the interval 'a loser' and returned a changed man, having 'taken something'.

The one-time Staffordshire policeman, sniffing an injustice, claimed Higgins was drug-tested and the 'test was mislaid'. Snooker officials have privately questioned this, chiefly because the sport only introduced a formal testing policy in 1985.

Floating this theory all these years later, with Higgins no longer around to defend himself, felt at best unfair. And if anything, the drugs that Higgins did take during his career surely hindered his overall progress, rather than helped his cause. Reardon might have had greater cause to fear a wholly straight-edge Higgins.

* *

With almost half a century on the clock, Reardon decided in early 1982 it was time to slow down and rein in the exhibition matches that were keeping him on the road. He took a poke in the Sunday Mirror at young players that, to his mind, had 'never done a day's work in their lives' and expected 'money for nothing'.

Perhaps this put him halfway towards yelling at clouds, but as a player he remained highly relevant.

The Reardon generation of potters – players who typically had come into the newly professional ranks of snooker after earning a living on civvy street – were being caught and in many cases passed by the new cue brigade, and it sat uncomfortably.

Yet when Reardon turned up to the Crucible at the end of that 1981-82 season, there was little holding back the man whose world titles came in a golden nine-season spell in the 1970s.

Reardon's steady slalom through the Sheffield draw spoke volumes for his unflappability. A hard man at the table, he often served up reminders of a playful touch to his character. This camera-pleasing side hustle as snooker's pantomime japester is often overlooked, but Reardon's slicked widow's peak and toothy grin were complemented by uncanny comic timing.

'We used to do an item – a "jazz" item at the end of every championship,' recalls Nick Hunter, the BBC's then snooker boss. 'We called them the funnies, or the bloopers, and the players would absolutely love them. They would wait to see the

78

bloopers, and several shots we had of Reardon were specially for the bloopers. He only admitted it afterwards. He'd do something that brought the house down, and he told me, "That was for your bloopers, Nick."'

Having served as a miner and a bobby on the beat, Reardon emerged as the dominant player in the first 10 years of snooker's colour television era, chalking up victory in the inaugural edition of the BBC's Pot Black show in 1969 and emerging as a fitting figurehead.

Reardon connected with the viewers, who recognised in him an everyman persona, a long-time amateur sportsman getting his big break in mid-life.

Few serious sporting careers begin in a competitor's mid-thirties, but Reardon's did. Fewer still are launched after the protagonist almost dies in a mining disaster, but Reardon's famously did that too, a pit roof at Florence Colliery in Stoke-on-Trent having collapsed on him on April 30, 1957.

He was almost fatally snookered that day but found an escape, the 24-year-old soon being encouraged by girlfriend Sue, whom he would wed in 1959, to find work above ground.

By the early 1980s, the likes of Steve Davis, Terry Griffiths, Cliff Thorburn and a raw Jimmy White looked to be taking over from snooker's old guard, and even the 1982 World Championship programme characterised Reardon as 'perhaps not the force he used to be'.

Yet Reardon had won the Highland Masters in Inverness just days before heading to the Steel City, sinking John Spencer 11-4 in the final after drubbing Davis in the semi-finals.

The 1982 World Championship began 25 years to the day after Reardon's brush with death beneath a mass of coal and rubble. It was as though he was fated to play no small part.

9: CALEDONIA DREAMING

SNOOKER HAD BECOME an obsession across the British Isles because of its small-screen prominence, much like wrestling and darts, middle-distance athletics and showjumping.

As rivalries simmered between the top names, sometimes spilling over, audiences at home were drawn in by the bombastic storylines before staying for the world-class action. It was happening widely across these newly exposed sports.

Giant Haystacks and Big Daddy were feuding former tag-team pals; Eric Bristow and Jocky Wilson were fierce foes at the oche but drinking pals later in the evening; and the perceived enmity between Steve Ovett and Seb Coe propelled both to new heights on the track. Ovett later contended the friction had been blown out of proportion, but any insinuation of a frosty relationship between the pair was hardly going to be bad for business, and the way they chased records and medals at the other's expense pointed to at least an intense eagerness for one-upmanship.

The top 20 cuemen in 1982 were primed to share £2million in the calendar year, the Sunday Mirror reported, and Steve Davis was creaming off easily the heftiest chunk of that cash mountain.

Beefs were big business, and if any snooker feuds began to froth up, it would hardly have been prudent from a business perspective to broker truce talks. Television audiences lapped up the Higgins-Davis rivalry and the Higgins and Thorburn hostility, along with the snooker-on-the-edge style of Jimmy White and Kirk Stevens.

Deep-pocketed sponsors – tobacco firms, brewers and bookies – flocked to the sport, and players who honed their skills in grimy snooker halls were suddenly living the millionaire lifestyle.

First Division footballers of that era were trousering average income of a little under £40,000 after bonuses and appearance money. Snooker's elite knew they could top that.

Reardon was said to be making hundreds of pounds nightly for exhibitions before getting off that gravy train, while Higgins and particularly the dominant Davis could almost name their price.

When Reardon began his 1982 campaign in Sheffield, on Sunday, May 2, a Scotsman stepped up as the opposition.

Jim Donnelly, who came from 7-3 behind to scrape past fellow Scot Eddie Sinclair 9-8 in the final round of qualifying at Sutton Coldfield, fondly recalls that first-round meeting with Reardon.

'It was my one and only World Championship and I was the first Scottish player to get to the Crucible,' Donnelly says.

Fellow Caledonian cuemen Stephen Hendry, John Higgins and Graeme Dott would go on to triumph in Sheffield, but Donnelly began the Scots' illustrious Crucible history.

Some 12 days before Higgins and Reardon would meet in the final, Donnelly was a witness to the two great combatants at close quarters.

Out of his poky dressing room and into the Crucible's backstage corridors shuffled Higgins at around 7.25pm on day four of the championship, short of snooker practice by his own admission.

The champion of 1972 had been swept aside by Reardon in the 1976 final, and in 1980 Higgins submitted to an urge to entertain, with the subsequent loss of intensity costing him the trophy match against Cliff Thorburn.

Higgins wanted a shot at a fourth final and a second title, and knowing Davis had already been sent packing felt as reassuring as a month on any practice table.

Ahead lay an evening session, as Higgins and Jim Meadowcroft began their first-round tussle. On the other table, behind the dividing wall, Reardon and Donnelly were playing to a finish.

Donnelly had ground to make up on Reardon, trailing 6-3 after their Sunday morning opening session, but the Glasgow semi-professional had cause to be distracted as the players waited to be called into the arena.

Higgins was on edge, hyperactive and unpredictable.

'There was Reardon and I behind the curtain, and there was Higgins,' says Donnelly. 'We were standing there waiting to be called through, and Higgins just couldn't stand still.'

As Donnelly remembers it, Reardon attempted to intervene and bring order to proceedings, the old policing instincts still intact.

'Ray said to him, "Alex, you've got to stand still." But he was walking about, he was near enough doing press-ups against the wall,' Donnelly says, 'and somebody, a female fan I think, had given him a lucky rabbit's foot, and he had that with him, taking it out and showing it to everybody.'

Donnelly's head was briefly scrambled by the antics of this overstrung player he had watched on television so many times. The 35-year-old Donnelly still managed a bright start against Reardon and cut his arrears by two frames to 6-5, yet the Welshman pulled away and reeled off four in a row to pass his first examination.

Over time, Donnelly gained more first-hand experience of the unpredictable nature of Higgins. He encountered both a generous spirit and a snarling, unaccommodating presence, never quite knowing which side of the personality would reveal itself.

'I've played him in exhibitions and there'd be 2,000 people in the hall and someone could go up to him and say, "Oh Alex, can I have your autograph?" and he'd be, "Sure, sure" and put his arm around them and everything,' Donnelly says. 'And then you'd maybe see him playing the following night in another venue, and you'd get someone going up to him and saying how great he is, the usual thing, and he wouldn't even look at you.

'He'd tell you to piss off, basically. He was one of these Jekyll and Hydes. One night you'd put your arm around him and think, "What is everybody talking about, thinking about this guy like he's some kind of a nutcase?" and then you'd go the next night and you'd realise why. Still, he was some man. To play him, even in exhibitions particularly, he played shots you'd never even seen, never thought about.'

The thing with Crucible one-timers is that typically they either become overawed and let the whole occasion wash over them, or they remember every last detail. Donnelly falls into the latter camp.

'I was living and working in Scotland. I still had a full-time job, as a sales manager for the German company Bosch. I was working for one of the distributors,' Donnelly says.

'I remember when I was sat with Reardon and the match was going on, in the session where it was eachy-peachy, and Ray was just narrowly ahead.

'They've shown it a few times when they dig out the archive footage, and Ray was standing at the side of the table, the top side where his chair was, and he has a beige suit on and he was looking at the crowd as if to say "Brrrr!" and they did the same back, as if it was cold.

'I was sitting, thinking, "I've got you worried."

'I pushed him in that match. You're playing the guy that was six times the world champion in his home territory, and I've come from basically a standard, average snooker club, with random, average snooker tables, different cloth, different balls, no under-table heating. Also, people don't realise that when you're playing on the television – I've always made a joke about it – that you don't want to be a slow player or you'll end up with a tan on the back of your neck from the heat from the lights.

'I've likened my experience to playing maybe for a Third Division team and suddenly someone comes along and tells you, "Come on, you're playing for England against Brazil at Wembley on Saturday." That was the difference between where I was practising and playing, and then going into the Crucible.

'It was good because I knew most of the players. I'd played Ray a number of times in exhibitions, and I was actually signed as the professional for the club he put his name to: Reardon's Snooker Centre in Glasgow. So that was one of the biggest clubs in Glasgow, with something like 28 to 30 tables, and they came on to me about taking on the job of being the resident professional player and doing some coaching as well, so I did that.

'Ray was coming up regularly, so I played him a number of times. I also had an event for Billy McNeill, the famous Celtic captain, who opened up a hotel out in Strathaven, just outside Glasgow.

'Normally what they had in those days was a black-tie boxing event, if they were opening up something, and they'd put in a ring and so on, but Billy McNeill was quite interested in snooker

84

and he ended up getting in touch with Reardon and asking if he would come to open up the hotel.

'And he asked Reardon who he would like to play from Scotland.'

Donnelly got the nod. He was a player of admirable class. In October 1982, Donnelly would even beat Higgins at the World Team Classic, helping Scotland through to the semi-finals.

Donnelly was particularly proud of breaking new ground for Scotland in Sheffield, even if Reardon had his number, and with signs of his snooker career flourishing he packed in the day job.

Bish, bash, Bosch.

* *

If Reardon had to tough it out in a series of tight frames against Donnelly, he was made to work every bit as hard against John Virgo in round two. Ultimately, the Welshman's guile made up for an absence of heavy scoring, Reardon going through to the quarter-finals as a 13-8 winner, with his best break of the tournament still only 74, which he had managed twice, once in each of his opening matches.

Reardon got past Silvino Francisco next, also by a 13-8 margin, and it was only against Eddie Charlton in the semi-finals that he truly scored heavily, putting together four breaks in the nineties.

'The Reardon progression through that tournament was quite solid,' says Phil Yates.

'But because of Knowles-Davis, and then the White-Higgins semi-final, everything was on the other guy really. Beating Donnelly was fine, and then he beat Virgo and didn't pull up any trees; then he beat Silvino Francisco who wasn't a fluent player, and then he played Charlton in the semi-final. It's hard to believe, but Reardon didn't make a century in the tournament, not one.

'Nowadays if you win the World Championship or get to the final, if you don't make around 10 centuries in the tournament it's a bit of a surprise.

'It really was a very, very different time. People will talk about the 1980s being a golden period for the game, and in terms of viewership in the UK it definitely was, but in terms of the standard on the table and its international reach, nowadays it's a completely different ball game.

'I think it shows how the game has not only developed but improved.'

What bears pointing out here is that snooker drama usually comes not with big break-building, but from those frames where players are battling to get the job done, often battling against their own shortcomings and the danger of mentally falling away. If a player can find a way to reach a final without making a century break, it speaks volumes for their tenacity.

Yates has every respect for Reardon's gritty run through the draw, and the longevity that meant this was not some sort of freakish performance.

Steve Davis went on an against-the-odds run to the Crucible quarter-finals as a 52-year-old in 2010 that was a highly enjoyable blip in an otherwise steady, long decline. He had long faded as a reliable force and was as surprised as anyone.

Reardon's performance at the age of 49 was a reminder of his continuing presence among the elite, underlined by his return to number one on the ranking list.

'Reardon of course remains the oldest ever ranking event winner at the age of 50,' says Yates, nodding to a win over White in the October 1982 final of the Professional Players Tournament.

'The game of snooker has gone through three phases: back then, it was a middle-aged game; then with the advent of Stephen Hendry and the players that followed him, it became very much a young man's game; and now it's reverted to what it was in the early eighties. Tournament winners and finalists in their forties have become commonplace again.

'Yet to get to a World Championship final at the age of 49, that really was an achievement.'

10: The Bear essentials

FOUR CANADIANS lined up in the main draw at the 1982 World Championship, and three of the names roll off the tongue.

Cliff Thorburn, Kirk Stevens and Bill Werbeniuk were such a powerhouse trio they would team up in October of the same year and drive Canada to victory over England – Steve Davis, Jimmy White and Tony Knowles – in the World Team Classic final.

And then there was John Bear, a tour rookie who turned up without a mandatory waistcoat, grumbled about Sheffield's cuisine, slipped out in round one and never returned.

Yet Bear, whose brother Jimmy later reached the World Amateur final, fulfilled a dream that originated on the hustling circuit. He fleetingly got to play top-tier snooker. Chances are, he played the World Championship more than you have.

Thorburn was not easily impressed by rivals, not when dicing with danger in shady clubs for quick dollars, nor later as a pro.

He knew when to tip the hat though, and Thorburn described Bear as one of 'the two greatest gentlemen I ever met in my life'.

This, then, is the story of John Bear.

*

'John was from Flin Flon, Manitoba. You end up, if you take the wrong turn and go about two miles, getting eaten by a bear.'

If the Bears didn't get you, the bears might. Thorburn is remembering his old adversary, the left-hander with the silky smooth action.

'Nobody looked better than Johnny over a cue,' says Thorburn.

In 2022, Thorburn successfully lobbied for his old pal to join Canada's Snooker Hall of Fame. Jimmy Bear was also inducted into this select band.

Thorburn had grown frustrated with nobody being added to the illustrious roll call since the early 1990s, saying: 'Nobody cared about it, but I care about it. I want other people to feel the love.'

Canadian snooker has been in the doldrums for decades, in the sense that nobody has made waves on the professional circuit, but its past will be celebrated for as long as Thorburn has a say. To his optimistic mind, tales of yore might just light a fire under present-day young potters. Those stories still pack a punch.

'There's two guys in the world that have busted me playing snooker and John was one,' says Thorburn.

This specific coup happened in Vancouver, in the late 1960s.

Thorburn says: 'I guess I must have been about 20 years old, and he took all my money, and then he gave me enough money to get back home to Victoria, to catch the ferry.

'John Bear was a really smooth master cueman: a lefty who had his own style. Jimmy was a righty and had his own style too. One was really aggressive and the other one was smooth. You had a crash-bang pro and a smoother pro.

'The other fella who busted me was Bob Checaloski, from Windsor, across the river from Detroit. He beat me playing snooker on a smaller table and he gave me money to go home as well. I'm not sure if it was because he didn't want to see me again.

Eventually, I got both of them.

'They were the two greatest gentlemen I ever met in my life because they got me home.'

In the cut-throat world of hustling, such generosity was rare.

Bob Checaloski did not make it to the professional snooker tour, but his brother, Don, remembers how Bob and Thorburn 'became great friends'. Bob, who later ran the Windsor Snooker Club, had been 'a young natural, with so much talent', says Don.

Hustling, whereby a player relies on deception or daring to lure top dollar, is notoriously a tough way to shake out a living. Thorburn would usually come away from clubs in credit and able to put a roof over his head, but not always, and not everyone had the generous spirit of John Bear and Bob Checaloski.

**

John Bear, tragically, had wrestled with hardship from a young age. He was just 15 when his father, Douglas Bertie Bear, died in appalling circumstances.

John was born in Kinistino, in the province of Saskatchewan, but did most of his growing up in the small mining city of Flin Flon, on the border with Manitoba.

It was in Flin Flon that as a teenager Bear played for the Elks, a local junior ice hockey team.

By October, summer temperatures are long gone in Flin Flon. Harsh winter conditions set in, with snow arriving and ice becoming a hazard.

The Winnipeg Free Press reported on October 3, 1959, that a blaze had broken out at about 3am the previous day at the Bear family home in a remote part of Flin Flon, with Douglas Bear's remains only found once the ruins were searched.

Wife Lucy had been babysitting at the home of one of her daughters that night, and son John had joined her.

The newspaper report stated: 'Another son, Edward, was at a neighbor's home. It was thought Mr. Bear was downtown or out visiting. When he could not be found anywhere, Edward entered the blazing building to find his father. Flames and smoke drove him out. The structure was a blazing inferno by the time the fire brigade and police arrived. They kept the flames from spreading to nearby homes.'

John Bear later spoke about the tragedy with wife Carol, whom he met in 1969 and married a year later.

'He lost his dad in 1959. The ice was so bad that they couldn't get any water, so he burned to death in his home,' Carol said. 'I remember the news.'

It was not the only horror that John Bear had to endure, for his mother Lucy died in a car crash in 1978, Carol recalled.

'It was a real horrible way for him to lose his family.'

John Bear died at the age of 62 in March 2007, in Victoria, B.C., leaving Carol a widow. John and Carol had two sons together and were proud parents.

Amid his tribulations, John Bear's life contained many a triumph. The woman born Carol Quocksister, whom he first encountered in Vancouver, later settling down there, was his great love.

'We met in 1969 at my grandmother's house,' Carol said.

'He was with someone else who was staying at my grandma's house, and after he left he kept coming back every Sunday and he would bring Grandma steaks. She had a houseful of kids to feed.'

There were grandchildren and great-grandchildren at the home, with Carol detailing a challenging family situation that meant Grandma was run off her feet.

'So John kept bringing steaks over because Grandma could barely afford to feed all the kids. He was playing a lot of snooker downtown, where he played for money, and he won lots of money and he always bought Grandma lots of meat.'

Carol was impressed. This was the ultimate meat cute.

'We got married in 1970; November 7, 1970, in Campbell River,' Carol told me.

'I was born in Campbell River, British Columbia. John was quite a character, with good manners, and he had charisma. He had a special thing about him. Everywhere we went, he knew someone. He remembered all the pool players he ever met, and they were always asking how he was. Even the Americans, they would ask after the "Crazy Canuck", which is what they called him.'

Carol laughed at this down the phone line, the happy laugh of somebody who had perhaps not told the story in a while.

As with many Canadians, Thorburn included, she pronounced 'snooker' as 'snucker'. For a while, John Bear felt like a snooker sucker, drawn in by a pro sport that kept rejecting him.

'John had a hard time entering into the snooker professional game,' Carol said. She believed he encountered racism along the way in his career, with the Bears being from an indigenous background, and credited Thorburn with banging the drum for his one-time rival.

'John had a hard time getting the door open to playing any kind of billiards. It was tough for him, but it was Cliff Thorburn who entered the picture and told them that they had to allow him to be a professional if he wanted to,' Carol said.

'All across Canada, he played snooker. John played in America in nine-ball and eight-ball. He played in many tournaments, he even played one-pocket. And he was a champion at everything, but for some reason they wouldn't allow him to enter the professional snooker ranks until Cliff told them.

'John had beaten Cliff at every game, even eight-ball. They

92

played nine-ball and John whacked him. He said that John was the best pool player he ever met and why wasn't he a professional at snooker. And John said they wouldn't let him. But after that the door opened and he started being allowed to play.

'Away from snooker he was a fisherman and, any kind of job someone offered to him, he would do it, even if it was just to help. He was very giving to people, and if it was to feed the family or whatever he would just help.

'He loved playing the game, and he had a few maximum breaks. After a while, nobody wanted to play him any more in Canada because he won all the championships.'

Snooker tournaments took place in Hong Kong and Australia too, at the point when John Bear got his break in the game, and Carol Bear recalled her husband calling home to regale with stories of where his money was going.

'He would tell me that a hamburger in Hong Kong was $10 a burger, and he actually played in Australia and a lot in America,' said Carol. 'He went to Chicago, a place called Pheasant Run Resort, maybe in around 1991, and played nine-ball there. He knew everyone; the pool players, he knew them all.'

Bear had begun his cue sports career in the time-old schoolboy fashion of cutting class.

'When he was a little boy, he didn't like school,' Carol said. 'He would walk in through the front of the class and walk out of the back and go to the pool room, and he had a little apple box that he would move all around the table to play snooker.

'I know he played with one of the biggest pool players from those days, and this was in Flin Flon, Manitoba, where he was raised.'

Freedman's Confectionary, with its backroom pool hall, was a familiar haunt.

'He would use the apple box to go around the table, and he would do this quite frequently, and after a while, the owners of the pool room would let him janitor the place so he could play for free because he didn't have the money.

'He looked after his mum until he was 15, which is when he decided to hit the road because he couldn't see his mum supporting him and that's why he took to pool, because that was his livelihood. He made money for himself, and he didn't have to bother anyone. They call it hustling among pool players. I was with him for many, many tournaments.

'After a while he said that I would kick him in the butt and make him play properly, because I would watch what he was doing. Sometimes he would lift his head too fast when he was shooting and he would miss, and I would say to him, "You're lifting your head too soon," and of course he would listen to me, and he'd put it back and then he would be so happy when he won a tournament.'

In early May 1981, Bear came from three frames adrift to beat Jim Wych 8-6 and win the Central Canadian Snooker Championship before a crowd of over 500 spectators at Winnipeg's Las Vegas Amusement Centre.

From 5-2 adrift, he knocked in breaks of 92, 87 and 115 on the way to seeing off Wych's challenge, the Winnipeg Free Press reported.

'When the Bears were around, you knew,' said Wych, some 41 years later. 'They commanded a presence that very few players I've ever seen command.

'Jimmy and Johnny shaped me along with a lot of western Canadian players. We were fortunate enough to grow up around these guys, watch them, learn from them and try to emulate them.'

A regional championship was not quite the Crucible, but Sheffield was on the horizon, with Bear beating former World Championship quarter-finalist Wych 9-4 in qualifying the following April to clinch a ticket to the main draw.

'He sure found it different in England. There was no salad. He said everything was pickled. And he said everyone wanted you to eat muffins all the time,' Carol remembered.

'He said they always ate tea and crumpets. He was just not used to the food. He liked eating his steak and the good food, so he was quite shocked by what was offered to him.

'He was a crowd-pleaser wherever he went. He got many standing ovations for his game. He was a very good representative for Canada. I hear about it and have pool players asking how he is, because it really wasn't too public when he passed away. He had a heart attack from diabetes. He was 62.

'It's been all these years since he's gone now, and we miss him all the time.'

An obituary for John Bear in the Vancouver Sun detailed that 'his game trademark was his "soft touch", "smooth stroke", and good nature'.

For all this acclaimed ability and conviviality, Bear seemingly did not achieve his snooker potential, and his World Championship dalliance ultimately struck little of a chord with the sports press in Canada.

That solitary Crucible appearance came in an all-Canadian tussle with Werbeniuk, with Bear managing a top break of a modest 44 in his 10-7 defeat.

The result was documented all too briefly back home. In Werbeniuk's native city, there was a write-up by the Winnipeg Free Press, albeit brief and in the Sport Shorts section, given equal prominence with local second division rugby.

Precedence was given to an exhaustive account of the Western Canadian Midget Volleyball Championships at Red River Community College – a junior event that saw the girls' title won by the Saskatchewan T-Shirts Unlimited team.

If John Bear had recoiled at the ritual of tea and crumpets at snooker's new potting palace, the culture change of going from being a hot favourite at home to a slim-hope shot in Sheffield may also have weighed heavily.

Once back in familiar territory, Jimmy's presence made the Bears twin tormentors, and at least in Canada the brothers were used to often having things their own way.

'If they were in a tournament, people would know who was going to be in the final,' Carol Bear said. 'Sometimes [opponents] would give up and not really play because they knew the two Bears would be there in the end.'

Jimmy Bear reached the final of the 1982 World Amateur Championship, held in Calgary at the back end of the year.

'If John had Jimmy's heart, he could have been invincible,' Thorburn said many years later. 'Those two were among the best brothers' doubles teams ever, up there with Joe and Fred Davis.'

In 1999, John and Carol Bear moved back to Campbell River.

Carol died in Langley, B.C., in November 2021, after a long battle with an incurable cancer.

I spoke to her in April of that year. She was generous with her time, charming company, and forever proud of John.

11: ARE YOU SITTING COMFORTABLY?

DAVID TAYLOR and his wife, Janice, had a wide choice of eateries near their Cheshire home, but a favourite weekend stop was the residence of Alex and Lynn Higgins.

As Taylor, snooker's 'Silver Fox', tells it, there was always the intriguing prospect of what bizarre discovery might be made.

It was anyone's guess what might be unravelling while roast potatoes sizzled in the oven.

'I got on well with him,' Taylor says. 'We used to go round to his place for Sunday lunch, because he lived just 15 minutes down the road.

'It was hysterical. You couldn't sit down on his sofa. You'd say to him, "This sofa is very uncomfortable," and he'd lift the cushion up and there'd be five or six hundred pounds stuffed underneath there. He just stuffed all the money from all his shows, his exhibitions, under the cushion. I think that's bloody awful!

'I went round one particular Sunday and a vase had smashed into a huge window, and Alex was trying to put the vase together again with glue. It was in a thousand pieces and he'd already spent six hours on it.'

Despite the friendship, hairdresser-turned-cueman Taylor was on the end of a tongue-lashing from Higgins in Derby just eight weeks before the 1982 World Championship, accused by the Hurricane of failing to make a sufficiently decent attempt at escaping from a snooker during a group match at the Yamaha Organs Trophy. Referee Len Ganley sided with Taylor, to the dismay of Higgins.

According to Snooker Scene, a bristling Higgins snapped at Taylor: 'Don't ever speak to me again. Don't speak to my wife or my daughter. Don't speak to my cat.'

Higgins lost the match 2-1 and, feeling wronged, went on to miss out on qualification for the semi-final stage. He and Taylor suddenly had a relationship to rebuild, and goodness knows what poor Mog would make of such palaver, but Higgins typically soon moved on to another controversy.

Three weeks later, on March 27, Higgins lost his rag with his own typically fervid supporters at Goffs during the Benson & Hedges Irish Masters. This was the famous County Kildare venue that also staged pedigree cattle sales.

On this occasion, Higgins was the bull, and the boisterous crowd dangled the red cape just long enough for his nostrils to flare. Higgins snapped 'Keep your traps shut' during what was a semi-final hiding at the hands of Davis, drawing a rebuke from referee John Smyth and a disciplinary charge.

Making his way home from that event, there seemed little hope of the 33-year-old Higgins recovering any sense of poise before heading to Sheffield.

It is March 2021 when I speak to Taylor. He and Janice have been running a smashing bed and breakfast, Ash Farm Country Guest House, for over 20 years.

This is their home in the tiny Cheshire village of Little

Bollington, but the usually thriving business has ground to an inevitable halt: the country is in lockdown, and there's only one thing for it.

'He's just watching the snooker,' says Janice, answering the phone.

Here's David.

'Yes, I'm just watching Judd,' he tells me.

It's the week of the behind-closed-doors Tour Championship at Celtic Manor, and Judd Trump and Barry Hawkins are contesting the last of the quarter-finals.

Old habits die hard, and Taylor, like so many, is appreciative of how snooker has barely left our screens during what by now has been a year of lockdowns and losses, tiers and tears, variants and vagaries, amid a remarkable time in our lives.

While many snooker buffs rushed to buy six foot by three foot tables ahead of the first lockdown, Taylor was in no such need.

Ash Farm is a bed, breakfast and baize establishment. Not only does it have its own snooker table, but the table is a part of the sport's legend.

'I got the one from the Benson & Hedges that Dennis won on,' Taylor says.

To be absolutely clear, that's the table from the 1987 Benson & Hedges Masters at Wembley Conference Centre, where Dennis Taylor came from 8-5 behind to beat Higgins 9-8 in a late-night nail-biter. At the time of writing, that remains the last major final to be contested by two Northern Irishmen, with Dennis getting one over on Alex.

Was this table on which history was made really delivered to the correct D Taylor?

12: TEEN IDOLS, AND THATCHER'S SMITTEN TOO

ALL ACROSS the British Isles, snooker was having a moment.

Even the Prime Minister was hooked in the early 1980s.

'I do watch television, golf, usually it's late at night, and snooker. Do you watch snooker?' Margaret Thatcher asked, mid-interview, on Thames Television children's show CBTV.

'You know this weekend it was absolutely fantastic. They make it all look easy, very, very easy.'

While Thatcher and husband Denis watched on from 10 Downing Street, a future First Lady of snooker was also keeping tabs on potting proceedings, when her studies and sporting commitments allowed.

Hazel Irvine, growing up near Helensburgh, in Dunbartonshire, was a high-flying pupil of Cardross Primary School and later Hermitage Academy.

The 16-year-old Irvine was a Barbra Streisand fan, and another great musical love were 'the Durannies' – teenage enthusiasm pours out as she mentions Simon Le Bon and co.

For Duran Duran, 1982 was the irresistible year of Hungry Like the Wolf, Save a Prayer, and Rio.

But sport was the passion that had truly captured Irvine's heart. She would swim most days, played netball and hockey to a high level in school, was a mean hurdler, and never turned down an opportunity to charge around a golf course.

While Scotland had yet to produce its great snooker champions, there was already a fascination brewing there, too. Some 20 years later, Irvine would be anchoring the BBC's Crucible coverage, holding down that role for over two decades.

'In 1982, I was just about to turn 17, just about to do my Highers, and I went off to university that autumn, off to St Andrews,' Irvine remembers. 'I was embroiled in studies.

'Snooker had always been a part of my family. I vividly remember my father, Bill, made my brother and I a six-foot table – he made it himself, and he covered it and did the cushions and stuff. That was when I was about 10 or 11, and he gave it to us for Christmas, and this would sit on our dining table, on top of a very, very thick blanket so we didn't scratch the table top.

'Particularly around Christmas times we used to play there all the time. I remember being hampered on the window frame in the dining room.

'So it was very much a part of what was a very sporty upbringing for me. I watched everything – I loved the Olympics, I loved football, I used to stop my homework to watch Scotsport, all that sort of stuff on a Sunday, Ski Sunday and all of that. TV sport was a big part of my upbringing, and snooker was a part of that, particularly the World Championship. I was always around to watch a bit of the final at least.

'I can't remember not being aware of it. I can't remember being a devotee of snooker more than I was anything else, but it was all part of the sporting landscape for me and I was genuinely interested in all sport. Snooker wasn't a particular passion, but when I think about it, the fact that I was playing every night after dinner with my brother and my dad, it probably was and I didn't even know it.

'We'd just bash it about and have a bit of fun, but it got a bit tasty at times, a wee bit of competition!

'I've still got the table, in fact. My mum crocheted the pockets. It needs a bit of TLC probably.'

**

Irvine was not the only teenager with an eye on events in the heart of South Yorkshire in 1982.

In Sheffield, the schoolboy Mark Watterson could hop on the number 53 bus after school and be at the Crucible before the interval in the afternoon session.

Just as importantly, he was assured of VIP access, with Mike Watterson, Mark's uncle, being the tournament's promoter.

Mike Watterson famously followed the clairvoyant vision of wife Carole who proposed the theatre as an ideal snooker venue after watching a play there. Her perceptive glance at the stage floor would be a game-changer. With nary an inch to spare, there was room for two tables and the bare minimum breathing space.

Steelworker's son Mike proudly drove a Rolls-Royce with CUE 1 plates, such was his success in staging snooker events.

He became chairman of Derby County Football Club in 1982, and devised and staged the first World Darts Championship in 1978, but it was the contribution to changing the face of snooker that was remembered as his most significant business achievement following his 2019 death.

Watterson was noted for his supreme selling of the sport to new audiences, along with managing top names and commentating on the game, but chiefly for giving its greatest championship a fitting permanent home after a long-nomadic existence.

There was plenty more to Watterson than his astute business brain though. He was even a classy semi-professional cueman, making a century in a 9-7 loss to Jim Meadowcroft in the final round of qualifying for the 1982 World Championship.

Nephew Mark was 14 years old in 1982, hooked on snooker. Forty years on, he modestly mentions how he 'came down a few times' that year to soak up as much of the action as he could.

School pal Nick Cavanagh joined him, Mark remembers, as the boys were allowed into the press seats for the semi-final between Alex Higgins and Jimmy White, literally one step away from the Crucible stage floor.

To this day, Mark Watterson remains captivated by the persona of Higgins, the player who was snooker's original rolling stone, long before an actual Rolling Stone, Ronnie Wood, became White's great buddy.

'He fascinates me, there's something about Higgins that fascinates me,' says Mark.

'He played my Uncle Michael at Bristol Redwood Lodge in November 1983 in the Professional Players Tournament.

'Michael beat him 5-2 and Higgins wasn't happy about it, and as they were walking down the corridor afterwards Higgins picked his cue up and just threw it at my uncle.

'It missed him, hit the wall, fell on the floor. Michael said he was fuming and picked the cue up and said, "Alex, you'll get that back when you apologise." He never apologised.

'My uncle knew Alex very well. Mike said he'd come in to venues and he'd be all, "Hey babes, how're you doing?" and he'd be all friendly and have a chat, and on other days he'd just argue with everybody in the venue more or less.

'The best time I ever met him was in 2005 when he did an exhibition of trick shots up at Hillsborough in Sheffield.

'He was an awkward character in reality. He was friendly enough and at the end of the night he wanted me to sit with him – I think he just wanted me to buy his beer for him, as there was just me and him left.

'But he was kicking off earlier in the evening. He was supposed to play eight frames and he'd only played one and then he insisted on an interval. We go to get a drink and someone said that Alex has changed his mind and he wants to continue playing, so we all come back to sit down. Then he starts the next frame and then says he won't play another frame unless all the balls are changed. It was just how he was.'

13: 'MY WIFE HAD A SOFT SPOT FOR HIGGINS'

ALEX HIGGINS, Jimmy White, Ray Reardon and co. were vying for the £25,000 top prize at the Crucible. Nice money if you could get it.

But in case anyone was unsure where the real power and the top money in the sport was to be found, Barry Hearn secured a £3.1million deal for selling 16 snooker halls to the Riley Leisure chain in the same spring of 1982.

Hearn retained only the Lucania in Romford, the club where he first encountered Steve Davis – greeting him with the line, 'I've heard a lot about you' – but the other halls were off his hands.

One consequence of the sale was that while a bricks-and-mortar empire shrank overnight, Hearn instantly had deep enough pockets to target major territory in the novel battleground of professional snooker.

Hearn signed up the 1979 world champion Terry Griffiths to the small stable of players he managed, in what was reported as a £1million deal.

This all marked a shift in Hearn's business tactics: having previously acquired snooker clubs because of their property value, suddenly he was identifying potting talents that could lead to even greater rewards.

Matchroom was born, initially as Barry Hearn Limited, and officially registered on April 23, 1982, with a nominal capital of £100,000.

There was no guarantee Hearn would find success as he explored the possibility of bringing in others to join the likes of world champions Davis and Griffiths.

Hearn has spoken of wanting to 'spread snooker's gospel', but he also wanted to monetise this gospel.

The nature of human fallibility meant these new assets were riskier than previous investment forays by the 33-year-old Hearn, but he was confident there was nobody within his ranks who could collapse the enterprise like a house of cards.

Which is why Hearn always baulked at the idea of bringing Higgins into the Matchroom fold.

'I was tempted loads of times, loads of times. It never really came that close because every time I was having a "shall I, shan't I?" moment he won, and he had so many opportunities that he didn't really need me,' Hearn said.

'When he needed me, then I was in the moment, in the mood, where I would think, "Oh, this bloke will be a disaster because I'm building something entirely different."

'So we never really gelled at the right time. As people, we actually got on very well, although there were a few rows. I think I had him up against the wall twice. I was going to knock him out a couple of times, even though it was objectionable.

'My wife always had a big soft spot for Alex Higgins as many women do, because Alex had that vulnerability that women liked.

'She would always say to me at the time, "He's never actually let you down, has he?"

'And truth be told he never, ever did. He caused me grief plenty of times when he was there though. And I remember this was epitomised in a challenge match he played with Davis over four days and nights, best of 65 frames, at Romford.'

When Higgins walked through the doors of the Romford Lucania in spring 1979, hired by Hearn for the marathon contest, he might have felt like a star turn. After all, he had been runner-up at the Masters just weeks earlier.

The match against Davis was to be played in the Matchroom, the Lucania's main hall. Lined with rows of chairs and benches, this is the room that begat an empire its name.

From outside, the Lucania was impossible to miss. Its sign had LUCANIA written in black, BILLIARDS in red and SNOOKER in yellow, green, brown, blue, pink, black and red.

Davis, then a gawky 21-year-old whose character was quite the opposite to that of the gregarious, outspoken Hearn, had already established a large local following. However, he had yet to play at his first World Championship, having only been accepted on to the professional tour in September 1978.

A full house for every session was guaranteed, and this encounter of the ego-led Higgins and the ego-free Davis did not disappoint.

This was work experience of the highest order for the rookie Davis. He has recalled being paid just £25 to play such matches.

'It was a classic, a classic. Romford Matchroom held about 300 people and there was only one door to get in and there was no fire exit and there were no windows,' Hearn said, glowing with a rebellious sense of pride.

'People used to smoke, of course, and they used to gamble. And Alex would come in and I remember to this day, he was on £500, for the eight sessions, just £500 – I always did a good deal – and the first thing he said to me was, "What price am I?" I told him, "You're 6/4, Alex."

'And he said, "I'm 6/4? Me? I'm Alex Higgins!"

'I told him, "Yes, that's the price, it's a good, generous price."'

What happened next might have surprised some promoters, but Hearn had seen it all before.

The story might be told with a pinch of dramatic licence, but Hearn recalls Higgins immediately laying down the £500 appearance money as a primary stake. The Hurricane was put out at being made odds-against, but he also sniffed an opportunity to come away with far greater reward than his appearance money.

'And we went through his pockets and each pocket had a pile of notes in,' Hearn said. 'And out of that, add it all up and I think it came to about £1,721, and he put his hands in his pockets and took out about 14 bob, and said, let's call that £1,722. So he nicked six shillings off me, and that was the bet.

'The standard of snooker people talk about, those that were there, it was 135 followed by 112, 140 followed by 108. It was fucking unbelievable. And it was nip and tuck through the first day, through the second day, and on the third day it all started going pear-shaped and Davis won frame after frame after frame.

'And he got to within two of winning I think – he had to get up to 33 frames, and he got to something like 31-20 with two more sessions to go. Alex hadn't potted a ball for hours, and all the crowd were giving him gyp, and he turned round – he'd had a few as well – and he said, "You pile of cunts can fuck off. I tell you something, you might have bought a ticket for tomorrow, but I fucking won't be here. Up yours, this is a toilet."

'And he stormed out. I was like, "What the fuck?"

'I'd sold all these tickets.'

Davis, in his autobiography Interesting, recalled it being 31-18 when all hell broke loose. He also remembered Higgins ranting and raving at Hearn out of sight of the punters, complaining of what to his fast-whirring mind was the most grievous of injustices: the home player having all the support. Hired hand Higgins had entered the Matchroom fortress and hated it as much as he found himself envying Davis. The People's Champion found that in this quarter of east London at least, there was a new lord of the baize.

Higgins marched off into the night.

'But he turned up in the morning, half an hour early, like nothing had happened at all,' Hearn said, his face incredulous at the memory.

'And I said to him, "You gave me a fucking sleepless night."'

'One thing Alex always did was he never came without losing all of his money, which was consistent. He had three or four challenge matches there, plus this game, and every single game he would say to me – because he never drove – he'd say, "You couldn't lend me fifty quid for my train fare home?"'

'And I always lent him fifty quid. Never saw it again, obviously, never wanted it.'

Hearn questioned his own stance on Higgins over the years, but always reached the same conclusion: a modern sporting business should find room for mavericks but steer clear of agitators, particularly the mad-dog breed. No serious regime can hope to reach its full potential with one so needy and disruptive.

Hearn has in his later years described himself as a 'benevolent dictator', but charity always stops somewhere. To Higgins' great frustration, Hearn kept him at arm's length.

'But there were times when we attempted – yes, because of the character and charisma – and had I been a bit braver, I might have [signed him],' Hearn said. 'But I was building something and I had very fixed ideas about what I wanted to achieve, and he definitely was a loose cannon.

'He'd have a fight with anyone providing there was someone close to drag him off. He knew, because he was quite a nippy little lad, that if he got the first one in, someone would stop it before he got beaten to death, and it always worked. He was quite smart like that.

'You can knock him or whatever, but the game would have been poorer to not have him in there. From my side, yeah, put it down to lack of bravery on my part, but it may have been common sense.'

Hearn said that 'Davis in particular' wanted the stable to have nothing to do with Higgins.

Matchroom Sport's group turnover for the year ended June 30, 2019, was £192.9m, with an overall profit of £23.4m. Of that profit, over £10million was generated by boxing, but some £1.4m came from snooker. The business had 'more than £60m in the bank', its annual report stated, and was well positioned to handle the approaching threat of Covid-19 to live sport.

The decision to leave Higgins' affairs for others to manage has not exactly been a ruinous choice.

On March 17, 2021, Hearn quietly handed over the business to son Eddie and daughter Katie, as he ceased being 'a person with significant control' and the company passed into the hands of Matchroom Holdings Ltd.

The end of an era was formally announced at the Crucible, with Hearn doing a final tour of duty as chairman of World Snooker Tour, the position he secured in June 2010, when he began an impressive rejuvenation of a sport that many felt was in serious trouble.

At the age of 72, Hearn decided it was time to take a back seat, several lifetimes' worth of missions accomplished.

Born to a bus driver father who died aged 44 after a series of heart attacks, and a mother who made a living as a house cleaner, Hearn had grand ambitions for his own working life and took his father's early death as a prompt never to waste a moment.

Leaving school with O levels, he received a big early career break when he joined the accountancy firm that looked after the affairs of an uncle's tiling business.

Hearn became a chartered accountant and an FCA – Fellow of the Institute of Chartered Accountants – by the age of 26. He understood how wealth was created, which roads led to fortune and which to folly and failure, and the observant young Hearn desired the lifestyle of a rich man.

In a quiet moment at the Crucible, Hearn explained how following the strategies and work ethic of one of the modern world's most successful investors drove his own business achievements.

'My great hero is Warren Buffett. I can't stop reading about him, listening about him. He's led a very focused life, at the expense of family and everything else, because, same as a snooker player, you've got to make sacrifices if you want to be a world champion,' Hearn said.

'I play with my grandchildren far more than I did my children, because I was too busy, and that is a price you pay. It's not a problem and hasn't caused me a problem. But Warren Buffett's attitude is all about focus, work ethic, and it's a game. For me, sport is just as much of a game as it is for the players who play the sport. Profits don't matter to me any more in my life, but at the same time they do matter because it's part of winning the game.

'I don't get trophies and belts and cups. At the end of each year I look around and ask myself, was it a great year, did I have a lot of fun and see some fantastic sporting moments? Did I make more money? Because it's a game.'

Hearn has been a feverish note-maker and described himself as being 'in love with numbers'.

'I like the game of sport,' he said, 'and I understand the dedication, and there is something that Steve Davis taught me more than anybody – Warren Buffett maybe second – but Steve had that attitude that the money comes second if you do a job right. It's pretty common sense.

'Perhaps there are some players around that have got to take that into account a little bit more. It's all very well jumping into your Ferrari and being a lad, but you've got to win, and winning is what sport's all about.

'Davis never asked me in his entire career what the prize money was at any event, but he knew that if he got his hands on a trophy it came with a big cheque. I get the feeling today that the money at a certain level can mean you get soft. Take golf, where there's a lot of golfers that'll never win a major that could have done, but they've become happy with making the cut. They've become happy on the US tour making $3million, $4million, $5million a year without having that many top-three or top-four finishes.

'The kids today are soft and they're getting softer, because life is sweeter, opportunities are great, prize money for failure is greater. People are settling for second best.

'If you're not getting the results, you've got two or three choices. One, you can say, "I'm happy, I've got a nice life." Another one might say, "I'm not good enough, I'm going to get a job." And the third one says, "I really want to win the trophy."

'The prize money might be half a million quid, but put that out of your mind, because a hungry sportsman is much more dangerous than a well-fed sportsman.

'One of the great things about the fight game is that most fighters know their career's on the line every time they go in the ring, so they're going to be as good as they can be.

'If a snooker player was as dedicated as me, trust me, they'd win the World Championship every year.'

The storied career of Hearn has seen Matchroom delve into an admirably diverse range of sports, from gymnastics to table tennis, pool to football, golf to fishing.

Ultimately, however, if Hearn and Davis had not struck up their unlikely bond in the mid-1970s, the modern history of sport, particularly in the UK, would read quite differently. There may have been no decade of dominance from the Nugget, no Brentwood mansion for the Hearn clan, and snooker may have fallen into an ever-spiralling decline. The most yakety sports promoter this side of Don King might have made his fortune elsewhere, in property perhaps, or he might have worked his knuckles to the bone trying yet failing to succeed.

Hearn estimates he enjoyed anywhere up to 20 lucky breaks in his career, and his delight at Davis winning the 1981 World Championship – the giddy charge across the Crucible floor followed by a bear hug – was that of a man who knew the gods were on his side.

As Davis said: 'If it wasn't for him, I don't think I'd have been as successful. Not because he gave me anything other than back-up. I learned from him in lots of ways. I fell on my feet and perhaps he fell on his feet when we met. It was a very strong partnership.'

Hearn echoed that, saying: 'Despite my sometimes overinflated opinion of myself, I know I would not be sat here today were it not for Steve Davis. He not only changed snooker, he changed my life.

'We were two kids from council house backgrounds and all we had was this dream, and we lived it out. I've put on sporting events all over the world for decades on end, but there's nothing that gets anywhere near that moment in 1981 at the Crucible. For me, that was the one. My life changed here in 1981.'

In 1982, it was a different story, the loss to Tony Knowles being a bump in the road, but it was one that Davis soon shook off. Hearn sarcastically chirruped 'Isn't life terrible' after that defeat, telling reporters it would mean Davis might only collect £500,000 in a year rather than £600,000.

Davis was already earning far more than any other player in the game, and more than almost anyone else in British sport, with Hearn brokering the level of commercial tie-ups that reached the ear of the likes of Higgins.

Like Torvill and Dean, Hearn and Davis have a special connection and affection for one another that has endured on a personal level and resonated with the public at large.

The man who thought snooker clubs were great value because of their prime city centre locations, and certainly did not acquire them out of any great love for the game, has come to be as much a part of the sport's fabric as many a world champion.

'You can't love and adore every sport out there,' said Hearn. 'It's like loving and adoring every single woman out there. Someone's going to be special, and snooker's always been special to me, because of what I owe the sport and what it's done for me over the years.'

14: Desperately seeking Silvino

IN THE DERBYSHIRE town of Staveley, the tanning salon Sun-Dayz is open every day except Sundays.

Staveley in August 2021 is that sort of place, where you feel things are not quite as they should be.

A once proud cinema-cum-bingo-hall sits derelict, empty since 2011, while the Elm Tree Inn on High Street is boarded up and a sorry sight: above its front door, the wall-mounted letters read 'The ELM T EE IN', its gable wall identifies 'The E M TREE INN'. Charity shops decorate much of the opposite side of the road, along with a William Hill bookmaker, the Raevenwulf Tattoo parlour and Door2Door Taxis, an operation that shares its front door with a carpet store.

This is a high street that is eerily quiet, in a town down on its luck, pleading for overdue investment. It's summer time, but the sun is not shining on Staveley.

When bidding for £25million of government funding, Staveley's submission in December 2020 described the town centre as 'struggling', its landscape as 'scarred', and noted how its 'potential is invisible and not yet understood by many'.

The Chancellor ultimately threw Staveley £25.2million in the 2021 Budget, with only Stevenage and Southport handed heftier lifelines among the 45 towns that sought support.

Bordering Chesterfield, this Derbyshire settling of 19,000 residents was once an industrial stronghold with iron and coal to the fore. Its residents learned a trade for life, but by its leaders' own recognition, Staveley in the early 2020s had become sorely lacking in skilled workers. Youth unemployment had climbed to 9.8% by March 2020, when the pandemic struck.

Four railway stations served Staveley in years gone by; now there is no such route out of town.

This dilapidated, rather sad corner of Albion is where a little sniffing around should lead me to Silvino Francisco, who arrived in England from South Africa in 1982 in search of fame and fortune and profited from both for a good while.

A terrific player for many years, particularly in the sport's mid-eighties popularity peak, by the summer of 1996 it was a different story. Francisco was in financial dire straits.

He and wife Denise had split, and the one-time cue master was said to be clocking in for shifts at a fish and chip shop to bring in much-needed cash.

This helping hand of cod wouldn't save Silvino from sliding further into trouble.

In a September 1996 Daily Mirror article, the 1985 British Open winner was quoted as saying: 'I wouldn't bet on things not getting worse.'

That was unknowingly foreshadowing the next dark chapter. In February 1997, Francisco was arrested at Dover docks with 47 kilograms of cannabis in his car. The haul, valued at £155,000, was such a find that Francisco was jailed for three years.

Since serving his time, little has been heard from Francisco.

His snooker career, as good as over before his crime, was plainly one that could not be resurrected, and the man who once lived a life of luxury had to start again in his early fifties, with a criminal record.

Has his life been on an even keel during the past two decades, when he has become one of snooker's missing men? The hope is that this story has a happy ending.

I'm in Staveley after following up a lead that Francisco played sporadically in a local snooker league and dabbled in coaching.

It is well known that he set up home in the Chesterfield area on first arriving in the UK, so it makes sense he has not travelled far.

On an overcast Wednesday morning, it's a pleasant enough stroll out of the town centre to where I understand the 1982 World Championship quarter-finalist is enjoying a quiet life. I pass a row of attractive detached houses, the sort that might just have space for a snooker room, but it is down a somewhat tired-looking street that I find the spot where, with a little luck, Silvino Francisco will open the door and hear me out.

If he turns me away, so be it. I'm prepared for disappointment.

Nobody's home. I hover for five minutes, check a nearby park, then knock again. Still no response. And then I try the bookies in town, and the supermarket, and most of the charity shops, and a pub or two, all in the line of duty, but there is no sign of Silvino.

Back to the house two hours later and again no answer to my rap at the door.

But is that a snooker trophy on the windowsill, a reminder of Francisco's glory years. It surely is. This is enough to tell me he's still in love with the game. I drop a scrawled note through the door, resolving to return. Silvino is within touching distance.

Lunchtime on September 8, and my mobile rings. It's an unfamiliar number, probably a junk call. I'm busy but pick up.

'Hello, this is Silvino Francisco. I'm sorry, I've been away.'

You don't say.

Silvino and June, his wife, whom he met locally, have been on holiday, enjoying a break on the Lincolnshire coast, but he has received my note. Let's chat, I suggest. Not now, says Silvino. He'll call me tomorrow, early in the day.

The call doesn't come, but when I ring, he's happy to talk. It's for a book about the 1982 World Championship, I remind him.

So Silvino, people want to know what you've been doing over these last two decades.

'Life is not bad. I've been here all this time,' Francisco says. 'I worked delivering school dinners for quite a time, at a place called Eckington, and that kept the wolf from the door before I retired.'

Retirement came about 10 years ago. Francisco is 75 as we speak, which makes him 11 years his wife's senior.

'I came over to England firstly in '82, a long time ago,' he says.

There is a long pause.

'That was when I really started my professional career. I qualified for the World Championship in a place called....'

Another pause. Is he still there? It was Stockport, I say.

'Stockport, that's the place,' he says. 'I beat Paddy Morgan, who was an Irishman from Australia, and I beat an Englishman who'd won the English amateur title.'

That was Chris Ross, an English-based Scotsman. Francisco trounced Ross 9-0 and Morgan 9-1.

'It meant a hell of a lot to me at the time to make it to Sheffield. It was brilliant to get there, I must admit,' he says.

Reaching such a big stage must have been quite an experience, eye-opening for a rookie.

Did he stay at the main tournament hotel, the Grosvenor

House?

'I stayed in a bed and breakfast,' Francisco says.

This will have been his first such interview for many a year, and Francisco seems not entirely at ease. That's entirely reasonable.

Mentioning his first-round Crucible win over world number five Dennis Taylor brings a touch more disco out of Francisco.

That 10-7 success was followed by Francisco seeing off a 19-year-old Dean Reynolds 13-8, with the Cape Town crusader immediately making a name for himself.

'It was a surprise to me that I went so far in the tournament,' he says. 'It was a big challenge to face Dennis Taylor in the first round. I'd already played some of the top players in a tournament in South Africa and I knew Dennis and Willie Thorne. I knew Willie quite well by then because he'd come over to South Africa.

'Dean was a very dangerous player by this stage, but I pulled out a 13-8 win.'

I ask him what he remembers most fondly from his playing days, and surprisingly it is not the British Open final win against Kirk Stevens in Derby, his lone ranking title.

Alan McManus, on retiring, said his own proudest moment in snooker was the day he turned professional. Francisco takes a similar view: his personal pinnacle was his first major splash in the game.

'I'm very proud of what I achieved. The highlight of my whole career was beating Dennis at the Crucible in 1982, because he was ranked fairly high when I came over,' Francisco says.

'I had beaten him in South Africa. He and Willie Thorne came over and I beat him, and he had a lot to say did Dennis. He said he'd get his own back when I came over to England. He made a big thing about that, and he wasn't very happy that I beat him at the Crucible. I beat him fairly easily, as far as I remember.'

Francisco had a 7-2 lead clipped to 8-7 by Taylor but saw it out.

It astounded Francisco that he had survived longer in the tournament than Steve Davis.

'I started on the day Davis went out. Davis wasn't very happy at all, I can tell you that,' Francisco says. 'He was not happy. Knowles just absolutely took Davis apart.'

Ray Reardon eventually ended Francisco's run, the longest he would ever enjoy in a World Championship, inflicting a 13-8 quarter-final defeat on the South African.

It was an eventful debut, to say the least, with Francisco's Crucible experience made all the more memorable by the revelation he had a notable regular practice partner: none other than Alex Higgins.

'I was the only bloke who would practise with him, nobody else would,' Francisco recalls.

'He came to ask me and I was happy to oblige. Our relationship was not bad, not bad. He was a real funny fella, very strange, very strange. He was not easy to get on with.

'A lot of people just ignored him, a lot of the players. I got on OK with him, I didn't have problems with him.'

I ask whether he was present when Higgins found an unorthodox use for a plant pot during a late-night practice session. Indeed he was, Francisco says.

'Yes, I was there when he ran into trouble,' Francisco says. 'It was the moment where he tiddled into the flower pot.'

15: HIGGINS' FILTHY FOUL

WHEN ALEX HIGGINS 'tiddled into the flower pot', round about the midnight hour as Sunday, May 2 turned to Monday, May 3, he must have known there would be splash-back.

That ill-minded indiscretion in the Crucible practice room was followed by a scuffle with a venue electrician, drawing the attention of the World Professional Billiards and Snooker Association, which already held a bulging file marked 'Higgins'.

The sport's judiciary had been due to pass judgement after the World Championship on Higgins snapping at the Goff's crowd; now, the Hurricane faced another rap.

Higgins' deliberate filthy foul had caused local outrage, so much so that on Tuesday, May 4, the Sheffield Star newspaper gave the incident front-page billing.

The Star's top story was the sinking of the Belgrano, an Argentine warship, as the Falklands War escalated. But beneath its banner headline was news of snooker's night of shame: '"Hurricane" in snooker storm!'

Within the newspaper, a somewhat speculative write-up claimed Higgins' 'future at the World Championship was in doubt', with an official complaint having been made to the tournament promoter and to the WPBSA.

It was quite a day for news, with the Sheffield paper also carrying details of a stand collapsing the previous day in Scunthorpe, at the filming of the popular TV show It's a Knockout, with more than 50 people taken to hospital.

Thankfully, for Higgins, it wasn't to be a knockout for him in Sheffield. A ticking-off, with the incident placed on file, would suffice while the tournament continued.

A day later, the Star had a snooker follow-up, quoting Higgins as having told the Crucible official to 'bugger off' when their confrontation occurred.

The report also said Higgins claimed the man's gripe had merely been with the lateness of the practice session. Higgins went almost so far as to play the victim, blaming the promoter for not pinning up rules to let players know at what hour they should vacate the building.

In the set-to, however, the venue official had seen his jumper torn, so perhaps Higgins was less the wronged man than he made out.

'We have settled our differences,' Higgins later said. 'I have apologised and shaken hands. I've offered him a new sweater, which he has said he won't take, but I'm going to insist. It was totally my fault, just the fiery Alex again.'

If Higgins felt oppressed by the authorities for large parts of his career, then he hardly helped himself. The most serious offences to eventually scar Higgins' record had not been committed by 1982, but the list of lapses was growing almost by the tournament, boozy bust-ups and rampant wrongdoing forming part of the Higgins notoriety. Violent, belligerent, alcoholic: at his worst, Higgins was not so much a flawed genius as almost beyond redemption. At his best, he could still be a charmer.

Emptying his bladder into the flower pot was almost a victimless crime, by his standards, however unedifying, but that lamentable leak and the subsequent ruckus was widely reported to have been considered when Higgins ultimately was slapped with a £1,000 fine for his Goff's outburst.

The Sheffield electrician emerged with the offer of a jumper upgrade, plus an anecdote for life.

* *

Ronnie O'Sullivan once claimed snooker was guilty of treating Higgins 'shabbily'. Many would agree, defending their man to the hilt. Such disciples argue that Higgins came with his faults, and contend that snooker's authorities, rather than helping him, caused him only agitation.

The panel that sat in judgement on Higgins after his 1982 Crucible triumph determined he had brought snooker into disrepute. Suddenly, he was the bad boy again.

Jason Ferguson, the long-standing and two-time chair of the WPBSA, found it awkward when the governing body came in for criticism after Higgins died.

Based on his own dealings with Higgins, prior to taking the helm of the governing body, Ferguson pointed to a tinge of regret at how the player he knew and liked came to encounter such long-running conflict with the players' own association.

'This comes to mind every year on the anniversary of his passing: that I know he had his ups and downs with the WPBSA, but as a person I actually got on very well with him,' Ferguson said.

'I remember he was in the qualifiers in Blackpool. I turned professional in 1990 and there he was, this hero that I'd been watching on TV while I was playing on this little table in my living room in Mansfield. And here he was, walking down the corridor of the Norbreck Castle Hotel, and I'm in the qualifiers and there's these huge stars walking around. But he was very nice to me, and I can tell you on a number of occasions I met him that he'd also been very decent to other junior players as well. It's not a story you hear a lot. A lot of people will talk about his disciplinary matters and things like that, but actually I had a good relationship with him.

'It's a real shame, his decline. He had crossed paths with the WPBSA before my involvement and he had a lot of problems with the WPBSA, and it was quite difficult for me at the time because there was a lot of animosity towards the WPBSA when Alex passed away, and actually it wasn't me, because there was no animosity between me and Alex. I'd only had good experiences.'

It was during those Norbreck days that Ferguson had his closest contact with Higgins, and those first impressions have stood the test of time.

'I wasn't one of those he'd despatch to the bar, but he'd always come over and say, "Has anyone got a cigarette?" or "Can you give me a light?"

'He was quite a character, and he was drinking at that time and he was a fading force, but you couldn't help but look back and think, "Alex, you gave us something magical on that screen."'

Ferguson is shouting up the unquestionably great elements of Higgins the snooker player and shot-maker and letting others take up the slack when it comes to looking at the bigger picture.

He compares Higgins to Judd Trump, and taking their adventurous styles of play in isolation, of course Ferguson has a point. Away from the table, they could hardly be greater opposites in terms of character: the mild-mannered Trump, ever since he roared to his first Crucible final, has kept a safe distance

124

from trouble. There is no Oliver Reed figure in Trump's life, no Rolling Stones, no drug issues, nor a booze or gambling problem. He attests to being fashion conscious but hardly tests the boundaries in the way Higgins would, with the fedora and various absurd accoutrements – rabbits' feet, his daughter's dummy – being all part of the showman's image all those decades ago.

Trump is thoroughly likeable, wears snazzy shoes, and as a crowd-pleasing potter of snooker balls he brings all the party-piece shots.

'You look today at how good Judd is and the level that Judd Trump's taken snooker to,' says Ferguson. 'He plays this slightly unorthodox snooker, he plays fast, he plays the odd shot where you think, "Wow, where's that come from?" But this was Alex back in the early eighties. Alex was mesmerising. My father, Thomas, was a big fan and would say, "This Alex Higgins, he's unbelievable, you should see the shots he's playing."

'He played the game differently to everybody else, he was unorthodox, but you know what? He was a genius at work, that we do know. Technically, tactically, he was so much better than people gave him credit for in my view. I had a huge respect for him.'

Steve Acteson, who followed his Press Association stint with spells at the London Daily News, Today and Daily Star newspapers, remembers the frosty atmosphere Higgins could bring to a room.

'He attacked me in a bar,' Acteson says. 'That was years later on from '82, but he'd just lost to Joe Johnson in the first round of the Grand Prix in Reading. We were in the bar at the Ramada Hotel, which was just 500 yards away from the venue.

'It was a big open bar and the tournament director Ann Yates was there. Higgins knew her from when he used to derisively call her a sash girl because she used to help out with the hospitality. And Higgins came from the North and Ann was from the Republic, being as he imagined some sort of hardline Protestant.

'Higgins started cat-calling across to Ann Yates because she had her niece with her, and Ann's niece had her boyfriend with her. And Higgins was calling out, "Oh Ann, I see you've got your niece with you, who's paying for her hotel bill. Is it the WPBSA? Ha ha."

'I just said to Alex, "Look, she's with her boyfriend, I guess that's who's paying her bill."

'I turned round and someone suddenly said, "Watch out!" and Higgins was storming across the room, going, "Acteson, fucking Acteson!"

'He grabbed me by the throat, but he was eight stone ringing wet, Alex. I got up and just shoved him away. He turned around and he started laying into everybody verbally.

'Alasdair Ross from The Sun and Dave Armitage from the Daily Star were standing at the bar. They were saying, "Calm down, Alex, pack it in," and he was having a go at them, and he picked up a glass ashtray. He was out of control basically.

'Ali took the ashtray off him, and Alex pointed at him and said, "See that, he's got a weapon, call the police." Well, it was Alex who caused the problem in the first place; if anybody's gonna get arrested it was him. But that was Alex. The temperature in the room dropped by 10 degrees when Alex would walk into it because you didn't know what Alex you were getting.

'Sometimes, like at [the Jameson International Open in] Derby, possibly that 1982 year, we'd be sitting there, and he'd be talking about cricket. And I remember him saying, "I can play billiards as well as I can play snooker, so why aren't there more all-rounders like Ian Botham in cricket."

'At other times, Alex could be absolutely charming.

'He could be quite fisty. There'd be one Alex Higgins who would pay a taxi driver £100 to drive him somewhere to a charity do, to support it. There'd be the same Alex Higgins who, back in Northern Ireland, I know of a chap who told me that he and his son queued up to get a photograph autographed by Higgins. Alex looked at this photograph from this 10-year-old boy and said, "It's not a very good likeness, is it?" and ripped up the photograph, threw it on the floor and walked off. So that was two fans lost.

'But he was such a mass of contradictions. He'd got a terrible cue action, and yet he was one of the greatest players ever to play the game. He'd play shots that other people wouldn't even dream of.

'It just left people standing open-mouthed, thinking, "How did you think of that one?" But, you know, unfortunately, through drink, through drugs, he was the architect of his own downfall. It was the caricature of Alex at the end. It was heartbreaking.'

The WPBSA said it gave Higgins 'considerable' financial help in his final years, as he fought cancer and suffered a long stretch of ill health. A benevolent band of players also quietly did likewise.

'You could see how much he was loved by some players, like Jimmy White. He loved Higgins,' says Acteson. 'I mean, Higgins totally exasperated Jimmy with the way he behaved, but they had some great times together, all sorts of stuff, and he idolised him.

'Jimmy was nobody's fool. He was a very savvy, streetwise bloke. He wasn't in awe of him so much, but he was a very good, close friend. People like Jimmy were heartbroken when Alex died. They all tried to help him. The WPBSA, who Alex was forever berating, they did as much as they possibly could to help him. But Alex is one of those people that just couldn't be helped.'

At Higgins' funeral, a tribute from White was read out, in which he berated his great mate for pushing aside many who tried to intervene. 'But that was Alex,' White added. 'He was an individual, his own man, he was the Hurricane. I will miss him to the end.'

White told me later it was important snooker paid a lasting tribute, and that came to pass when the Northern Ireland Open winner's keepsake was named the Alex Higgins Trophy, the renegade's name adorning a showy piece of cut crystal once more.

16: The show must always go on

THE MORE THE global political and cultural landscape changes, the more the World Championship bubble remains resolutely impermeable.

Take the death of Al-Qaeda leader Osama bin Laden, the man on whom blame for the 9/11 attacks in 2001 was widely pinned.

Not long after play ended on day one of the 2011 Crucible final between John Higgins and Judd Trump, news broke of the CIA-led armed raid on Bin Laden's previously secret compound in Abbottabad, Pakistan.

It was going to take something extraordinary to turn conversation away from that day's dramatic action on the baize, and with dramatic timing Barack Obama played his wildcard as news emerged of the death of the world's most wanted man.

This news was the buzz of the Mercure St Paul's bar for at least five minutes in the unruly early hours while players, pundits and punters gathered and gamely attempted to drink the place dry.

The dramatic end to Bin Laden's decade-long game of hide-and-seek had registered, yet discussions soon reverted to how Higgins might fend off boy wonder Trump in Monday's action, or whose round it was next, and given it was long after 3am perhaps it was also time for bed.

Having lasted 16 days of snooker's spring jamboree, it was commonly felt there could be an invasion of little green men in the neighbouring Peak District and this preoccupied corner of Sheffield would carry on, business as usual. One more day, then home – only one war of the Worlds to be concerned about.

Had there been an impending nuclear assault on Sheffield, as imagined by Barry Hines and Mike Jackson in the nightmarish 1984 drama Threads, the question at the Crucible might have been whether another frame or two could be slotted in before the apocalyptic moment of detonation and devastation.

You don't have to be an obsessive, but it helps.

**

Sheffield in the spring of 1982 is a city jolted, and there are more tremors on the way.

Local unemployment is through the roof (officially, it surges from 13,273 in May 1979 to 42,554 by October 1982, in Sheffield's travel-to-work area), with the steel foundries rivalled only by the pits when it comes to misfortune frowning on the workplace.

Those wishing for sporting succour will see Jack Charlton's Wednesday agonisingly pipped at the post for promotion to the First Division. United are about to be crowned Fourth Division champions, but what were they doing down there to begin with?

Unfulfilled potential peppers the city, but hope is not lost.

The Human League and ABC, formed in Sheffield and twin beacons of glamour and ambition, are racking up sales at record shops from Broomhall to Brooklyn.

New Romantic, post-punk and goth movements are taking a grip on disenfranchised factions of the city's youth, the generation who can and will paint this place a brighter future.

130

Fashion and music fuse as the artistic communities strike back. Resilience will be in plentiful supply. This city will march until its feet blister against cuts perceived to be callous, with the municipal council's radical model of local socialism at least offering a glimmer of hope for sunshine days ahead. (The left-wing local authority's conspicuity soon leads the district to be labelled a 'People's Republic' – by both critics and supporters.)

Beyond Sheffield's brutalist facade, its emptying factories, and the poverty so many are enduring, there is obstinate charisma serving as a stirring counterpunch. Early eighties Sheffield is bouncing back, but there will be blows along the way.

* *

Showtime is beckoning at the Crucible on May 4, 1982, with Willie Thorne and Terry Griffiths about to resume their first-round match in an afternoon session.

Eight thousand miles away in the South Atlantic, an Exocet anti-ship missile is despatched from an Argentine navy Super Etendard strike fighter aircraft and crashes into the starboard side of HMS Sheffield.

It tears a savage hole in the hull, reaches the ship's galley, and 20 men die, a devastating blow to the UK during the Falklands conflict. Soon, the warship known as 'Shiny Sheff' will sink.

At home, news emerges slowly. That evening, Defence Ministry spokesman Ian McDonald reads a statement to television news cameras, soberly detailing the sequence of events.

He says: 'In the course of its duties within the total exclusion zone around the Falkland Islands, HMS Sheffield, a Type 42 destroyer, was attacked and hit late this afternoon by an Argentine missile. The ship caught fire which spread out of control. When there was no longer any hope of saving the ship, the ship's company abandoned ship. All who abandoned her were picked up. It is feared there have been a number of casualties, but we have no details of them yet.'

Those that deliver bad news rarely get a positive public reaction. In more recent times, consider England's Covid-era chief medical officer Chris Whitty.

Duly the updates from McDonald on the Falklands crisis draw a sour reaction from some.

A letter printed by the Daily Mirror, attributed to a 'Wing Cdr. G. McMahon, DFM (retired)', describes McDonald as possessing the personality of 'a mortician's assistant, with the verve of a depressed snail'. This same correspondent duly concludes that 'the effect on public morale must be disastrous'.

In Sheffield, meanwhile, there is great grief at the Royal Navy's first loss of a warship in combat since the Second World War.

HMS Sheffield had been launched in 1971 by Queen Elizabeth II and the Duke of Edinburgh, who travelled to Barrow-in-Furness on the duke's 50th birthday to perform the ceremony. Propelled by four Rolls-Royce engines and kitted out with surface-to-air missile launchers, Sheffield was a mighty 410-foot warrior of the ocean, a vessel at the vanguard until its defences were undone by a stealthy enemy.

Services are held in Sheffield to mourn the loss of life. The city's cathedral holds a memorial where speakers include Reverend Frank Curtis, Lord Mayor Enid Hattersley and Sheffield Attercliffe MP Patrick Duffy. Duffy served in the Second World War and survived a plane crash in the Orkneys that left him with burns so significant he was read his last rites, later serving as Navy minister in Jim Callaghan's Labour government. He is rather well qualified to offer commentary on such matters.

Come recent times, there is no obvious record of how the tragedy was marked in Sheffield's Crucible theatre, or indeed whether there was any official moment of silence.

I ask those who might remember, but nobody recalls the Falklands losses being noted at the World Championship.

If there was no such observance, consider that such mournful silences at sporting events were not quite so commonplace as they have become.

Also, as a reminder, Sheffield's snooker marathon is such a law unto itself that most news that penetrates the theatre's dense, breeze block walls, no matter how desperate, is often considered as belonging to another world, to be given due consideration only once out of the building or once the day's play finishes.

The Falklands conflict was all over in barely 10 weeks. Within days of the snooker finishing, photographer Simon Knott captured a striking shot of Sunday newspaper boards on Fitzalan Square, a two-minute stroll from the Crucible. In Knott's picture, the News of the World declares, 'Argys are on the run', while the Sunday People proclaims, 'Britain on road to victory'.

Aged four (and a half) at the time, I can recall glimpsing burning ships on television news bulletins when visiting the home of a nursery school friend. The gravity of that situation and the political significance of the war naturally washed over us.

Or perhaps it was just me it washed over. Many years later, this boyhood pal received an MBE for his own armed forces service.

* *

The Crucible's thrust stage, taking the drama practically into the laps of the audience, made it ideally suited to snooker.

Its layout was championed by revered theatre director Sir Tyrone Guthrie and designer Tanya Moiseiwitsch. Seating for the audience on three sides of the stage was unusual, and in 1971 nobody had an inkling this would lead the theatre to become better known as a home for sport than for the performing arts.

Mike Watterson described the Crucible, based on his first inspection, as resembling 'a dropout's hangout', going so far as to label it 'an embarrassment to the city'.

Watterson complained of discovering 'beatniks' dotted about the theatre when snooker arrived in 1977, six years after it opened its doors, and Steve Davis remembers such grumbles.

'Mike told me that even though it was made with the arts in mind, it quickly fell into disarray, with the type of people that were hanging around in it,' Davis says. 'I wouldn't say snooker has salvaged the place, but perhaps early on it gave it a sense of identity that it was losing.

'Sheffield was more of a concrete jungle then and nowhere near as pretty as it has become.

'The Crucible is certainly a focal point in the city, and that happened overnight I think, from 1979 when Terry Griffiths won. That was the first year when everyone was watching on television. I think that was the first year the BBC showed the tournament in its entirety – blanket coverage. My only stroke of luck would be that I hit the ground running at the right time.'

John Airey, as a paying punter for over four decades and a tournament season ticket holder for much of that time, is well placed to offer a sense of the venue in its early days.

'It was completely different back then in the arena,' says Airey.

'You used to be able to see the smoke come gradually down from the ceiling. Probably 20 per cent of the crowd was smoking, and as the session continued you could see this fug descending. And people could take drinks in, so you'd get lads walking in with trays of pints.

'Every tournament in those days, someone would fall over carrying one of those trays and there'd be a crash-bang-wallop moment.

'And there'd be illegal bookies lurking nearby because you had to pay tax on your bets in those days, nine per cent, so there'd be a guy around the corner from the Crucible with a suitcase of cash and he'd offer the same price as the bookies but with no tax. Higgins would be out there, putting bets on the nags.'

Initially perceived by many as a snooker automaton, Davis was so focused on his craft that he barely had any time to indulge his other great love: music.

Sheffield had been experiencing a creative surge, with the likes of a fledgling Human League, Cabaret Voltaire, ABC and Heaven 17 at its vanguard, surrounded by a curious array of talented acts that never quite troubled the charts, the likes of They Must Be Russians, Mein Glas Fabrik and Surface Mutants. There would have been plenty to tempt the Davis taste buds as clanging sounds of the Steel City burst from rehearsal rooms, often in deserted former factories, if only he had been listening.

Music offered escapism to many. In the late April days leading to the 1982 World Championship, Sheffield played host to Thin Lizzy at the City Hall and The Cure at the Polytechnic's Phoenix Hall. Altered Images hit the Phoenix on May 8. U2 performed at the Lyceum – next door to the Crucible – in October 1981, while Johnny Cash walked the line at the City Hall in the same month.

Sheffield newcomers Pulp were featured in Melody Maker, a January 1982 interview with Frank Worrall describing the band's live show as 'a carnival of lunacy'. They had already recorded a session for John Peel and would bring their razzmatazz to the Crucible stage in October 1982, performing at the Stars on Sundae event in the venue's compact, secondary studio theatre.

'We just want to get on to Top of the Pops as soon as we can,' an 18-year-old Jarvis Cocker told Worrall, who noted the remark was made with 'tongue firmly in cheek'.

Cocker and co. would have to wait for their big break. On June 2, 1994, Pulp finally made their Top of the Pops debut, and for the next four years they would be mainstays, their subcultural tendencies having eventually led to mainstream success.

In May 1982, the Human League were touring North America, being described by the New York Times' Stephen Holden after a show at Manhattan's Palladium concert hall as 'the most melodic, as well as the most intellectually edifying' of English synth-pop bands.

They were riding high on the success of the album Dare and the global smash hit Don't You Want Me, a Sheffield export to make a song and dance about. The single would hit number one in the States in July, having already been a UK Christmas chart-topper.

Lead singer Phil Oakey had spotted teenage pals Joanne Catherall and Susanne Sulley dancing at Sheffield's Crazy Daizy nightclub barely 18 months earlier, instinctively inviting them to join his hitherto heavily experimental band as backing vocalists. It was this chance encounter, and the instant chemistry of the new-look band, that saw the Human League shoot into pop's Premier League.

Back home, there were precious few waitresses working in cocktail bars. Unemployment in South Yorkshire stood officially at 11.5 per cent, but the Daily Mirror reported how local sources suspected the real figure to be around 20 per cent, albeit quoting a Department of Employment spokesman as denying the lower figure was inaccurate.

In April 1982, Sheffield City Council leader David Blunkett described the jobs situation as 'a disgrace' and claimed the government's 'monopoly' on statistics meant it was using that privilege to save money.

It was a time of heightened political tension, unease, fear and outrage, in Britain and overseas.

At Sheffield City Polytechnic – since rechristened as Sheffield Hallam University – the Phoenix Hall that staged The Cure would be renamed later in 1982 as the Nelson Mandela Building, to honour the then-jailed South African anti-apartheid radical activist.

At the University of Sheffield, meanwhile, a teenage Helen Sharman was studying chemistry. For the former Jordanthorpe Comprehensive schoolgirl, this was one small step towards becoming Britain's first astronaut just nine years later.

Another Jordanthorpe student was Brendan Moore, who has yet to see the Earth from outer space. He has, however, been one of the chosen few to populate snooker's inner sanctum as an arbiter of the beautiful game.

A huge boyhood fan of snooker, Moore had a reasonable talent with cue in hand but not one that would take him anywhere close to the professional ranks, so a career in white gloves, dinner jacket and dickie bow was an appealing alternative.

Moore, still at primary school in 1982, never gave it a moment's thought that he might become a snooker referee, one who would go on to take charge of World Championship finals.

By this stage of his life, at the age of 10, he had yet to step inside the Crucible.

'If we ever went to the theatre with school, we used to go to the Lyceum, for pantomimes or plays,' Moore says.

In May 1982, Moore still had a year left at primary school in Lowedges, which like Jordanthorpe can be found at the southern tip of Sheffield, and like many children up and down the country he was gripped by the new phenomenon of computer games.

The Commodore 64 was months away from going on sale – a moment that still evokes vivid memories for Moore.

Thanks to a Sheffield shopping institution dating back to the late 1800s, there was a pocket-money paradise in the centre of the city. It also offered window shoppers a cinematic experience.

'The one thing I miss from Sheffield as a kid is the shop Redgates. It was the eighties' version of Toys R Us basically, but bigger,' Moore says.

'It was spread over three or four floors, back when computer games were new. When the Commodore 64 first came out they had this game called International Soccer and they played it on the big screen in the shop window. Me and my mate – this is how sad we were – at 10 years old we sat there, went to the fish and chip shop, and just sat there watching it being played because we'd never seen anything like it.

'They had a section for Scalextric, another for Subbuteo, then your girls' stuff with your dolls and Barbies, and your boys' toys like Action Man. And I don't know why it went, or what happened to it – probably pretty much what's happened to Toys R Us now – but it made Toys R Us look bad.'

The family owners of Redgates sold up in 1986, and the chain that inherited the prime location, Zodiac Toys, pulled down the shutters for the final time two years later.

'We had another shop called EMK that was the bargain basement for computer games, and they had the games for the Spectrum on cassettes, and they were 99p or £1.99,' Moore adds. 'I was both a Spectrum and Commodore boy, and all these years later I'm still a gamer. I've got the modern stuff.

'I always played snooker though. I had a six-foot table at home when I was six or seven and we used to play at the transport club where my dad was a bus driver, and I'm now captain of the snooker club there from when I was a bus driver too.

'We had one table in there that was full size and you had to be 14 to play on it. There was a nine-hole golf course at the club too, and my dad would go off to play golf and say to me, "Whatever you do, do not go on that snooker table." He knew what was happening though. Me and my friend would shut the curtains, and he'd see that and walk in and say, "What did I tell you?"

'But he let me carry on playing. I've always played. I've made centuries in practice but my highest ever in a match is 63.

'My first time here at the Crucible watching snooker was when I was 23, 24, and it was Jimmy White. I finished a bus-driving shift and came straight to the box office, asked if they had any tickets, and they did, and I was two seats in from the centre on the front row, so I had a view of both tables. After that, I came every year.'

In a city split by football allegiances, Moore is an avowed Wednesdayite, always eager to visit Hillsborough when at home, but his commitment not always so clear-cut.

Moore's father, Derek, died on Christmas Day in 2021. Derek was a Sheffield United fan but had a soft spot for Wednesday too, and Moore remembers 'going to Bramall Lane one week and Hillsborough the next with my dad'.

'If they played each other, he'd probably just prefer United. I was like that when I was a kid, but then I started going to Wednesday with my friends who were all fans,' Moore says. 'The only thing I remember about football in 1982 was the World Cup in Spain, and me crying as a 10-year-old when Italy beat Brazil 3-2. It was all Brazil then. Me and my mates all had Brazil shirts.'

Sheffield has undergone a large-scale facelift in Moore's time, particularly close to the Crucible, with a shabby car park outside the theatre replaced by the paved piazza pomp of Tudor Square.

The giant greenhouse of the Winter Gardens beyond, attached to the Mercure hotel, represents an aesthetic upgrade from its former state: here stood the brutalist precast concrete-fronted

'Egg Box', an inelegant extension of the Town Hall that looked gloriously voguish for perhaps all of five minutes.

Moore fondly recalls the 'Hole in the Road' roundabout, just along Arundel Gate from the Crucible.

This was where pedestrians would navigate a shop-lined underpass, an audacious exercise in bringing a new trading culture to Sheffield, with doomed pretensions to grandeur. A giant fish tank became cultish, a popular meeting point, yet this cool-cat Hole soon withered to a rathole, graffitied and occupied by murky characters of the type that would have stalked Mike Watterson's angstiest dreams if they ever stepped foot in snooker's hallowed home up the road.

Built in 1967, the once-futuristic sprawl was filled with rubble in 1994 and sealed to allow Supertram tracks to run over its site.

Sheffield has undergone a handsome makeover, but Moore would still love to revisit the homestead of old, warts and all.

'I miss the old city,' says Moore. 'Don't get me wrong, I like Sheffield now, but that was how I grew up with Sheffield.'

The world changes, though, and standing still invites trouble.

Epochal moments in history pass, the next chapter begins.

Moore left snooker behind in 2023, taking up a new job in pool. Snooker may one day leave Sheffield, though that would be a sorry day, given the sport and city have forged such a tight bond.

Today, snooker's adopted home is a good, sturdy city. Its door swings open for mis-shapes and misfits; it keeps us feeling fascination; its biggest nights soar to giddy stratospheres.

For these sing-song factors alone, snooker's ragtag and bobtail 1970s tribe stumbled on a perfect match in the Steel City.

But the foundries, the factories and the mines were meant to last forever, and we know what happened there. Sheffield might do well to brace itself for a shock to the system again.

17: 'HE'S GONE, AND HE'S GONE, SO I'M IN THE FINAL'

EL-HADJI DIOUF, Jennifer Ellison and Willie Thorne walk into a bar.

And before that delicious set-up surrenders a punchline, Jayne Torvill and Christopher Dean roll in too.

It is the evening of April 24, 2012, or at least it was when the press pack entered the fray. Strictly speaking, it is now the morning of April 25, and the lounge of the Mercure St Paul's is bustling.

As well as the usual snooker crowd, this city centre hotel is the chosen tavern of Torvill and Dean's Dancing on Ice stars, fresh from performing at Sheffield Arena. That explains the presence of the eponymous hosts and the soap actor turned showbiz lifer Ellison, joining the greats on skates. Quite what former Liverpool footballer Diouf is doing here – quite separately and with a pleasingly peacocky entourage – is less obviously apparent, although he is now playing for nearby Doncaster Rovers.

Star of the show, however, is unquestionably Thorne. This is his fiefdom, his personal stage. The great WT. Mr Maximum. The 1985 Mercantile Credit Classic champion. Everyone wants a bit of Willie. And over the decades he has gladly accommodated glad-handers, autograph hunters, anyone wanting to chew the fat about the day's snooker, or the racing.

'No one enjoyed being the centre of attention more than Willie,' said Cliff Thorburn.

Being in the close company of the garrulous Thorne lasts only so long this time. By 1am, he has disappeared off to bed, another day of commentary for the BBC just hours away.

It occurs to me this is a practised routine: Thorne has been coming to Sheffield in the spring ever since 1977; he loves the place unreservedly, despite the Crucible being the stage for what he describes as his 'biggest failure'.

That false step, Thorne wrote in his book Taking A Punt On My Life, was a squandered opportunity to win the 1982 World Championship, a tournament he considered there for the taking.

With Steve Davis, Terry Griffiths and Thorburn bundled out in the first round – Thorne accounting for Griffiths – glory beckoned, at least in 28-year-old Willie's eyes.

'Willie used to say, "Right, he's gone, and he's gone, so I'm in the final,"' David Taylor remembers.

Thorne died on June 17, 2020. A leukaemia diagnosis came in March of that year, as large parts of the world went into lockdown. That crushing blow was followed by Thorne being put into an induced coma shortly before his death, caused by respiratory failure. Septic shock followed, as Thorne lost his battle for life and snooker mourned one of its best-loved figures.

Silvino Francisco was heartbroken by the passing of a long-time friend.

Francisco lost contact with most of his snooker rivals and colleagues after his playing days ended, but he recalled that he and Thorne remained close.

'I stayed in touch with Willie. How he died, I just can't get over that,' Francisco says. His mind then revisits peak Thorne.

'He could have been a world champion, without a shadow of a doubt. He was a tremendous potter and all-round player; he really was good.'

Thorne broke his right leg in a go-karting accident in August 1981, also suffering major damage to his left foot, yet eight months later he sniffed the opportunity of a lifetime at the Crucible.

After scuttling former champions Griffiths and John Spencer, Thorne was lined up to tackle another previous winner, Alex Higgins, in the 1982 quarter-finals.

At the table, Thorne was in great shape. Away from the baize, Thorne had been keeping himself busy by having an affair with the wife of a friend.

On the opening day of his clash with Higgins, that liaison was exposed, and the tabloid coverage was hardly ideal timing for Thorne. He later admitted feeling doubly scrutinised by the Sheffield crowds: judged for his snooker alongside his playing away, all the while as he fought to tame the Hurricane.

As Thorne battled to focus, Higgins, unusually, had a clear sense of destiny in Sheffield. It was all for young Lauren, a father's gift to his daughter. Higgins was so consumed by this dewy-eyed ideal that he was barely eating, but on May 10, the morning of the Thorne match getting under way, he devoured bacon and eggs. After days of getting by on stout, long glasses of milk and vitamin pills, this time Higgins went full throttle on a full stomach.

The lowdown on their tussle is that Thorne trailed 5-3 after day one but grappled back to 6-6, helped by a 143 break. The total clearance ranked as the second highest break in the tournament's history at that moment.

'Willie pots a fantastic pink, goes up and down the table a few times and sinks the black, and at the very end he goes to sit down and Higgins blows his fag in his face,' remembers snooker super-fan John Airey.

Higgins, who gallantly paired a red shirt and yellow collar with cream trousers and waistcoat, got himself a lead again and ultimately dug in for a 13-10 victory, a considerable obstacle cleared on the path to the final.

Thorne's tournament was over and he would only reach the quarter-finals one more time, in 1986 when Thorburn emphatically had his number.

David Taylor, who had a semi-final run at the World Championship in 1980, was particularly close to Thorne.

After stunning Griffiths in his 1982 opener, Thorne spoke of his debt to Taylor, suggesting it was the Cheshire man's calm-headed influence that had set him on the right track.

Quoted in the Sheffield Star on May 5, 1982, Thorne said: 'I've had chat after chat with David Taylor and he convinced me that you don't have to get the big breaks to win. He has helped me tremendously. I also went to a hypnotist to sort out a few things. Everybody tells me how well I can play. I just didn't know how to win.'

Four decades years later, Taylor recalls how Thorne even sought his counsel on where to stay in Sheffield, and how he accepted the suggestion of eschewing the bright lights of the Grosvenor to head into the nearby Peak District, west of the city, for a little peace.

'I stayed at The Castle in Castleton,' says Taylor.

'Willie Thorne said to me, "You got to the semis, where did you stay?" which was a strange question, but typical of Willie. I told him we were at Castleton and he finished up staying there as well. It was only 15 minutes out from the Crucible. It was good to get your head out of the bubble and it worked for me in 1980, but it didn't work so well after that.'

Taylor, being 11 years Thorne's senior, pushed hard to rein in the all-or-nothing instincts of his younger, easily persuaded buddy.

'Willie and John Virgo were my big friends. We had some good times. Willie played Doug Mountjoy at the World Championship a year earlier and he was going out, but he had a great chance of beating Doug in my view,' Taylor says. 'It just wasn't going to happen, though, because Willie saw half a chance of a pot and he went for it. Doug was too wily for him.

'I just started saying, "Let's just go through a few safety shots," and eventually he lost, but he came back in his career. He had so much talent that man, it was unbelievable. He had all the credentials to be a world champion and was a great player.'

The schoolboy Ken Doherty, keeping tabs on the championship from his Dublin home, remembers Thorne pushing Higgins hard, and the 143 break told the young Doherty he was watching a special talent.

'Breaks like that were scarce,' says Doherty. 'There hadn't been a 147 yet at the Crucible. Cliff Thorburn made the first in 1983, so breaks of 140-plus were a real rarity. Doug Mountjoy had a 145 there once which was a huge thing. Willie was a class, class player, and he had a wonderful touch. He used to study how the pack would break and would be always making wonderful little cannons. He was a very, very classy player, Willie Thorne, and he's sadly missed.

'I played Willie a few times and had some great moments in his company, not only playing him but working in the commentary box with him for the BBC.'

Three years after Thorne's first notable Crucible run, he sprinted 13-8 ahead of Steve Davis in the 1985 UK Championship final, only to miss a gimme blue in the next frame, lose all momentum, and slide to a 16-14 defeat. True greats are defined by their titles, and sadly Thorne does not belong to that class, as skilled a player as he was and as popular as his repartee became to television viewers. Still, it takes serious potting prowess to even get into a position whereby you can miss such opportunities as that defining blue, and Thorne will not be forgotten in a hurry.

'I think when he lost in that final to Steve Davis, that was a big turning point in his career,' says Doherty. 'If he had beaten Steve Davis in that final and won the UK Championship, who knows? Willie Thorne had the capabilities, the potential, of going on to win the World Championship as well. Losing that final to Steve sort of knocked him for six, knocked a bit of confidence out of him, and although he would still often be at the business end of events, it didn't quite happen.

'He used to beat me, and I used to beat him. Going up against him at the Grand Prix in Bournemouth was one of the first professional matches I played when I came back as world champion in the 1997-98 season, and he beat me that day. He was a wonderful player, he had a great touch and a great knowledge of the game, and he was a really top-class break-builder.'

How might Thorne's story have turned out had he landed the 1982 world title? A compulsive gambler already, that terrible addiction would not have been cured by sudden wealth. So much in his life appeared entangled with the struggle to resist a bet, but the prestige of being a world champion never harmed anyone, and it may have provided succour in his darkest moments.

There were gloomy moments, no doubt, but sunshine and bonhomie were also plentiful in Thorne's life, and Thorburn recalled him once marching into the Crucible green room, clocking the assembled cream of the crop, and barking: 'Right, who's the second best player in here now that I'm here?'

Thorne went bankrupt twice because of the gambling illness that drove him to despair, the absence of self-control causing damage to relationships inside and outside snooker.

'He was a very naturally talented player and probably didn't fulfil his full potential as a player, maybe because of other things going on off the table,' says Jason Ferguson. 'It's well documented, his life, and also there were some great players around back then.'

Nigel Bond describes Thorne as 'probably a little bit of a nearly man', but Darley Dale's 1995 Crucible runner-up was in awe of the Leicester man's talent.

'I always got on great with Willie,' says Bond. 'He had beautiful cue ball control. In and around the black he was so fluent, so natural.'

I first interviewed Thorne in 1997, when he was complaining that although his form on the practice table was mesmerising, for whatever reason he could not consistently transfer that fluency into the match arena.

He was stumped and it was gnawing away at him, because when it came to talent, Thorne had it all.

'He was a player ahead of his time, with the way he played,' says commentator David Hendon.

'He was far more attacking than most of them and he'd do well in this era.

'Now there are 70-odd players who've had 100 centuries, but he was the sixth or seventh to do it, in a different era. Also, he obviously had certain flaws which stopped him winning tournaments.

'So, when Davis and Griffiths went out in '82, because they'd dominated the season I think everybody fancied their chances. It was suddenly wide open, but there is something to be said for having won it already, and obviously Higgins was a former champion.'

There are sorry stories of Thorne borrowing money from friends within sporting circles and failing to come good on returning the cash. Barry Hearn has spoken of writing out a £25,000 cheque in 2017 for a desperate Thorne and never expecting to see the money again.

What is firmly on the public record is that Thorne borrowed over £450,000 between March 2012 and March 2015 while insolvent and without having the means to pay back that money. Many have been left out of pocket, with Mr Maximum unable to repay the bare minimum, to his great regret.

Gamblers Anonymous describes addiction as 'an illness, progressive in its nature, which can never be cured, but can be arrested'.

Thorne found it tragically difficult to press the stop button.

It falls to a player who also fell on hard times to shower the Thorne story with a little empathy.

Francisco was declared bankrupt in 1996 amid difficulties in his private life and diminishing returns with cue in hand. All these years later, he looks back affectionately on his friendship with Thorne, wishing his old chum's story came with a cheerier ending.

'We got on really well. The only problem with Willie is he was a bad gambler,' says Francisco. 'I think that knocked him a bit back with his snooker. Money was like water to him and that was his big problem. I think he would have been a much better snooker player if he didn't gamble like he did.'

18: Even Mr Perfection falls early

For John Virgo, who stumbled out of this World Championship after a second-round loss to Ray Reardon, the stars never quite aligned in Sheffield.

They called him Mr Perfection – perfectionism being an astrological hallmark of a virgo – but a semi-final run in 1979, the year that he won the UK Championship, was as close as JV came to an imperial performance on the Crucible baize.

Like his close friend Thorne, Virgo fancied the look of his own chances when the seeds began to scatter in 1982, only for hopes of a big win in the Steel City to be derailed by a major success elsewhere.

With his round-two slot secured by a 10-4 saunter against Mike Hallett, Virgo took himself out of the bubble and away to Chester races. A big gambler then, he claims to have pocketed more by backing Dawn Johnny and Walter Swinburn for the Chester Cup than he would have landed for potting snooker's biggest prize.

But Virgo's head was suddenly wobbled, distracted by this sudden racecourse windfall, and he felt he bungled an opportunity against Reardon, sliding to a 13-8 defeat.

'Virgo is another who could have been a world champion,' says David Taylor.

'I remember John going to India. He'd won the UK Championship and went out there, and he said to me that he was practising out there and Steve Davis came along and said, "I'm playing today, can I have a few hours with you," and after two hours Davis said, "John, I'm going to practise by myself, I've not had a shot yet."

'John Virgo was that good, he really was special and people tend to forget it.'

People forget this because as good a player as Virgo was, he has become an even better commentator.

In September 2021, Virgo caused a stir when he told Talking Snooker he was being shuffled into retirement from the BBC booth. This came during well-intentioned efforts to bring in fresh voices, but was it not too soon to say 'Goodnight JV'?

Forgoing Virgo's expert voice would have meant giving a kiss-off to the worldliness and shrewd eye for a shot that had built during his 50 years in the game, the wisdom that he relayed to viewers with that warm Salford brogue and teasing humour. It was a popular decision, therefore, when it emerged during the 2022 World Championship that he would be kept on.

Virgo was famously caught swearing on mid-afternoon BBC coverage of the World Championship in 2016, when during a slow-going semi-final between Mark Selby and Marco Fu he could be heard remarking: 'I wanted to watch a bit of racing this afternoon. I'll be lucky to watch some fucking Match of the Day.'

He had enough credit in the bank for that magnificently outspoken quip to be laughed off and quickly forgotten, with an apologetic Virgo having been convinced he was fully off-mic. It was a blunder I was compelled to report, but which everyone was glad caused no serious repercussions. It was classic Virgo, if not intended for a wider audience.

Virgo's presence is an assurance of old-school charm, brilliant off-the-cuff anecdotes and streetwise sense, having been involved in the game well before the 1980s boom.

Gambling got him into financial trouble for a while, but a rescue route emerged in 1990 when his Big Break arrived, Virgo talent-spotted to play the sharp-witted foil to presenter Jim Davidson as game-show snooker took over Saturday night BBC television.

In his early days, Virgo, like so many others, had needed money to be riding on his matches, even in practice.

'Terry Griffiths, after he turned pro, would go into his snooker room with a flask and his sandwiches and play all day, but I always had to play for something,' Virgo said.

'Snooker clubs, before the professional game, were already hugely popular. The pro game in the late seventies and early eighties became very popular on television, but before that, every main town that you went to there was a snooker club and someone in there would be having a bet on this, that and the other – it's a completely different culture to what it is now.

'I see the snooker clubs today and most of them, like the betting shops really, are full of one-armed bandits and things like that. There used to be card tables. In my day, down at the snooker club you either played for money or you backed someone else. The centre of attention was that snooker table and the gambling that was going on.'

Virgo likes to use the term 'a den of iniquity' when visualising such a club, having remembered his father describing them that way.

A while ago, Virgo wrote a book about his friendship with Alex Higgins, and the experiences they shared. Just as he was able to attend Thorne's funeral during the pandemic, as both had been living in Spain, so Virgo was present to see off Higgins on 2 August 2010, when thousands lined the streets of Belfast for a final farewell to the Hurricane.

Among fellow mourners for Higgins were Thorne, Jimmy White, Stephen Hendry, Ken Doherty and Joe Swail. At the time, there were questions about why the likes of Steve Davis, Barry Hearn and Ronnie O'Sullivan had not been spotted at that send-off, but it smacks of pettiness to judge anyone by their non-attendance at a funeral.

Those in snooker know the debt they owe to Higgins, whether or not they liked the man or wished to be part of that day.

Virgo got to see Higgins' rise and fall. Others only witnessed the aftermath of his best days.

'Alex was a little before my era and I don't remember his matches at the time,' said O'Sullivan, 'but I do remember going to Blackpool when I was 16 and he was in the qualifiers, and we shared some games on the practice table.

'I used to go and get him his Guinness. When he was playing his matches it was like I was his slave – it was "Go get me this", "Go get me that". And I was quite happy to do that because he was a legend, you know.'

This was what happened in 1992 at the Norbreck Castle Hotel, where legends in decline would brush shoulders with rising stars, and where far-fetched dreams of making it in the paid ranks would be savagely shattered week after week. Beside the seaside, in this vast and turreted tourist lodging, the boy O'Sullivan won 74 of 76 matches in the summer of 1992 to ink himself into almost every main draw in the season ahead, with Eddie Charlton and Fred Davis among those he brushed aside. The Norbreck is where the notion of professionalism might be challenged by behaviour that could stray into 'lads on tour' territory, the weeks and months on end spent away from home causing some to lose touch with reality. Survive and thrive at the Norbreck and you had broken the back of cracking the game. While Alex Higgins toiled, a decade on from his Crucible triumph, snooker's Class of '92 was born, with teenagers O'Sullivan, Mark Williams and John Higgins breaking through.

Alan McManus described snooker's Norbreck days as a 'maze of malpractice', writing evocatively on his blog of 'halcyon days of mayhem'. Avoid the pitfalls of that mayhem and you might just launch – or relaunch – a future on tour.

* *

Nigel Bond was glued to any match featuring Hurricane Higgins in the late 1970s and early 1980s. In 1979, the 13-year-old Bond was taken by dad Graham to watch the first session of the quarter-final between Higgins and Terry Griffiths at the Crucible. Higgins sprinted into a 6-2 lead, helped by two centuries in the opening three frames, but would up losing 13-12 to the eventual champion.

Facing Higgins for the first time in a European Open qualifier at the Norbreck in 1993 should have been an occasion to cherish, yet Bond finds it hard to look back with much fondness at what transpired, despite his 5-4 victory.

'It's sad really that towards the end of his career – and obviously I played him towards the end of his career – he was a bit bitter,' Bond says. 'I remember beating him at the Norbreck, and my mum and dad were there watching me play. There were only about 20 seats and when Alex was playing, everyone was craning their neck in to get a look.

'He said to my mum, and she didn't like this: "You need to learn your son the etiquette of the game." And that was because he was just bitter. He was telling the referee where to stand, and he was telling me to sit down in my chair. It was sad really because it was my hero I was playing.'

Gary Wilkinson, who reached number five in the world, joined the tour in the late 1980s and soon encountered a rancorous Higgins, detecting 'a bit of bitterness in him'.

'A lot of that was to unnerve players,' says Wilkinson, 'and as we all know, as long as you pot more balls than the other player, that's all that matters.

'We've all had a taste of it now. You know your career's coming to an end, and most players, when that does happen, they've got nothing else to fall back on. Snooker was Higgins' life, so it's not excusable but you can understand some of the antics he did get up to.

'You were always on edge playing him. He had such a presence, loaded with nervous energy and fidgety. I wouldn't say it was an enjoyable experience playing him. I wouldn't say I was scared of him, but it was the utmost respect because he could do anything with a white ball. A lot of us met him at his downwards spiral, but he was still gifted. It was just nice to be on the same table.'

Being in the company of Higgins could also be a hoot, as a young Bond discovered on a snooker trip to the United Arab Emirates.

'I remember us playing the Dubai Classic and we always had a day off where we played a golf day, and I got partnered with Alex,' Bond says. 'He was driving the buggy, and at every watering hole he was having a beer. At one point I thought he was going to turn the buggy over. He didn't have a driving licence – the guy couldn't drive – but those are the sort of memories I'll take, the ones that are funny situations.'

John Airey presents a fan's perspective of dealings with Higgins, starting from an encounter all the way back in 1982.

'I remember seeing him in the Grosvenor. We were stopping there; most of the players did too,' Airey says.

'He came across to us once and he was all dressed up in his suit and he had his fedora on, and I was a bit of a Higgins fan, to be honest. I was about 14 then, and he came across and said to me, "Do you like my hat?" So I sort of mumbled and said to him, "Yes, it's a very nice hat," and he sauntered off. Great conversation!

'You'd need danger money to be a minder for Higgins. I got the impression in the morning before he played, he was a charming guy. I didn't know him and he talked to me. But the number of people who've told me that when he had a drink he was just a horrible piece of work...

'I met him a second time just shortly before he died, and he was an absolute nightmare the second time, and I thought, "What a contrast!" He was charming when I was 14 but all these years later he was a horror. He was playing Ian McCulloch in an exhibition in Carlisle, and I was refereeing, and I put my drink on his table and he hissed, "Get your fucking pint off my table." He was about six and a half stone wet through then.

'He played McCulloch in three exhibitions, and this was when Higgins was ill.

'McCulloch loves his car to be clean and he picks Higgins up from the airport, and Higgins immediately puts his feet up on the dashboard, starts smoking a fag.'

Airey has been reliably told about an episode of Higgins being taxied back to an airport from such an exhibition match.

'Alex says to the driver, "Just take a detour and pull round by this house." Alex got out and threw a brick through the window, and got back in and said, "Take me to the airport, drive on!"'

19: BEST-OF-63?

BY 1982, CAROLE Hersee had just about the most famous face on British television, as ubiquitous as Selina Scott, Paul Daniels, the Two Ronnies or Terry Wogan.

But hang on: Carole who?

The British public of a certain age remember Hersee not by her real name but as the 'test card girl'. A still image of an eight-year-old Hersee, perched by a blackboard and mock-playing noughts and crosses with a clown doll, was officially titled Test Card F, and this would occupy hour after hour of air time during gaps in the BBC schedules.

Debuting in 1967, the test card remained a familiar sight into the 1980s and beyond; however, you would have been forgiven for thinking the test card girl took her holidays during Crucible time.

Her small-screen absence was a matter of pride for Nick Hunter, the man who created quiz show A Question of Sport.

Hunter went on to become the BBC's snooker executive producer, and at the dawning of the Crucible era he approached the head of BBC Two, Aubrey Singer, with an offer the corporation could hardly refuse.

'I went down to him in 1977, or 1978 it might have been, and I said, "Would you like more snooker?" because the figures had started to rocket,' Hunter recalled. 'And he said, "Well, I can't afford it."

'So I said, "Yes, you can. You put a picture up of a nice girl as a permanent fixture when you're not on the air as a test card; I can give you the snooker instead of a test card."

'He said, "Well, that'd be great, but how much?"

'And I said, "It's free, it'll cost you nothing."

'He insisted there must be a catch, but I said, "There isn't a catch, because I've got to record both tables in case something happens and we're not on the air with them – which to me would be a disaster – so every frame of every match is recorded."

'They had to be sent to London, the recordings, as we had a production team in London that did a lot of the editing, so the pictures were being made anyway, and all they've got to do is be connected up to presentation and we're away.

'He agreed to do a good many hours extra, and the audiences then really took off. People would just sit there and watch the whole tournament and we didn't have to cut out at important moments. Snooker's not a respecter of time.'

The hours of exposure surged. Snooker was suddenly a sport for mass consumption in the blossoming colour television era, but you could still have too much of a good thing.

If Fred Davis had his way, Crucible finals would have been best-of-63-frame behemoths, and ideally even longer.

Davis was an eight-time world champion in the nascent pro era who once won a final 84-61 – that's frames, remember, not points. He remained influential into the 1970s and presented a more-is-more prescription for snooker on television.

The vision Davis had for snooker was flushed away by Hunter.

Pot Black had thrived as a quickly digestible product, snackable content for the Morecambe and Wise generation, and small-screen tournament snooker could hardly turn its back on that hard-won audience.

'I was responsible for all the BBC stuff, and before it kicked off I said that I could only work on it if they agreed to make some changes, but not huge ones,' Hunter said.

'Fred Davis thought the World Championship final should not be less than 63 frames, so I said to him and Rex Williams, "Bye bye." I thought I was pushing my luck already.'

The men returned to the discussion table, and Hunter recalled: 'They sort of said, "Whatever you want to do, run it past us and if we reckon we can cope with it then we'll do it."

'The first thing I did was say the World Championship has got to be open to the world, otherwise you can't call it that. But Rex Williams then said to me, "No amateur player will ever beat a professional." To that, I said, "Well you never know, do you," and before long Terry Griffiths came up from the amateur game and won in Sheffield at the first attempt as a qualifier.

'Anybody could enter, this is the point. I didn't say to them, "This is what you're going to bloody do." We had conversations and I think it was persuasion.

'For the first match I did, which was 1976, we were going into Grandstand... we did the final where Ray Reardon was playing Alex Higgins, and we joined it live with Reardon so far ahead that short of him having a heart attack he'd won the damn thing.

'It didn't make very good television because you couldn't ask whether Higgins could get back into the match because the answer was no, clearly he bloody couldn't, and it was all a bit of a disaster.'

The BBC's World Championship coverage, with snippets having also been shown in 1973 and 1974, may have got off to a false start, but there were glory years – decades even – to come.

'We went from doing two frames into Grandstand in 1976 to five frames of the semi-final and then the final in 1977. By 1979, we were able to do the whole lot,' Hunter said.

In February 1982, Hunter's snooker production was nominated for a British Academy of Film and Television Arts award. The BAFTA for 'actuality coverage' was a four-horse race, with two of those horses being steeds from the royal wedding of Prince Charles and Diana Spencer – ITN and BBC both getting a nod.

The third horse was ITN's broadcasting of the crisis in Poland that saw martial law imposed in that country in December 1981 to combat anti-communist momentum. The fourth, and the outlier, was 'international snooker', with Hunter and his team in the picture for a second successive year, having lost out previously to ITN's coverage of the Iranian Embassy siege in London.

Again, Hunter and the snooker crew missed out on the award, but this was the esteemed company they were keeping. Snooker was not only a hit with audiences; the members of BAFTA recognised its enormous impact too.

By the time the 1983 BAFTAs came around, coverage of the Falkland Islands war and the raising of the Mary Rose, a warship from Henry VIII's navy, squeezed out snooker from the nominations.

Hunter revealed the BBC almost got snooker shambolically wrong.

'In 1976, with the final in Manchester, I had to get the place lit and sorted for Grandstand, and Ray Reardon said, "I can't play under these conditions,"' Hunter said.

'And I said to him, "Well, what does that mean?"'

'The answer was: "Either the BBC improves the conditions so I can see what I'm doing, or we'll all go home." So that focused my eyes, I can tell you.

'Anyway, we moved things a bit and he said it was better and he would play, and he duly smacked Higgins and it was all a bit of a disaster.'

It had taken Mike Watterson to detail to Hunter how the BBC's stage lighting set-up had made life hellishly uncomfortable for the players at the Wythenshawe Forum.

Too hot. Too bright. There would need to be a radical rethink at the Crucible if snooker really wished to take a leap into the sporting mainstream.

Together with Hunter and others, including lighting engineer John Crowther, Watterson helped the cosy Sheffield auditorium provide an unsurpassable stage for the drama that snooker would throw the public's way year in and year out.

'Watterson was an amateur snooker player and he said Reardon couldn't see what was going on in Manchester because the lighting was wrong, in the wrong place on the snooker table,' Hunter said.

'We went to the expense of putting a table up under proper conditions, although we weren't going to pot a ball in anger, and he showed me. Everything was done by spotlights in those days, strip lighting hadn't happened yet in snooker. They'd all got spot lamps around the table, and I had said I wanted to be able to get close-ups of the players when they were off the table.

'So that meant there had to be extra lighting and that meant the place was bloody hot and Reardon couldn't see what was going on. Watterson showed me that by lowering the lights around the table that were used by me for idents and the like, it had wrecked his view of the ball. When you lifted the lights up, it cleared, and he demonstrated this to me and it was like a curtain being lifted. Reardon was absolutely right.

'With the extra lighting we'd put in, far from increasing and improving the lighting around the table, it actually made it much worse. John Spencer said he could fry an egg on one table he played on.

'The standard of play improved and the players were happy. They were happy particularly that we had taken notice of what they wanted and what they couldn't cope with and I had done something about it. So the conditions they were playing under in 1977 were much, much better, and Reardon was proved right, and I was bosom pals with Reardon for the rest of his career.

'We didn't make that many changes at the time, once we'd started and got on the air with the better-positioned lighting and the cooler arena, once we'd got rid of the spot lamps. The strip lamps were the idea of John Crowther. He, I and David Vine all worked together.

'Very soon the television audiences absolutely rocketed, and I would never have believed the audiences would have gone the way they did, and I certainly didn't think there would be 10 million viewers in the second week or 20 million for the 1985 black-ball final at midnight. I would have said, "No, very silly, but we'll do very nicely."

'The whole point of snooker is that it gets on the air at length. It can be termed by the people who don't like it as a very slow drag. I often thought about Fred's 63 frames and internally laughed. Sixty-three frames!'

Bradford-born Singer – the man into whose lap so much snooker conveniently fell – had previously been the BBC's science and features man.

His successor as controller of BBC Two was former Panorama

editor Brian Wenham, who stepped up to the role in 1978 and happened to be a huge snooker fan from the get-go.

Hunter could hardly have hand-picked a more supportive channel boss.

'He was the man accused of just running a snooker channel,' said Hunter. 'Brian told me he would come and watch the snooker until hell freezes over. He would leave his London office at half past five and drive up to Sheffield, watch a few frames of snooker, and then drive back for the next day's work on BBC Two.

'When you've got a controller who's that interested in snooker, you're not going to do too badly. He gave us transmissions all day and every day. If there was a gap in the schedule, the snooker went into it, automatically.'

Wenham stayed in charge at BBC Two until 1982 and is said to have boosted viewing figures by 50% in that time. Snooker played no small part.

Hunter, working all hours during Crucible time, wanted the players to know he was firmly in their corner.

Strong relationships off camera would only strengthen the on-camera product.

As well as becoming great friends with Reardon, Hunter, who also produced the BBC's World Darts Championship coverage, was fond of Higgins.

For all the havoc that could encircle Higgins, Hunter always felt he and the Belfast buck shared some serious common ground.

'I got on absolutely fine with him. I got some lovely autographs that he did for me, especially for me. We got on really well,' Hunter said. 'I did a couple of times stay out of the firing line, because there were times particularly when he drank that he'd be looking round for somebody he could hit.

'If that person had been me, he'd have hit me.

'I once interviewed him on air because David Vine couldn't for some reason, and he went round the Crucible for about two days saying the head honcho had interviewed him. There were times when his behaviour affected us. Once or twice, there were problems with the referee and that did have an effect on us, but I never went in and challenged him.

'He knew whose side we were on; he knew bloody well we were working on the sport he loved and were making it bloody popular. He was as amazed as anybody when we turned in audiences of 15-16 million. He once said to me that he pissed himself when he saw the figures for his matches, he simply couldn't believe it, thought there must have been a mistake.'

20: HEARD IT THROUGH THE GREAT VINE

HAZEL IRVINE is choosing her words carefully.

The Pope is celebrating Mass. Yogi Bear is toileting behind a Jellystone pine. It's raining in Manchester.

Of course Hazel Irvine is picking the right words. It's what she does better than just about every sportscaster.

Irvine, the BBC's excellent snooker anchor, came off duty an hour ago but hasn't switched off.

In fact, what I'm hearing – the delivery, the knowledge, the enthusiasm – is comparable to those one-take Irvine monologues on the final night of Crucible campaigns.

You've seen those in recent years, I'm sure. While many others are found flagging come that Monday, Irvine always holds back something a little special.

This is what David Vine would always shoot for, too. And tonight, ahead of the evening's play at the World Championship, we're talking about Vine, the long-time BBC snooker helmsman.

Irvine has taken what she has learned from Vine and others and run with it, throwing in her own ideas, and in time someone else will take the baton, and the process will begin over again.

Vine died in January 2009, having retired from broadcasting nine years earlier.

Irvine has since earned her stripes and become an audience favourite, an ever-terrific broadcaster who asks the right questions, makes it her business to connect with the right people, and brings great sense and sensitivity to the studio.

How does she measure up to her long-serving predecessor, who skilfully shepherded the snooker coverage from 1978 to 2000? Many would say the succession has been seamless. Irvine takes the comparisons bashfully in her stride and has been doing ever since stepping up to the Ski Sunday top job, another long-standing Vine preserve, in late 1996.

Today, she's spent the afternoon on air, but Irvine has had thoughts of Vine knocking around in the back of her mind.

'I remember having a conversation with him when I took over on the skiing and he was very generous and chattered away,' says Irvine. 'I had a conversation with him when I was taking on the snooker, too. I wasn't exactly stalking him, but...

'David called the shots in his career, quite rightly, and the fact he said "Right, I've had enough and it's time for someone to take over" was a brilliant opportunity for me.

'I always admired him, and I did work with him on the 1996 Olympics in Atlanta. He was doing the weightlifting commentary at that point, and that was when women's weightlifting first came in actually. I think the weightlifting probably summed up his talents. He was a brilliant storyteller, and he could make it sound so exciting, just as he could skiing.

'We always tried to incorporate some of Viney's lines, and even when I was starting out on the snooker, Ray Stubbs and I, Ray would go in and do some of the interviews in the arena in the early days, and on the night of the final he always did David's "It's pay day" line, always. So we always try and reprise that now, whether I do it or Rob Walker does it, and it's an unspoken nod to the greatness of David Vine and his legacy.'

Irvine casually brings up 'the guys', and she is talking about Steve Davis, John Parrott, Stephen Hendry, Ken Doherty et al, the former world champions who are now her BBC colleagues.

'I've spoken to the guys many times about it and they have great respect for Viney, particularly his fearlessness in those interviews at the end of finals,' says Irvine.

'In the days when you had the players standing side by side, the winner and the loser, interviewing is a very difficult thing to pull off when one is glum and the other wants to jump up and down. But David always did it, and you always got a laugh out of him.

'Viney was a really great storyteller. He was pithy. It was his measured economy of language which was always very impressive. Even his links were very well structured, and they conveyed the right information.

'I know he had a very set way of doing things: he was very strong on the technical detail, when you had to be, at a time when the technology was different and a little less forgiving than it is now. That's the beauty of good technical operators: they don't make it look like they are good technical operators; they just make it look simple and smooth and only people in the industry know your feet are charging about beneath you.

'What you learn from someone like David is information, and he would craft a link which would give you the world ranking, the age, where they're from, without even blinking, so you knew everyone.

'He was a permanent fixture in snooker for such a long time and a very hard act to follow in that respect. If you just tried to do what Viney did – do the basics as well as Viney – that's half the battle. But to try to do it in his style, you wouldn't stand a chance. You have to formulate your own style for there to be a point of difference, because you're never going to follow someone successfully by doing the same things exactly.'

Mike Ganley remembers Vine as a titan of the Crucible.

'David Vine was a major part of the tournament. He wasn't officially in charge, but he was always in charge,' says Ganley.

'Someone would say, "We'll do it this way," and he'd say, "No, I think we should do it this way." And David would probably get his way. Nick Hunter was in charge of TV then, but Viney was a real proper journalist and he knew his stuff, and his delivery was as good as it gets. They were great people.

'Back in the early 1980s, Embassy had their hospitality room upstairs in Sheffield. Del Simmons had the WPBSA room – that's the Champions' Lounge now – and it was invite-only, serious invite-only.

'Anyone who went in there without an invitation would be kicked downstairs. And it wasn't a competition between the two, but they invited the likes of Viney up, and it was a very social environment – very social.'

Simmons was a power-broker at the heart of the sport as business-world heavyweights queued up for a slice of sponsorship and tournament action, hopping on the fast-rolling snooker bandwagon. He would have recognised the importance of keeping Vine on side. Embassy, likewise, would have doubtless enjoyed showing off TV favourite Vine to their guests.

By the time the 1982 World Championship rolled around, Vine was a colossus, known not merely for presenting the phenomenon of televised snooker and skiing but as a man for all seasons who had hosted programmes as diverse as Miss World, Wimbledon, A Question of Sport, and It's a Knockout.

'The phrase that comes to my mind is "a big beast",' says Talking Snooker's Nick Metcalfe.

'You used to hear a lot about big characters in the eighties, with political figures. Certainly, in the Tory party you'd have people like Ken Clarke and Ken Baker and Norman Tebbit. They were all Thatcher's "big beasts" – it's a compliment really, they were such enormous characters, and David Vine was probably one of those. He was just such a powerful presence. I can see David Vine running the show and being this big, all-consuming kind of presence.

'He almost was snooker on television, to some extent, certainly with the BBC.

'When he died, Shaun Murphy put it very simply: that it's sad because when you switched on television, growing up, you knew most of the time, certainly on the BBC, you'd be watching David Vine.'

However high the on-table drama escalated, ringmaster Hunter was always convinced that in Vine he had a professional on camera who would take it all in his stride. Could he handle Alex Higgins? Could Higgins handle Vine?

Vine once faced down John McEnroe at Wimbledon, after a 1981 blast from the American at an umpire, famously asking the fiery American after the match: 'What right have you got to call anyone an incompetent fool?'

If he could take on Superbrat in the land of strawberries and cream, Vine could eat Higgins for breakfast in Sheffield.

'He was a very nice guy as well, good to work with, a good pro,' says Hunter of Vine. 'We worked on the darts together and of course he was the first presenter on A Question of Sport. So there was darts, snooker and A Question of Sport, and I did all three with him.

'David did the first half dozen Question of Sport series. To my fury he went and skied in the bloody winter and I had to go and find somebody else; luckily David Coleman wasn't a bad shout! Not a bad alternative, just as long as you didn't say 'alternative' in Coleman's hearing!

'David Vine was one of these guys that listens to his producer. He was keen to see if television worked with snooker at length, and then we sort of gelled, and it became perfectly obvious that he ought to work on the whole championship.

'I wanted somebody who I knew editorially had the same sort of view of things as I had. There are times in the championship where you have to sit there and think aloud, and your link man must be able to realise what you're thinking.'

Hunter recalls the time, in 1983, when he and Vine dutifully stayed to the 3.51am bitter end of the second-round slog between Cliff Thorburn and Terry Griffiths, on the middle Sunday of the tournament – or rather the early hours of Monday.

'David Vine and I were there watching. To be fair it was ridiculous. I had said that there would never be a frame I didn't record, and that cost me, because in the end I couldn't get a crew to stay on until four in the morning,' says Hunter.

'There's a limit to what they'll do for you, even if they want to, so I had the suggestion that they pull stumps. So my boast that I've never missed a frame went out of the window. When you looked at who was playing, Thorburn and Griffiths, we looked at each other and said, "Oh, bloody hell! This could go on."'

Reflecting on the championships of that era, Hunter assessed the player line-ups as an 'extraordinary cast of characters'.

'I don't know how they do it sometimes, those boys, looking down their cues. God almighty,' he said. 'It would give me the yips just thinking about it.'

It would have taken an extraordinary turn of events to fluster Vine, who was 20 years into his on-screen career by the time the 1982 World Championship came around.

At the age of 47, Vine had seen it all in sport, from the surreal with Superstars all the way up to the Olympic Games. This was a man who had watched Jackie Stewart compete in weightlifting, Colin Bell take on pistol shooting and Bobby Moore run a steeplechase.

The headmasterly Vine was a commanding figure in a treacherously difficult job, sharp of mind and ever ready to react.

'He had a great voice, brilliant,' says Rob Walker. 'You're born with your voice, but then it's the way you use language, your intonation, and Vine had a really authoritative and warm voice.

'If I instinctively think about David Vine, funnily enough it's the sound of his voice that comes to me more than his face. He was an iconic figure. It was a clever place for him to position himself, because Coleman was the main man but Vine wasn't far behind him.

'Coleman couldn't be at every event all the time, so Vine got his niche with Ski Sunday and snooker. He did it very well and the other bits and bobs came, because he was clearly a classy and safe pair of hands on a live broadcast. You can tell that he liked snooker and he engaged with it, so his relationships came through with the people he was having to deal with, in nice circumstances or difficult circumstances.

'If it looks easy, if it looks like he's just wandered on to the set and said whatever he felt like off the top of his head, and it felt like he was just talking to a best mate, you can almost guarantee that a lot of work would have gone into that.

'I'm not saying he wasn't instinctive, but the mark of somebody who's really good at what they do is they take something that is quite complicated and make it look simple. Vine had that, and if you have the luxury of being able to use 500 words instead of 50, you can waffle, but if you're using 50 words you have to think extremely carefully about exactly the phrases you're using, your language and the intonation you've got, to deliver extremely succinctly the salient points. And he was really good at that.

'In my opinion, and this is where Vine was really good, the most important thing with television is you've got to be genuine, and it's so obvious when this isn't the case. You have to believe what you say. Not everyone's going to like you; it's not a green light into everyone's living room. You're still going to annoy certain people because life is subjective, but the one thing you don't want is for people to be able to say, "This guy doesn't mean what he says."'

Vine had a deep affection for snooker, that was clear, but his task was to provide compelling and enlightening company through the sporting spectacle, and you would be hard pushed to find a more capable figure for the job.

Broadcaster Michael McMullan grew up admiring Vine's precision-trimmed presentation.

'I often wonder with David: did he ever use a script? And I mean that as a compliment because I don't think he needed one,' says McMullan, a Eurosport and Matchroom reporter.

'He was just so good at it and so natural, and he could afford to be natural because he didn't need to contrive anything, he didn't need to force anything, because he was so on top of the brief all the time. He had a wonderful economy with words.

'If you look back at any of the old snooker broadcasts from that era, generally about 60 to 90 seconds into the programme you're watching people playing snooker, and that's because he was able to sum up so much with very few words in very little time. He would give you the context: here's who these players are, here's how they got to this round, here's how it fits into the tournament, and off you go. He was just wonderful at that, which for me is the number one skill in broadcasting, certainly sports broadcasting: to be able to fit a lot of information into a small number of words and a small period of time.

'There were some great television people around in that period: Des Lynam, Steve Rider, Dickie Davies – I thought they were all wonderful at that, but nobody more so than David.'

McMullan began his snooker journalism career in the late 1990s, in the twilight years of Vine's time on television.

'With David, you didn't really see him much at tournaments because he was in the studio all the time, but he would come into the press room now and then,' McMullan remembers. 'The only time I met him properly was in 2005, and it was the last year of Embassy, and they always used to put on a big dinner after the final. So clearly in 2005 it was bigger than ever because it was the sponsor's last year, and they'd invited back a lot of faces from the past, people who had been associated with the Embassy years.

'I remember it being late in the night, and the Shaun Murphy-Matthew Stevens final had finished late because it was 18-16, so by the time the media got to the dinner it was probably well after midnight. It must have been about two in the morning, because the speeches were already over, and I looked over and saw two men sitting at the table in the corner, and it was David Vine and Ted Lowe. You'd struggle to find the words to explain what big figures they were in my early snooker experiences.

'I'd seen them both around venues, but I'd never really spoken properly to either of them. So I thought to myself that this chance is literally never going to come up again, because they're both retired, they're only here because it's the last night of

Embassy. And it was great; I went over, got a picture taken with them, spoke to them both, and there was no attitude, no airs and graces about either of them, which was fantastic to see. I found them both to be very ordinary guys who were just happy to be there and reflecting on the wonderful life they'd had in the game.'

Devon born and bred, Vine began his career in the written press, initially with the North Devon Journal Herald and subsequently the Western Morning News in Plymouth.

After that crucial grounding, a short spell in regional ITV was followed by a long BBC career, beginning in 1966, that great lift-off year for English sport.

A BBC profile of Vine, upon his retirement, stated: 'The 64-year-old has not so much been one of the charismatic strikers of the BBC sports team, more the safe pair of hands at the back.'

To the uninitiated that might read almost as a slight, yet Vine did indeed offer safe hands, and he was not showy, just always classy.

'I think he was basically a consummate professional, really, in every single way,' says Nick Metcalfe. 'He was totally authoritative with a great precision about him. He just had this great presence on screen, and he had a real gravitas, he oozed gravitas. He had it in the sixties or seventies, it's like he was just made like that. It's like when you see David Dimbleby in the seventies, and you see he had that gravitas then – it didn't come with age, he just always had it, which I love.

'I like those all-rounders, and you don't get it so much now. Mostly you get specialists. David Vine was the first presenter of A Question of Sport, but people don't remember it because David Coleman was the most famous. David presented It's a Knockout, but again, people don't really remember it because it became a Stuart Hall thing. He presented showjumping a lot, he'd do the nightly Wimbledon programme, he did Grandstand and Match of the Day and the Olympic weightlifting.

'But when he got the skiing and snooker gigs, that's when he became synonymous with particular sports really. I almost can't separate those two because he became so synonymous with both. His run on Ski Sunday was legendary television. There are different arguments whether the skiing or snooker was more important to him, and on some levels it was skiing, because he did everything on that programme. He was like Brian Moore when you see the old football matches: he'd present it, he'd commentate on the race, he'd do the interviews afterwards, and he'd say goodbye.

'It could have been called "Ski Sunday with David Vine", but in a different sense that was only on for, what, 45 minutes a week, whereas the snooker was on hour after hour and so you'd see a lot more of him.'

There was a winning old school charm about Vine that appealed across generations.

'For example, he called it the United Kingdom Championship,' Metcalfe says. 'He never called it the UK Championship. And he wouldn't have called it the World Championship. Instead, he'd have begun, "Good evening from day two of the Embassy World Professional Snooker Championship."

'Everything about him was just fashion from yesteryear really.

'In a funny kind of way, David Vine was almost as famous as the players. Probably not quite, but he was along those lines.

'He had that sense of being very much in charge, total authority. I think you knew where you were with David Vine, and I think TV viewers like that: we like knowing where we are.'

21: A LOWE MOMENT FOR SNOOKER

WHILE DAVID VINE was peerless at shrink-wrapping bundles of detail into pocket-sized packages, it was quite a different skill set that was the hallmark of the other great voices of the early Crucible years.

For Ted Lowe, commentary was all about a slow drip-feed of narration, his sparse observations being peppered with pearls of wisdom, rarely a word wasted. His method was not to present a play-by-play account but to chime in with observational missives and sufficient brass tacks basics to engage the viewer, perceptive at times but often simply reactive.

Those interjections and asides would reach living rooms across the land, even if occasionally there was cause for wondering if the old sage might have nodded off, taken himself off duty.

Lowe would then spark back into action, before stepping back from the mic once more, letting the pictures tell the story.

Nobody asked for more because they had never known more.

'They didn't talk very much because they were told not to,' says David Hendon. 'The analysis of sport hadn't really happened by then. They were there in the background as company almost.

'Commentators weren't there to criticise, so you'd never hear criticism of shots. They were there to add context, but they stayed in the background because that was the style. Sky probably changed all sport with the way it's done now, and some people would say there's maybe too much analysis now, but times have changed.

'Back then, they were friendly voices in the background. Ted had the perfect voice for snooker. He had to whisper because he sat in the audience in the early days, but he had a lovely manner. It's a bit like being sat there with your grandad.

'They were all unobtrusive, but if you watch it back there's a lot they could have explained to the viewer but they didn't. You could watch it for literally five minutes and there wouldn't be a word spoken and all sorts of things could have happened, and now they'd be showing replays, they'd have the touchscreen, but then they went unremarked upon because that was the era. I'm not saying one's better or worse, but that was the era.'

Snooker was seeing spectacular viewing figures long before 18.5 million tuned in for the 1985 final between Steve Davis and Dennis Taylor, and the hushed tones of Lowe made his voice one of the best known in sport, certainly in the UK.

Jack Karnehm and Clive Everton were BBC television's other principal snooker broadcasters by 1982, both canny operators. Everton was later to supplant Lowe as the consummate wise owl of the commentary box, yet for a long time the number one voice was that of Whispering Ted, the man the public had already taken to following the success of Pot Black.

'The thing about Ted was that he was very different to Clive, in that he didn't have the background in the game,' says Michael McMullan. 'This was a time when people didn't know very much about snooker yet, because in the early 1980s it hadn't been big

176

on television for long. What they needed was for someone to give them a basic grounding in the context, the drama and the players, and I think in a way Ted not being quite as knowledgeable as Clive made him ideally suited to be the man for that role.

'He was giving people more of an introduction to snooker, setting the scene and giving people a basic education in the game. It was later on, when the general knowledge among the public had grown a bit, that Clive's slightly more advanced style then became more appropriate.

'So I think they both excelled in their own ways, in slightly different eras. People call him Whispering Ted Lowe, but I never thought he was particularly whispering, just that he spoke very softly. There was the fact that Ted was the voice of so many big early moments. All those first world finals, Ted was the voice of them, and I don't know anyone who was around and following snooker in those days who doesn't look back on Ted with a lot of affection, and a little bit of sadness at that lost innocence that you feel for anything from that long ago.'

Rob Walker, the World Championship's long-standing MC, has been a recent addition to the BBC's snooker commentating team. Already an Olympic Games-level athletics broadcaster, making the leap from full-tilt track and field to the sometime snail's pace of snooker required plenty of diligent homework, genning up on what has made great snooker orators past and present so special.

For Walker to be the gregarious hype man in the arena one minute, then a reliable performer behind the mic in the booth the next, requires a versatility that should not be underestimated.

He has learned from the likes of Hendon and Everton, knowing a snooker match is rarely an evenly paced or predictable race.

'You absorb such an amount by osmosis because you listened to it as a child and you're aware of the main nuances,' Walker says.

'What I made a conscious effort to do in snooker is to become comfortable with leaving big gaps, because the last thing you want in snooker is for someone to be talking all the time. I think you've got to follow your own instincts, and enough of what you've heard those greats doing would sink in.

'The main thing you're thinking about is doing the players justice. It's not about you. When you're in that box, your job is to sell those players and sell the sport, and remind people there are great characters in snooker.'

British television was a three-channel small world in early 1982, with BBC One and Two running alongside ITV in its various regional guises, but the seeds were being sown that would lead the way to a startlingly different future.

Four days before Tony Knowles and Steve Davis got the Crucible action under way, the ambitious and unsubtly named newcomer Satellite Television began broadcasting in parts of Europe. By the summer of 1983, media mogul Rupert Murdoch had bought a majority stake and Sky Channel was soon born, a first step towards the Australian-American becoming the most powerful individual in British television, and by extension arguably the most powerful person in all of sport.

In the battle for audiences in 1982, snooker was in a strong place. On the second evening of the World Championship, however, it had competition from the first UK showing of the US hit show Dynasty, on BBC One. This gold-leaf soap opera was a sassy imported alternative to the hair curlers and cobbled streets carrying-on in Coronation Street, with Dynasty being deliciously touted by the Illustrated London News as a 'torrid "sex & oil" series'. How could snooker compete with that?

Dishy Dennis Taylor versus smouldering Silvino Francisco was the alternative over on BBC Two, both broadcasts beginning just after the watershed.

The Americanisation of the networks was happening before our eyes, but in Thatcher's Britain, and in Northern Ireland, there was still room for folksy, native light entertainment. That arrived in the homespun charm of Terry Wogan's eponymous chat show, Wogan, which was launched on the evening of May 4, 1982 – Bruce Forsyth and Paula Yates his guests – and in the fact a Saturday morning children's show, Get Set For Summer, could feature a segment billed in newspapers of the day as 'motorbike scrambling with David Essex'.

This was pleasingly naive broadcasting compared to the modern day. Snooker, similarly, was still finding its way. Blinding the viewer with the science of the sport would have been a turn-off, so it made sense that Lowe's easily followed observations and bons mots should be piped into living rooms across the land.

'If you'd have put the evolution of commentary the other way round, with the likes of Dave Hendon, myself and Clive before Ted and Jack, it wouldn't have made sense,' says Phil Yates.

'I wouldn't diminish Ted and Jack, because they were involved in what were still snooker's very early days as a television sport, even in 1982. It was nothing like it is now. Jack had two major things going for him: one, he had a really good voice; and two, he had quite good timing, as evidenced by his "Come on, mate!", the 1983 line when Thorburn was on the 147, and timing is so important.

'I'm full of stats, but you'll never find me talking about stats when the players are on the colours, or if there's a frame that's tight. The commentary wasn't worse, it wasn't better, it was just very different back then.'

Snooker as an overall televisual experience to UK viewers was a wholly different animal to what it has become.

Today, Eurosport will give the tournament blanket coverage, while the BBC has gone from dotting sessions or half-sessions into empty slots on the schedule to making the World Championship a multi-platform experience, available not only through its core channels but via its red button, iPlayer and website. There's nary a reason to miss any of the action. Not even Nick Hunter could claim to show every ball live, but the digital age has created this possibility. The eighties were great in their own way, as the hours of exposure rocketed, but wall-to-wall snooker was still beyond the broadcasters.

Now we are thoroughly indulged. It is these that are the good old days, make no mistake, at least for the armchair viewer.

'Back in the early days, you were excited when the snooker came on and didn't seem to mind if they said they weren't coming back for another three hours,' Hendon says.

'You couldn't really find out what was happening without listening to the radio or perhaps Ceefax. You're not going to learn the score unless you're going to go looking hard for it. People think it was live all day, but it wasn't. There was plenty on, but there's more now.

'Now, because there's so much analysis, Eurosport and the BBC would stay on after the final, we wouldn't be rushed off after the ticker tape and all that. That's why seeing what happened after the 1982 final was so special, because it was new and it was spontaneous.'

It was a gift to snooker that the likes of Lowe brought a deft, occasionally light touch to proceedings.

Lowe was brought up in a horse-racing environment, his father being head lad for Derby-winning trainer Ossis Bell. But the gallops weren't for Lowe, who as a young man in the 1940s became a manager at the Leicester Square Hall snooker parlour.

A long and winding road that would lead to the Crucible was set from the night Lowe took over commentary duty for a televised match when the regular man on the Leicester Square beat, Raymond Glendenning, took ill. There was no booth as such for the man with the microphone, with Lowe so close to the action he had no option but to keep his voice down.

Nick Metcalfe, who co-presents Talking Snooker with fellow snooker writer Phil Haigh, considers the early 1980s a remarkable starting point for his own lifelong passion for televised sport.

'John Virgo said it quite well when he said that Ted Lowe wasn't a massive expert on snooker. But it didn't really matter because he did everything very well, really,' says Metcalfe. 'He had a voice that I think was symbolic of the time. There were others like that, be it a Dan Maskell, a Henry Longhurst, a John Arlott.'

Maskell, Longhurst and Arlott set standards that commentators in tennis, golf and cricket would strive to match long after those denizens stepped away from the microphone for the last time. That said, rarely is a mimic required in this demanding industry. Anyone not moving with the times gets left behind.

Broadcasting styles change, shuffling along on the coattails of our fast-moving culture. There is fanfare attached to televised sport in the 21st century, with an onus on those calling matches – snooker, football, all across the spectrum – to be present and insightful. Going effectively AWOL on air simply won't wash.

'Somebody would expect me, as an old-timer, to say I liked them quiet, but they were too quiet in the past really,' says Metcalfe.

'With Ted Lowe, you'd sometimes wonder: is he there? But then he'd pop up with something very relevant. He was always the colour person really, he just did enough to keep us informed of what's going on. There was no real analysis, but that was the culture then anyway, and calling the shots, if you can use that phrase, definitely came later. Suggesting a player wanted to get on a certain side of the blue or put a bit of side on, that never used to happen in a million years really.

'You might very occasionally have something along those lines, but now they call every shot. But the thing about Ted Lowe that I always come back to is the cry of "No!" when Davis missed.'

Lowe's instinctive gasp of incredulity when Davis over-cut the black in the 1985 final against Taylor – a yowl of amazement doused in received pronunciation – has become much-parodied over the years, not least in the Crucible press room.

'It's funny that "No!" would be so meaningful, but it was so perfect, because we were all saying the same thing,' Metcalfe says.

'Back then, they were all selling the game, they were all salesmen, in a funny kind of way, and Ted Lowe was part of that. Ted had to sell the game, and I think he did a good job of doing that. He had a great nickname too, and that is important.

'Clive was a great voice, but the original voice of snooker was Ted Lowe really.'

Everton, a leonine figure in snooker's modern history, was working as a journalist at the Crucible when it was announced on the morning of May 1, 2011, that Lowe had died. Lowe was 90, and news of his death came on the first day of the final between John Higgins and Judd Trump.

Edwin Charles Ernest Lowe, gone but forever a huge part of the rapid rise of snooker. As Everton wrote in a Guardian obituary, this was a sport where Lowe found many friends, rising from his days in Leicester Square to becoming its much-loved head narrator, and duly 'always on the alert to do it a good turn'.

The same might be said of Everton, who racked up 50 years as editor of Snooker Scene magazine in 2021, a staggering achievement. His decision to step aside in 2022 prompted an outpouring of admiration. Clive's influence has been felt in many ways during his remarkably long innings, notably in print when calling out those who by his sober reckoning had not been acting in the sport's best interests, and not least when providing astute judgement and scrutiny on live television matches.

From 1978 to 2010, Everton was a staple member of the BBC broadcasting team, and many consider him the sport's greatest wordsmith.

'The person I was drawn to, in terms of being impressed by his abilities, was Clive,' says Yates, who first met Everton in 1988 and has worked closely with him since, including as a chief scribe for Snooker Scene.

'Clive was the one I aspired to be like. Clive had three things: a deep understanding of the circuit and the game as a whole; he'd got an extraordinary vocabulary and was a brilliant writer, so he'd got words; and something which none of the others had at the time – he had information, background information. I always looked to him as one of my favourite commentators because he was the same kind of mindset as I was really.'

Hendon also worked closely with Everton for many years on Snooker Scene and was at one point referred to by his magazine mentor as its 'editor in waiting'. It is no coincidence Hendon, like fellow veteran Snooker Scene scribe Yates, is such a modern-day master of imparting expertise on paper and on air.

'Clive was the best of them all and he probably got the fewest matches of them all, because there was a pecking order,' Hendon says. 'He was a player, but he was also a journalist so obviously words were his thing.

'Clive and John Spencer are probably the two I like listening to from the early days. But I liked Ted. Ted, when you're young, just seemed like a nice old man, and funnily enough the first time I came here to the Crucible, which was in 1990, we saw Ted in the street and my mum ran to get his autograph. He was a massive star and people were flocking around him.

'Today, I've just walked in through the same stage door and people couldn't care less, but Ted was as big a name as the players.'

Lowe was undoubtedly an important figure for the sport.

Yet McMullan, just like Hendon, considers Everton brought a unique and hitherto unmatched array of qualities into the commentary box.

'There's the ongoing debate in sports broadcasting about where you strike the balance in using people from a journalism background and those who are players and ex-players,' McMullan says. 'The thing with Clive, virtually uniquely in the world of sport, is that he came from both backgrounds equally.

'He was a very accomplished amateur player and he did have a brief professional career, but by the time there was a professional circuit worth joining he was past his best as a player, so he was never really going to accomplish much, but nevertheless he was good enough at the game to play on the professional circuit, so we got that technical knowledge. But perhaps even more so he came from the journalism background because he'd been working in that field long before he was a professional snooker player. He brought the knowledge of the game and a wonderful command of the language.

'For me, the single best thing about Clive is he was able to commentate in a way that engaged the more knowledgeable spectators. He would still have something to say to people who knew a lot about the game, but also he would not go above the heads of people who were more casual followers.'

There were others who served, including Vera Selby, who briefly featured at the 1982 World Championship, but for many years the commentary box was dominated by those three lead voices: Everton, Karnehm and Lowe.

'They were part of our lives. It was so much comfort,' says Nick Metcalfe. 'We often need telly for comfort, and we often need comfort in life full stop, but it's nice to have that sort of comforting background noise.

'It was a wonderful era when we think about it. These were great voices, really special voices. We remember those voices and how they just didn't talk as much. I don't quite know how and why the culture changed; I guess someone involved in TV sport, or a few people, just thought actually it's not right now, the world's getting more fast-paced.

'Dan Maskell in tennis would literally be silent for minutes. Now if any commentator goes silent for 10 seconds, you're worried.'

22: Everton, Acteson and the 'reptile house'

It was Clive Everton who blessed the World Championship with its 'marathon of the mind' badge, and minds have been lost, blown and even occasionally broadened while going the distance in the confines of the Crucible press room.

To spend 17 consecutive days in this austere chamber – or 18 days including previews day – is tantamount to masochism. But those who inhabit the tucked-away lair do so readily, arriving each year braced for the helter-skelter ride that will reveal its twists and turn both inside the arena and off camera, ready to be dealt another thrashing.

This is a room where large television screens show the spectacle unfolding on the other side of a couple of whitewashed breeze block walls, and where intermittently those writing about said events will pay it undivided attention. It is where late-night drama is sometimes not so much lapped up as resented, newspaper deadlines going by the wayside as a pair of tenacious potters add to the weary journo's workload. Another rewrite, another call to the sports desk to explain that, no, it's honestly impossible to say when the match will end, so please stop asking.

It is an open prison, a place where the language can be coarse and the usually good-humoured small talk can take a turn and cut close to the bone.

The wardens – the doughty and snooker loopy press officers who work all hours – cop as much of the brunt as anyone.

Nonetheless, you would need to travel far and wide to find greater camaraderie. It typically holds true that the inmates who return to this high-ceilinged penitentiary year after year would rather be nowhere else than locked up in this curious quarter of Sheffield. Because notwithstanding the griping, the sniping and the whole lot of typing, those who report on snooker tend to do so out of a deeply held love of the sport.

Life-long friendships are established, drinking sessions begin once the last balls of the night are sunk, or often long before, and you sense the ghosts of yesteryear would heartily approve. In the Embassy days of sponsorship, cigarettes would be dished out like candy to the journalists, and just like many a newsroom of the day, a tobacco haze would fill the air. Those who were there tell me this. My own press room debut came in 2009, the last year this room of scribes and radio reporters came appointed with its own staffed and stocked hospitality bar room.

A pint to help the morning's early frames pass by? Certainly, sir. Help yourself to a bag of nuts and regale me with your charming banter. Hair of the dog, is it?

It usually was.

Terry Griffiths, always a welcome visitor to the press room, would stroll through and take a J2O, a saint in a sinner's den.

Clive Everton, a great friend of Griffiths, rose above us all in the press pack, of course. Sober, shrewd and steady, Clive was the grown-up in the room. He would take any mocking of his old-school ways on the chin, having seen it all and heard it all before.

'Who's in the chair?' would be his much-imitated opening gambit as he checked in with the Guardian sports desk before lunch, seeking an audience with the office top dog. To hear Clive later in the day deliver his crisp, informative, accurate and often ad-libbed postcards from Sheffield to a copy taker was to hear a master storyteller at work. We all knew it.

We were in the company of perhaps the ultimate witness to professional snooker's history, with Clive's idiosyncrasies a hallmark of his must-read journalism. He was this press pack's lone survivor from the 1982 contingent.

Whoever happened to be 'in the chair' knew what they were getting from this righteous sage of snooker: a froth-free and definitive write-up of the day's action.

* *

Steve Acteson is on the other end of the phone line, calling from Kent, where the former snooker and darts correspondent is enjoying semi-retirement, spending as much of it as possible on the golf course.

We are sharing memories from contrasting press room eras. Steve had revelled in a world of plenty in those early days; I still recall the revolt on the morning the drinks fridge – which replaced the bar – sprouted an unexpected padlock on its door.

We concur that Everton was a formidable newspaper chronicler of the sport, whatever the year.

'In my day, Clive Everton obviously was the doyen,' Acteson says.

Acteson came through the ranks of sub-editors at PA and jumped at the chance to get out of the office, making his Crucible debut in 1982 and sticking as closely as he could to the beat during the heady days of that decade.

He later served as a snooker writer for the Times, Today and the

London Daily News, before taking up a senior role on the Daily Star sports desk.

Joining Clive and Steve in the Crucible press room in 1982 were the likes of John 'Tex' Hennessey (Daily Mail), John Docherty (Daily Record), Terry Smith (Daily Mirror), Janice Hale (Everton's Snooker Scene assistant editor), Ronnie Harper (Belfast Telegraph) and a 29-year-old Alan Green, a rising star of BBC radio.

However genial the atmosphere might have been, there was inevitably a rivalry for stories among these comrades.

'Later, Terry Smith and I were up against each other when I was Times and he'd moved to the Telegraph. He was always desperate to know what I had, even if it didn't matter,' says Acteson. 'He'd still get upset if he felt I was hiding something.

'Terry was the only man I know who managed to break both arms falling over playing football, both arms at the same time. But he was a lovely guy.'

Smith later edited the Benson & Hedges Snooker Year Book, while Hennessey wrote the terrific Alex Higgins tome 'Eye of the Hurricane'. Docherty reported on 25 World Championships, while Harper, along with Everton, belonged to the select few who witnessed Higgins landing the world title both at Birmingham's Selly Park in 1972 and at the Crucible a decade later. Harper, who also briefly managed a young Higgins – and dumped him over an exhibition no-show – died in October 2018.

These characters served their time in a formative moment for snooker, and a collective passion for narrating the sport's multifarious sagas did all concerned a great favour.

Mike Ganley recalls: 'When you were going to Sheffield you had top sports writers from around the country turning up – your Tex Hennesseys, John Docherty from Scotland; later you had

Dave Armitage from the Star. In those days you would have all these top sports writers at the Crucible from day one. Maybe some of that was down to the social side of it as well. But those guys were actually there and putting a lot of words into newspapers, and the back pages, and to be fair it was different to now, because you didn't have social media and people with camera phones, so you could relax, whereas nowadays the players can't go for a walk without somebody taking a picture of you or knowing what's going on.

'And it wasn't that this protected them, but the players could relax a little bit more around people. There was a respect between the players and the snooker press guys in that they knew what they had to report on. Obviously when there's news, we all have to step our game up. In those days, to get the sort of stuff they wanted from the players they had to play the game with them, so you had to have a relationship and if you broke that relationship down you didn't get anything. In those days, journalists were real journalists, not bloggers or the like. It was the newspaper men, the Press Association, and not everybody got in and that was a good thing.'

Ganley's starry-eyed assessment of the newspaper men is that of the snooker fan that he was at that age, and he remains a buff at heart all these years later in his tournament director role. Objectively, though, it is an unintentional distortion of reality.

To portray the Crucible press corps as Fleet Street elite is a stretch, then and now. Hennessey's day job had been that of a sports sub-editor at the Mail rather than a feted, big-bucks reporter. He covered snooker on his days off and used annual leave to keep up a presence on the tour. His was probably not the bumper salary and stature of an England football writer, a cricket chief reporter or a globe-trotting boxing columnist. Docherty was a cornerstone of the Daily Record's sports team for a quarter of a century, and covered as many Wimbledons as he did Crucibles.

Yet these were not the Brian Woolnoughs, Hugh McIlvanneys or James Lawtons of the sports writing world. With every respect to such titans, snooker ought to be thankful for having had its own merry band of hacks. This is a sport where journalists tend to arrive as devotees, already subscribing unconditionally to the notion of this pedestrian pursuit being sport, spellbound by the prospect of one-on-one, cue-in-hand combat between what has always been a fabulously knotty set of personalities.

Time management is perhaps the most underrated skill of the Crucible journalist. After all, it takes tremendous expertise to make room in the day for 12 to 15 hours on duty, plus a lengthy late-night pub debrief/speed-drinking session, and sufficient a window for the necessary sleep to sustain the body during a 17-day run of repeat performances.

Somewhere amid this daunting routine comes the task of identifying the upcoming day's likely best story angles and pushing those merits to a sports editor. If a writer can build relationships with the players while prising reaction and teasing stories from them, then all the better for the prospect of future scoops. Snooker rewards those who persist, who return year on year, who work those long hours and go the extra mile, who refuse to see the sport as a poor relation to those perennial page-fillers: football, rugby and cricket in the early 1980s, but typically football, football and more football in the 2020s.

While this is a sport that welcomes the besotted, there have been certain writers who have spent much of their time during the World Championship in the nearby hostelries, resting down their pints for just long enough to smash out 500 words for the next day's newspaper. Confession time: many a moon ago, I filed an overnight story from a bowling alley. Four hundred words of pin-sharp copy.

Players and press, by and large, are essentially kindred spirits, united by affection for this strangely beautiful game and the mental warfare lurking within. The media room has become a haven for those that savour both the face-value potting contest and the cerebral rascality that often comes into play in the arena.

All of this is not to say the media are apologists, willing to give an easy ride to the authorities, or to any player who goes rogue.

In particular, the likes of Everton and, more recently, Hector Nunns, have been year-round close scrutinisers of the politics of snooker as much as the potting. The fourth estate and the sport's powers that be exist uncomfortably side by side on occasion, and whoever the temporary custodian might be at any time, they can be assured beady eyes will always be kept on their performance.

Come the World Championship, it is usually events on the table, and the post-match press shakedown of the players, that dominate the agenda.

Tabloid hounds turn up their quirky tales, frisking down the players and bringing a little streetwise straight-talking to press conferences, scenting for scandal, gunning for grudges. Some over the years may have struggled with the value and potting order of the colours, but snooker coverage would be much the poorer without such story sniffers. Any mug can describe the ebb and flow of a match, but it is another skill entirely to root out the human interest angle – the acrimony, the pathos, the comic line.

'In the heyday, Steve Davis used to come down to the press room and watch matches on the screens, relax and read the paper, or read a magazine, because he didn't particularly want to be in the players' room,' says Acteson.

'I think he didn't like the atmosphere in there, where there used to be a lot of bitching going on, not necessarily about him but he didn't particularly like it.

'He felt more comfortable in the press room, oddly enough. The fathers used to sit in there too. Terry Griffiths' father, Martin, was regularly down there every time Terry played, and there was Bill Davis and Tommy White, Jimmy's dad.

'There was a kind of unspoken rule with the players: if they were in the press room, we didn't really bother them.

'I once asked Steve if I could have a chat, but I had to do it formally. It wasn't the case that "you're in the press room, you have to talk to me". You had to do it right.

'I remember at Preston that he and I used to go on those Space Invader machines. It was all friendly in those days. The press and players, we used to mingle all the time at hotels.

'There was mutual mistrust that came later on, especially them mistrusting the press.'

Not every snooker player felt an affinity with the journalists in the early 1980s, and a number of authority figures were already cautious about dealings with those sniffing around for potential page leads.

Over time, a certain level of disdain is said to have crept in, with those in blazers increasingly inhospitable towards the reporters.

'The press room became known as the reptile house, which we thought was very unfair because we were the people putting the game on the map by giving it media coverage, but that seemed to escape them,' says Acteson.

* *

Most national newspapers had an assigned specialist correspondent early on, but it was the chivvying of a chap named Chipp that pushed snooker towards the provincial back pages.

David Chipp had an unsung role in snooker getting column inches in scores of local papers, from Aberystwyth to Aberdeen, Belfast to Brighton.

Chipp, who died aged 81 in 2008, lived a remarkable life. He suspected he was conceived in the grounds of Kew Gardens and knew for certain that is where he was born, his father having been a live-in assistant director of the estate, and Chipp would serve in the Middlesex Regiment from 1944 until 1947, at which point he began to read history at King's College, Cambridge.

In 1950, Chipp joined the Reuters agency as a sport reporter and worked in that capacity at the summer Olympics in Helsinki two years later, before myriad twists and turns led to him becoming a news correspondent in China. He is said to have been the first non-communist reporter to set up shop in Peking – now Beijing – since the revolution, and later titled a memoir The Day I Stepped on Mao's Toes.

Chipp was later news editor at Reuters and subsequently, from 1969 to 1986, editor-in-chief of the Press Association in London.

PA has long served as a backbone for the news media industry across the British Isles, with its wire service pumping a rapid and diverse flow of news stories – politics, crime, sport, entertainment, business, even TV and weather listings – into the newsrooms of its subscribers.

Many a newspaper would be lost without PA. Yet by the early 1980s, Chipp noticed there was a chink in its armour: snooker was going stratospheric, and PA lacked a correspondent.

'I was put on snooker because we had a very far-sighted editor of the Press Association,' Acteson says. 'David Chipp was very old-fashioned, a gentleman. He was Tie Man of the Year, that sort of thing.

'He said to our then sports editor Nelson Fairley, "Nelson,

snooker and darts seem to be becoming very popular. And I think we should put a man on to cover them. What do you think?"

'Nelson said, "Yes I think we should, and I know just the bloke."

'I'd gone from news to sport as a sub-editor and made myself quite unpopular because I was forever trying to get out to cover matches, because at that time I'm desperate to become a reporter and not a sub.

'So Nelson gave me my big chance. I did the Jameson International at Derby, and then I did my first World Darts Championship, where the defending champion Eric Bristow was very much the number one, and he got knocked out in the first round by a lad from Northern Ireland, Steve Brennan.

'Then I went on to the Crucible for the first time, only to see Davis get knocked out in the first round as defending champion.'

Acteson quickly caught the snooker bug.

Chipp's intuition from his editor-in-chief mountaintop meant PA would be along for the ride in snooker's glory years, rather than lagging behind, and regional sports editors would be able to keep pace with their rivals on the nationals.

Snooker was such a goggle-box fascination that in the space of barely three or four years, its profile shifted from ponderous pastime to preoccupation of the nation.

'The world starts getting different round about then,' said John Virgo.

Few got as close to Alex Higgins as Virgo, who was three years the senior of the two men. They would knock around together in the snooker clubs of Manchester and Salford in the early 1970s, typically at Potters in Broughton. Mark E. Smith of The Fall was growing up locally, still a few years away from first bothering John Peel's mailbox; John Cooper Clarke, the punk poet, was milling about similar streets and haunts, living on the breadline.

Those that became allies to Higgins would have to cope with the mood swings, the drinking and the incendiary streak that coursed through his very being.

Mike Ganley, whose father Len would face up to chiding in many Higgins matches, served his time in the press room before becoming the professional snooker circuit's on-site big kahuna at events. He questions whether reporters could ever hope to get affably close to Higgins.

'Anybody having a relationship with Alex would have been a miracle worker,' Ganley says. 'You might have had one, but it wouldn't be for long because you'd write something he didn't like and he'd come in and tell you. And that's just the nature of that beast.'

In 1982, Phil Yates was an economics and politics student at Bradford University, on the way to a 2:1 result, six years away from embarking on a career in snooker but already deeply invested in the sport.

'I first saw Higgins in an exhibition,' Yates says. 'I was dressed up in a suit and was only about 14 at the time. My dad had dressed me in this suit, and I'll never forget that Higgins said I looked like an actor.

'So I'd seen him two or three times, but the first time I should have spoken to him was in September 1989. I'd just started to work as not even a junior for Clive – the junior junior, I was the guy who got the tea for the junior.

'John Dee was working for Cue World at the time, which was Snooker Scene's sister publication, and he was also a freelance journalist – so Clive said to him, "Can you take Phil up to Stoke?" It was to Trentham Gardens, for the first tournament of that season, it was a chance just to get involved. I wasn't doing any work up there, but it was a chance to understand the ropes.

'John picked me up that day and Higgins was playing, so I'm really excited to be in the presence of the great man. Anyway, he lost to Mark Johnston-Allen, who became a great mate of mine, and Alan Hughes, who was the MC, came in, and there was all this kerfuffle because Higgins hadn't turned up for his press conference. What you've got to remember then was, even at the lowliest tournament, there was a big press corps at every single event and each newspaper had its own correspondent. And it was all, "Where's Higgins? Where's Higgins?"

'Alan burst into the room, and said, "Gentlemen, Alex has said he will not be attending the press conference because he's got a bad foot," and he read this prepared statement – "I've got a bad foot and the kid played well" – so I never got to meet him then.'

Yates would come to see 'an awful lot' of Higgins in action when tournament qualifiers were staged at Blackpool's Norbreck Castle Hotel.

'You woke up, and you thought, "Oh dear, Higgins is playing today,"' Yates recalls.

'They used to put up an assignments list, and there were 24 tables so all the referees were craning to see who was refereeing his match. It's like if you go to a sixth-form college and there's that day in August when you get the A Level results and everyone's looking and you'd get all these reactions, and it was like that when these guys were looking to see who'd have to referee him. Because it was a daily occurrence: he was having massive goes at referees all the time and saying very personal things to them.

'That's why I say he was very cruel. If you had some sort of weakness, he'd mention it. Say you had a bad complexion or you're overweight, something he could have a go at, he'd pick up on it and really hit below the belt.

197

'At the qualifiers, you've got day upon day upon day of matches, and we just went up for the end when it was newsworthy and you could get a few quid out of the local newspapers.

'Myself and Trevor Baxter were there as the two press men, and Higgins was playing and he was going to lose. He was 4-1 down and well behind in the next, and the people in the tournament office said, "Do you need to speak to Alex today?"

'Normally we would have said "Yes" but there'd been a couple of good stories, there'd been a 147 that day and I think some other controversy, and I didn't need to speak to him. And we'd been speaking to him all week because he'd been playing a lot of matches, so we said, "No, no, we won't have him today."

'And I'll never forget that the response was, "Well, he'll want to speak to you." I said to Trevor, "We'd better go to hide here," so we hid in the room behind the press room. Anyway, he lost and we heard him come in, and he shouted, "Come out, come out, wherever you are!"

'Then the press guy told him, "Alex, the press don't want to speak to you," and he replied, "But I want to speak to them." He wanted to have a go about something. It was a ritual: he had a go about playing conditions, he had a go about the referees, about his opponent's etiquette, everything basically. It was just ridiculous.'

My Crucible press room debut came roughly six months on from PA telling its regular snooker freelancers it would no longer be taking their coverage, electing to produce reports in-house. These would often stem from television coverage or a World Snooker website write-up, rather than unfiltered from a reporter.

Uproar ensued among the freelancers, who were stunned to lose a long-standing source of income and, as might be expected, noisily claimed the shift would mean snooker receiving half-baked coverage.

The call had been taken significantly above my pay grade and it wouldn't behove me to point fingers or pass judgement now, out of great respect for colleagues on both sides. Needless to say, though, I feared a frosty reception in Sheffield. Would the likes of Clive Everton, who wrote derisively of PA's cost-cutting step in a Snooker Scene editorial, hold it against me in Sheffield?

If he did, he kept that to himself and was only ever pleasant and helpful. Whatever sense of grievance Clive may have felt towards PA did not spill over into the personal, and I thank him for welcoming me warmly, as others who were similarly hit also did in that first year and thereafter.

To observe Clive in action was always a privilege. With a battle-hardened sense of humour and unmatched snooker acumen, he might have been the old man of the press room by the time I arrived, having seen it all before, but his enthusiasm for the day's fare was invariably unmatched.

In 1982, Everton's Snooker Scene magazine promoted a dial-a-score service for the duration of the World Championship. This was a results and information hotline, such was the challenge in a low-tech world in finding out precisely what was happening in Sheffield.

He was ahead of the game then, identifying and feeding a hungry market, a canny businessman as well as a fine journalist.

Michael McMullan grew up listening to Clive on the BBC and first encountered him face to face in 1998 at the Crucible.

'I'd been to a couple of stagings of the old Irish Masters at Goffs, and I'd met Phil Yates there, and for my first World Championship I arrived quite early in the morning. There were only a few people in the press room and Phil as ever was one of the first there,' McMullan remembers.

'He said, "I'll introduce you to Clive when he comes in." And my feeling was that this is just so exciting. I was excited enough to be at the Crucible for the first time and then to be meeting Clive was great. Phil introduced me to him and Clive has always been someone who has shown a lot of interest in new people coming in. He doesn't like to see people trying to comment on the game who don't have a knowledge of it, but if a young person arrives in the press room and clearly does have a knowledge of the game and a love for it, I've certainly found Clive has been massively encouraging of that.

'I didn't speak to him a huge amount that week because he was so busy: he was still doing all the TV commentary and he had various newspapers and was writing most of Snooker Scene at that time as well. So it was probably really the following season where I was going to tournaments regularly that I got to know him properly.

'This was someone I'd grown up admiring so much, and he seemed to be as genuinely interested in listening to me as I was in listening to him, and I always remember and always appreciate that.

'He's always been encouraging. I know he was the same with Dave Hendon. He spotted early on that Dave was someone who had a lot of ability and knew a lot about the game and Clive encouraged that.

'I know Clive has had his critics and his enemies in the game, there's no doubt about that, but when he identifies someone coming in who shares his passion and enthusiasm, I've always found him to be extremely encouraging of that, and it's something that I, and I know Dave and Phil, have always appreciated over the years.'

200

23: HE CAME FROM THE JAMPOT, HE'D HAVE YOU ON TOAST

AN OXFORD GRADUATE, a Jampot juvenile and a YMCA whippersnapper, Alex Higgins was wending his way from one Belfast snooker hall to another in the early 1960s, topping up his classroom education with some real-life learning while dishing out a few lessons along the way.

Later in life, he was astute enough to polish off the Daily Telegraph's cryptic crossword, his general knowledge and puzzle solving having been gifts from the streets given the young Higgins was not averse to a little truancy.

In Belfast, to skip school would be commonly known as going on the beak, or mitching. And Higgins, though a bright boy, became drawn to the prospect of regular mitching soon after starting at Kelvin Secondary.

The Jampot snooker club, just off Donegall Road, was a regular haunt; the Oxford, a billiards hall smack at the heart of the city centre, was another spot where the young Higgins would leave grown men humbled on the baize from an early age; the Mountpottinger YMCA was where Higgins won the All-Ireland Amateur Championship in 1968, shortly before his 19th birthday.

All have long since closed their doors, and it is the Jampot that has particularly become central to the Higgins legend. Myriad myths surround the club, and precious little hard evidence of its existence remains, beside a handful of photographs showing its scruffy side-street exterior and an interior with snooker tables surrounded by archaic arcade machines, and a queue of women in fur coats primed for a big night... of bingo.

The Crucible it was not.

Cecil Mason can attest to that. He later became the Jampot's owner, but in the 1950s and early 1960s he was a regular visitor to the club, and he knew the Higgins family well, having gone through school with Anne, Isobel and Jean.

'Alex's sisters all went to school with me, and the Higgins children all went to the same school,' Mason says. 'I knew him from an early age, and he was 11 going on 22, always with the older boys, and always ahead of the game.

'He could play with the older ones because he was a good player. I knew him, his mother, his father and his sisters, the whole kit and caboodle.

'He was a real artful dodger from when he was 10 years of age, full of devilment.'

Mason was in his mid-twenties when he and Higgins first crossed paths, and he stood by the Hurricane through thick and thin. He was the dark-suited gentleman in the crowd who greeted Higgins at the immediate end of the 1982 World Championship final, kissing his own hand and planting the hand on Higgins' temple as the champion returned to his chair.

Mason also accompanied a distraught Higgins to Churchtown in County Cork for the funeral of hellraiser extraordinaire Oliver Reed in May 1999, comforting him that day over the loss of the big-screen great and swarthy old soak. Reed died at 61, just as Higgins would.

Mason was loyal to the end with Higgins, too, tending to his ailing younger friend as those final days beckoned.

The Jampot became more than a hangout for Mason, but as a business venture it was hardly a goldmine.

'Television had just come in during the early 1960s for common people, cinemas all began to collapse – the Majestic, the Regal, the Windsor – and when it came to snooker halls suddenly nobody was interested,' Mason says. 'Colour came along, everybody was watching TV and there was a great decline in snooker.'

Mason savoured seeing the 18-year-old Higgins become the youngest winner of the Northern Ireland Championship in 1968, before landing the World Championship four years later at John Spencer's expense.

The Jampot was fated to lose its lustre as a snooker venue, though memories come flooding back as Mason paints a picture of the club that has found its own fame down the years.

He explains how there were 14 tables, with number eight being the most prestigious, where only the local elite would be given the nod to play.

Park any thoughts of romanticising the Jampot. Mason's warts-and-all testimony suggests it would be long forgotten, were it not for the Higgins legacy.

'It was a big, long room, just a complete state,' Mason says.

Playing on table eight was beyond the reach of Higgins initially, given the hierarchy in place, but the scrawny youth was not one to hide his light under any bushel, with the raw talent that would take him to the top becoming as evident as his precocious self-confidence.

Higgins just needed to be given a chance, and it was in these inauspicious surroundings, where only the strongest survived, that his game first flourished.

'Harry McMullan owned the Jampot before me,' said Mason. 'He didn't mind the kids coming in and playing. It was only fourpence for half an hour.'

For Mason, some of the charming tales of how the young Higgins picked up the game have been embellished beyond recognition.

'I've heard these stories where people say Alex used to stand on an apple box and things like that; it's all a load of crap,' Mason says.

With Higgins tearing off and away to England, building and then squandering a fortune, in time Mason decided he had had enough of being the Jampot's proprietor.

'I tried to change the Jampot to partly bingo when the snooker had fallen away. Then I sold the place for £600,' he says.

Ten of the tables went to building merchants Macnaughton Blair for £100, Mason explains, detailing how the timber was considered desirable because it would be reappropriated for fireplace surrounds.

'And I gave four tables away to boys' clubs,' Mason adds.

He can recall heady days in England in the company of Higgins, staying at Reed's home as well as appearing on This Is Your Life in 1981, the primetime show that celebrated celebrities by rolling out faces from their past and present, with endless handshakes and succinct tributes the order of the day. It was Higgins getting the red book treatment this time, caught unawares by Eamonn Andrews in London, and Mason was sufficiently significant a figure to join in the jamboree, alongside a cast of admirers so eclectic it also featured former Liverpool FC captain Emlyn Hughes and Devil Gate Drive glam rocker Suzi Quatro.

Then there was Sheffield in mid-May of 1982. The World Championship final, day two.

'Oh yes, I was in his dressing room and with him all the day,' Mason remembers.

'I had a small financial interest also, so it was a great day! There were five or six over from Belfast and Alex got us tickets through his manager Del Simmons. Alex booked us into the Hotel St George. From 1980 onwards we stayed in the same place.

'Absolutely there was a party afterwards.

'He could have won the World Championship lots of times, but he liked to take unnecessary chances. That's why they call him the People's Champion, because he wasn't boring, there was none of this tip-tap stuff, he went for his shots.

'I've got photographs on my walls of those days. I was with him all the time at the big snooker tournaments.

'He was drawing crowds when he was a teenager in England, even then, and I can't understand it... he should have been a multi-millionaire. He could've been. Like Ronnie's said, there are three geniuses in sport: Paul Gascoigne, George Best and Alex Higgins.'

Higgins frequently gave off the impression that to stand still for even a minute would be beyond him. Woman to woman, town to town, home to home, there was always somewhere else to be, or someone else to be with. By his own account, he spent a week living in a row of dilapidated terraced shacks in Blackburn around the time of his 1972 World Championship success, carrying his few precious possessions out of one front door and in through the next one along as the demolition men arrived to pull down a house each day. Make up your own mind on the veracity of that tale.

Those who knew him from a young age, like Mason, are best placed to comment on the Higgins myths and legends. There are so many contradictory tales, and pulling together the full story is a patchwork effort that may have some mistakenly placed fabric among its truths.

Of course, the boy Higgins needed playing partners in his early days, so what became of them?

It is September 2021 and Arder Lavery is enjoying retirement in Adelaide, South Australia. He moved away from Belfast with teenage sweetheart Alice in 1968, with the aim of kickstarting a football career on the other side of the world. When the Troubles made a return to Northern Ireland far from appealing, the land down under became a permanent home. Arder and Alice married not long after moving to Australia, and in 2019 celebrated their golden wedding anniversary.

Arder Lavery did much of his growing up in north Belfast – the childhood home was a terrace on Strathroy Park; family included sisters Eileen, Roseleen, Geraldine and Anne, and brother Jim, plus parents Ella and Arder. Mother Ella died when the young Arder was 11 years old, and it was around this time that Alex Higgins first crossed his path.

'I was a Catholic from a Catholic district and I got thrown out of home, so we were renting a house, my sisters and I, just up the road from where Alex lived, up the Donegall Road,' Lavery says.

The spot where the Lavery clan were rehoused was an almost uniformly Protestant district of south Belfast, across the city from their former home. They moved to Lecale Street, close to the Windsor Park national football stadium, in Higgins' locale.

'I only ever went to the Jampot once, ever. It was down a little lane, and trains went underneath. I used to walk from Lecale Street, which was nearby, past where the Jampot was,' Lavery remembers. 'I came from the other part of Belfast, Ardoyne, so instead of going all the way to school, I decided to go into town and to the snooker every day, and the club was called the Oxford. They had 23 snooker tables, and I'd go in there every day.

'And then one day down the Donegall Road, I looked in the laneway and all the kids were coming out of this laneway, and it was the Jampot. I went in there and there was this one little kid standing on a milk crate playing snooker, so I had a game with him and he was brilliant. I told him what I did, how instead of school I'd go to the Oxford every day, so we arranged to meet the next morning instead of going to school, and we walked in the Oxford. And we played nearly every day for about a year. I was 12 when I met him and he was 11. We were only kids, but we used to beat most of the people there, most of them men.'

Lavery has been a regular contributor to the Belfast Forum website community, presenting his memories of the city in the 1950s and 1960s there. As he recalls it, this is how a small part of the Higgins story happened: that the schoolboy potter and his Catholic pal bonded over a love for hustling working men every once in a while for just a little of their hard-earned cash, and going on the beak. Six decades have passed since Lavery and Higgins formed this class-dodging alliance.

'We just got away with it. A lot of kids did the same, they just didn't go to school. My excuse was that I lived too far away from the Catholic district and couldn't walk there anyway, but I managed to walk to town every day,' Lavery says.

'We used to beat everybody, but we usually couldn't afford to play for money, and if we ever did it was for thruppence or sixpence. When you walk in the Oxford, there were about 10 tables downstairs. One was by the bar, and they used to have Alex and me playing all the time there. We were little celebrities, little kids.

'The majority of people who went in there were bus drivers or bus conductors, and they would leave you money to go next door to put the bets on. We were only kids, but they let us go in and put the bets on for the bus drivers.

'I remember Higgy and I had a book, somebody gave us this book once, and it was called How I Play Snooker by Joe Davis. The book told you how to stand and do this, that, and the other, but Higgins and I never did any of it, you know. We just thought, "What a load of shit." It said to "stand straight and keep your arms straight", but if you watch Higgins play he didn't do any of that.

'If I hadn't taken Higgy down to the Oxford, he would have hung around Belfast. In Belfast, you stay in your own district and you don't move, but because I was thrown out of the house and had to walk down by where he lived, that's how we got to know each other. To get to my school, I'd have had to walk through the top of the Shankill, which was a bad area, from where I lived off Donegall Road, so instead of doing that I just walked into town. But my sisters, who I lived with, thought I was going to school.'

The friendship with Higgins that Lavery recounts so vividly was one that was lived out almost entirely in snooker halls in the early 1960s.

'Although there was no Troubles in those days, you didn't want to get stopped by anybody. Because I was a Catholic from the other side of Belfast, I wouldn't go into people's houses on that side of the city,' he says.

'What happened after that was we parted ways for a while. Soon before I left for Australia with Alice, we went down the Donegall Road to the pictures, and Alex jumped on the bus, and I couldn't believe it was him. I was like, "Jesus, Higgy, how you doing mate?"'

Higgins turned 19 in March 1968 and had already tried and failed with his first tilt at a sporting career, unable to make the grade as a jockey at trainer Eddie Reavey's Berkshire stables. Armed with a teenage self-belief that verged on delusion, it had hardly bothered Higgins that he possessed no meaningful experience in the saddle, but it came back to bite him.

By the age of 17 he was back in Belfast, having been denied his romantic dream of riding winners by abundant factors: for one, he could not keep his weight down. It was also claimed Higgins became too tall to ride, and that he was more enthusiastic about backing horses than riding them.

Lavery recalls Higgins telling him of playing snooker at the Mountpottinger YMCA, a grand four-storey building on Albertbridge Road, across the River Lagan in east Belfast, and how making his fanciful ambitions known there had led to the Reavey apprenticeship. Today, the building houses a Pentecostal church but still bears its old insignia above the front door, Mountpottinger YMCA's name enduring in capitalised and vintage serif lettering against a pale, mosaic tiled background.

As Higgins left for England again to pursue sporting fame and fortune, this time having demonstrated actual prowess before catching the ferry, Lavery headed to the other side of the world.

'It was after I left that all the Troubles really started,' Lavery says. 'One of the first to be killed was a good friend I grew up with, and I've been back three times, most recently when I heard all these stories – he's dead, he's dead, he was shot. Thank God I got out of it.

'The reason my girlfriend and I got out was that we ran away to Australia. I'd been in England and had a contract with Crystal Palace. I left that, went back to Belfast for a few months. When I got back to Belfast, I had this letter saying I would be going to

Australia to play professional soccer for a club called St George Budapest in Sydney, so that got me cleared right away.

'We went to Australia without her parents knowing. It turned out OK after all the years and we're still married. My wife remembers Higgy because she remembers that moment on the bus. She always remembered meeting the bloke. He was all friendly. There was a do up here in Queensland a few years ago, after he passed away, and he had a sister (Isobel) who lived in the Gold Coast.'

Arder and Alice were followed in emigrating to Australia in 1970 by Pat 'Paddy' Morgan, another son of Ardoyne who in 1974 would beat Cliff Thorburn in round one of the World Championship in Manchester. Morgan also defeated Higgins 13-6 in the World Professional Matchplay Championship in 1976, played at the Nunawading Basketball Centre in Melbourne.

In the early 1970s, news could be slow to travel to Australia, and Lavery recalls hearing first from Morgan that the debutant Higgins had won the 1972 World Championship, quite some time after the event.

'He said to me, "Did you know your mate won the world title? I'm meeting him tomorrow at the airport,"' Lavery says.

'So me and Paddy went down to pick him up from the airport. I'd booked Higgy into a motel at a place called Liverpool, just outside Sydney, and he borrowed 100 dollars off me. I don't know what he'd done with all his money. I was involved pretty heavily in snooker in those days and I arranged a couple of nights for him. The first of them, we went and he was drunk as usual, and he went to the toilet and a bloke came over to me and said, "Look, can you go over and talk to your friend, he's having a wee-wee outside the door of the toilet." It was shocking, shocking.

'So we talked about old times and he played another time on that trip at a place called Lithgow, in the country outside Sydney. On the way we stopped at Parramatta and he had to have a couple of whiskies; then we stopped at Penrith and he had more whiskies, and we were two hours late in the end coming into the club, which they'd set up for him. The show had been cancelled because he hadn't turned up on time. But a friend of mine said he'd get everyone back in. Alex couldn't even stand up, but it was the best he'd ever played in his life, he never missed a shot.'

Higgins met his first wife, Cara Hasler, in Australia in 1973. Both racing fanatics, their relationship combusted in 1977 and Higgins went on to start a relationship with Lynn Avison.

'The second time I met up with him in South Australia, he just wanted to get drunk all the time, you know. It's just a terrible thing,' says Lavery.

'He hadn't changed, he just wanted a drink non-stop. He had money coming from somewhere, I don't know where it was, but there were no big games for him over here, so I don't know how he got paid.

'He'd grown a bit of course, because when I knew him he was 11 and I was 12, and he was very, very small.'

The chaos that followed Higgins around – the Hurricane leaving wreckage in his path – was in stark contrast to whatever light breeze followed in the wake of Australia's own 'Steady' Eddie Charlton, a player who achieved plenty in the game but whose plodding style could have a soporific effect on audiences.

'The only bloke we had over here in Australia was Eddie Charlton, and I did a bit of business with him, but as a player he was very boring,' says Lavery. 'Shocking.'

For all the many faults, an accusation of being 'boring' could never be thrown at Higgins.

24: Outlaw recognises outlaw

JOE SWAIL has tremendous affection for the city, but the description that springs to mind when he considers the Belfast of his youth is that of 'a horrible, dark place'.

Swail was raised in the Markets, a principally Catholic area of Belfast. He recalls barricaded streets, barbed wire barriers, soldiers, bombs and bullets, with mum Josephine and dad Billy attempting to give him the best start in life regardless.

'I remember, growing up, when I was only about seven or eight; we lived in a house, the whole family of us, and the toilet was in the back yard. That's the way it was back then,' Swail says.

A humble man, befitting his background, Swail has a quietly spoken manner and the memories of his childhood are flooding back as we meet backstage at the Barbican Centre in York.

It is December 2018. Earlier in the year, in March, Swail lost his father, his most ardent supporter. A long-term struggle with tinnitus is compounding the stresses of life as a pro for Swail, and as we speak the clock is ticking on his snooker career.

This will be his last season on tour, but that's no cause for upset. After all, Swail, who is partially deaf, can reflect proudly on

212

almost 30 years in the paid ranks.

Twice a Crucible semi-finalist, losing to Matthew Stevens in 2000 and Ronnie O'Sullivan a year later, Swail has come an awfully long way since weekly doses of Pot Black on the small screen gave him the snooker bug.

'I had to go to bed about seven o'clock, eight o'clock, as a boy. But I was allowed to stay up certain Tuesday nights to watch Pot Black, because I loved Alex Higgins,' Swail says.

'Everything was happening in Belfast and I started loving snooker. I loved watching Pot Black and all the other players, but Higgins just stood out, every Tuesday night, and I was very disappointed when he lost, and that's when he became my idol, you know. Then I became hooked on snooker.

'I got to meet him one time in Cork, back in those early days. I went down to meet him for a competition, I must have been about 14 or something. Alex had won the world title in Sheffield by then and I went down with my friends and obviously I'd never met him before. So I went through the bar to get myself a cordial and water, an orange, and he happened to be beside me.

'With him being my hero, I was too shy to speak to him. Something always stuck with me from that day though, because he must have known I played a wee bit, I was starting to come through the amateur, junior scene. I found out later on he was always following the results of the junior players.'

Swail, at the time, was floored to learn Higgins knew of him.

'That day he was doing a crossword and he was really struggling with a question and you could see him stuck, so he turned round and said, "What's tha', what's tha'?"' Swail recalls.

'And he said to me, "There's no point in asking you, you're from Belfast as well." I just freaked out, completely freaked out, and after that I went back to my friends and didn't know what to do, what to say. But Alex was just carrying on as normal.

'He had such an aura about him, and a lot of charisma. But you never knew what mood he was in, and of course I started coming through the ranks, and while I was coming through he was falling off the tour. He got banned a few times and probably didn't do himself many favours; however, I loved him, I loved him.'

To address the Troubles, we should mention news fatigue, which is that flighty human condition whereby an audience becomes weary and, in some cases, desensitised by what it once considered shocking, where stasis sets in and the extraordinary becomes the depressingly ordinary. Global and local Covid-19 death rates sparked horror for many as the pandemic first took hold; but, as the tens of daily fatalities became hundreds and the hundreds became thousands, and the death count kept ticking along, the impact perhaps surprisingly fell away for many beyond those directly affected.

It was easy to become quickly numbed, such torment becoming merely another part of one's quotidian routine.

Those that lost loved ones were visited by personal tragedy, but the collective grief of communities and nations began to subside. The news bulletins were vibe killers and consequently millions zoned out or tuned out. Anxieties faded; interest waned. Another day of 1,500 Covid deaths across the UK in January 2021 passed by, soon to be almost forgotten. On January 21, the day after 1,820 Covid-connected deaths were announced, which by the end of the year remained the highest daily figure yet recorded, almost every national newspaper in the UK splashed with the inauguration of US president Joe Biden. Communities had become inured to the killer virus in their midst, editors and journalists too. More of the same eventually becomes a turn-off and it was ever thus.

The bombings and torrid stories of life at the sharp end for innocent civilians in Baghdad, Kabul and Raqqa, to summon three examples from recent times, have dominated the global news agenda before sliding off the front pages and television bulletins. Another family home razed to the ground, another slaying of the inculpable, another war crime. Another mass shooting in America.

By 1982, the Troubles had been rumbling on for 14 years, within Northern Ireland and beyond. On May 17 of that year, the day after Alex Higgins lorded it over the snooker world in Sheffield, the front page of the Belfast Telegraph led with news from the trial of an accused in the killing of leading unionist and former Stormont speaker Sir Norman Strong, and his son James. The man would later be cleared of involvement.

Prominent on that same page were stories about Belfast's first curry house being named the city's top restaurant, the death in a road collision of a local punk band's drummer, Falklands peace talks at the United Nations, industrial action on the railways, and a fraud conviction. Proud parents Elizabeth and Alex senior celebrated Higgins' 'night of glory' at their Abingdon Street home and were pictured with a bottle of champagne and the 1980 Coleraine Cup trophy, presumably at the behest of a photographer keen to have silverware, anything faintly resembling the World Championship trophy, in shot.

This is a front page that gives the impression it may have been a quiet weekend on the streets of Northern Ireland, yet page four of the same Monday newspaper is topped by a report headlined 'Double terror attack on home', which discloses that a bomb blasted a hole in the gable end of the house of a security forces member in the town of Magherafelt, with another device discovered under a nearby car. The same report mentions four petrol bombs being thrown at a police Land Rover, as well as the fire-bombing of a sports centre clubhouse in Enniskillen.

These were stories from the weekend that might have warranted front-page coverage at any other period in Northern Ireland's history, yet here they were, tucked inside the newspaper, having become the everyday reality. Page four fodder, alongside a long write-up of a salty schism in the poultry farming fraternity, as one flock of exhibitors displayed their birds at the Balmoral agricultural show while others carried on their fowl affairs at a rival event.

On the day snooker's World Championship began, Friday, April 30, you had to turn to page three of the same newspaper to find a chronicle of chaos: police coming under a bomb attack in Derry; another device packed with nails detonating outside a shop; some 170 rounds of .30 calibre ammunition falling from a chimney stash in north Belfast; two crates of petrol bombs discovered in a cupboard.

The chilling single column appeared adjacent to an entertainment guide that showed life was carrying on. Saturday night in Belfast would feature an Ulster Orchestra concert at Ulster Hall, Bernie Winters and Leslie Crowther bringing the Sid Colin musical Bud 'n' Ches to the Grand Opera House, and the life story of Oscar Wilde dramatised in the play Speranza's Boy at the Lyric Theatre.

A multi-national judo tournament was taking place at the Valley Leisure Centre in Newtownabbey, an Irish folk dancing festival at McNeill Hall in Larne, motorcycle road races in Tandragee. Second-year pupils at St Patrick's High School in Maghera had raised £800 – no small sum in 1982 – through a sponsored silence to help a leper colony in Nigeria.

People needed an escape, and to the 12-year-old Joe Swail, what occupied him most during Crucible time were the goings-on in Sheffield. Would Higgins, the self-made boy from Sandy Row, deliver another sporting triumph for Northern Ireland?

'I'll never forget his 1982 win,' says Swail. 'There was the second-round decider against Mountjoy, and I remember when it got to the semi-finals and he cleared up against Jimmy.

'We didn't have a TV in the house and so it was the case that myself and a lot of mates had got together, and we went down to the town in Belfast. And you've got to remember it was always full of armoured cars and there were soldiers everywhere, and we were all outside this Granada shop that rented TVs. We all congregated outside, watching the end of the clearance that Alex made against Jimmy. We were all getting excited. None of us had TVs, and we were all shouting and screaming at the window of this shop. It seemed that Alex wasn't in control and that's what made it so exciting, to keep doing what he was doing.

'It was unbelievable, never to be seen again. Then he went on to beat Reardon. For the final, we rented a TV and we never gave it back. So, good memories.

'It was a dark place and we'd had so little to shout about. It was a horrible, dark place, it really was, and then when Dennis Taylor won in 1985 it was another celebration, it was brilliant once again and everyone came together. We were lucky to have these great sportsmen, Alex and Dennis, Barry McGuigan, Joey Dunlop, and when those guys won it allowed us to have great times, because otherwise we had nothing. It gave us something to shout about.

'I think in Belfast we're fighters. A lot of these sportsmen had to go to other countries to make the grade. It was tough because if you grew up in Belfast, unless you got the opportunity to go outside the country, and excel at your sport, it was grim, it was very, very dark.

'We all remember where we were in 1982. Everybody remembers where we were when Alex won it, and I was watching in my living room. My mum let me stay up that time.'

At this point, Swail laughs at the memory. It's the happiest laugh, too, sparked by thoughts of family, the salad days of youth, and the moment it dawned on him what he wanted out of life.

Swail is as affable a character as you could wish to encounter, with his nickname of 'The Outlaw' a whopper of a red herring, stemming as it does from the Clint Eastwood movie 'The Outlaw Josey Wales'.

'I don't forget those times long ago because they make you what you are,' Swail says, 'and I'm sure Alex and Dennis were in the same boat when they were young – brilliant, good proper fighters.'

Swail rightly points to the early 1980s being a heady time for sport in Northern Ireland. In 1982, Billy Bingham's Green and White Army were heading to the football World Cup in Spain, Dunlop was the fastest thing on two wheels, and future featherweight world champion McGuigan won five fights before April was out. The great Tom Kiernan coached Ireland to Five Nations and Triple Crown rugby success at the start of the year, with Ollie Campbell the star of a team only denied a Grand Slam by a Serge Blanco-inspired France in Paris.

Michael McMullan, who hails from County Antrim, highlights how sport was far from a frivolity amid turmoil on the streets.

'At that time, there were two things that unified the communities in Northern Ireland: one was that neither community trusted the English, and the other was sporting success,' says McMullan.

'So when things like that happened – Alex Higgins, Barry McGuigan, the football team, and obviously Dennis Taylor in 1985 – that was something that everyone was on board with, and nobody had any regard for the fact that Alex was a Protestant and Dennis was a Catholic.

'Everybody got behind them and wanted to be a part of it because there wasn't a great deal else for everybody to cheer about at that time.'

On the cusp of his teenage years, Swail was already displaying serious snooker talent.

'I never played at the Jampot though. It was a wee bit before my time, and I never went there,' Swail says.

He would have jumped at the chance. Like Higgins, Swail hoped his snooker might bulldoze any political or religious walls.

'The thing about Alex was that he'd travel anywhere to play snooker. The political divide in Northern Ireland didn't bother him. He went up to the Falls Road, to Shankill. I'd like to think I could do the same thing,' Swail says. 'You've got to remember it was very, very tough. Alex didn't care and he just went and played snooker – he'd take on anyone, anywhere for money.

'I learnt a lot off him. It's like footballers learning off George Best and other icons. Players learn from his mistakes. The world would be boring without Alex and George. They were something else.

'Although I never got to know Alex very well in his early days, I got to know him later on in life, just before he died.

'I didn't really get to know him to begin with because of his character, but we had a couple of good nights out before he passed on, and he said a couple of things to me that I'll take to my grave. I'll never forget that, and it made him just that bit more special in my eyes.'

25: 26 SHIRTS, FIVE TUXEDOS, NO NONSENSE

BECAUSE SNOOKER had for so long been an underground concern, it was entirely fitting that a London Tube train driver should referee the first Crucible final.

Dublin-born John Smyth had not quite given up his long-held post on the Piccadilly Line at the time he took charge of John Spencer's 25-21 win over Cliff Thorburn in 1977; despite the packed theatre and BBC television coverage, some suspected the rush of interest in snooker amounted to little more than a fad.

Punk rock, disco, Daisy Dukes and snooker. Were these just fly-by-night fashions, or would such late-seventies trends endure?

Smyth was certainly not among the sceptics, but he had them in his ear.

Yet by this point snooker had Smyth firmly in its grip, and after commandeering that landmark title match, it was a matter of time before this middle-aged cog in the subterranean system swapped carrying London's commuters on rolling stock for a very different professional journey.

Was he swapping a safe meal ticket for a roll of the dice? When Smyth became a full-time professional referee in 1978, the year that he turned 50, he was willing to take that chance. As it happened, he was signing up for a trip through snooker's gold rush era, and it would be another 18 years before he retired.

Smyth was also chosen to referee the 1982 World Championship final, selected from the pool of officials that also featured Jim Thorpe, Len Ganley, Gus Lilygreen and John Williams.

'Smythy was a good bloke, a lovely old boy,' remembers Mike Ganley.

'Him and his missus, Val, they went everywhere together.'

In 1984, Smyth was the referee when Kirk Stevens made the first maximum 147 break in Masters history, and the nearest person for the Canadian to hug in delight after sinking the black to complete the clearance. Opponent Jimmy White was second in line.

In 1990, Smyth was among a handful of snooker figures on the guest list for the wedding of Steve Davis to Judy, with that a telling sign of his place right at the centre of the game. Five years earlier, the then heavy smoker Smyth had a heart attack while on a lucrative exhibition tour with Davis.

The man who moved to England in his early twenties, spending almost three decades working beneath the streets of the capital, would not be fortunate enough to referee a third Crucible final. However, he took charge of five Masters title matches, taking turns with John Street, as Smyth ran the showpiece at Wembley Conference Centre in the odd years from 1979 to 1987.

Like most referees of his era, Smyth had at least one head-on collision with Higgins. A noteworthy altercation came at the 1986 British Open, where Higgins suffered a miserable early exit at the hands of Jack McLaughlin, a fellow Northern Irishman.

Smyth told Higgins to keep his language in check during the

contest, prompting the beaten man to launch a tirade at refereeing standards afterwards, the age-old distraction technique for a humbled sportsman.

Higgins' dry wit could drift towards the acerbic, but his response to Smyth this time must have raised a few smiles.

'All I said was I would feel safer on a tube train if he wasn't driving,' Higgins said.

**

One of the few aspects that is uniform about snooker referees is... well, it's the uniform.

Stylistically, the referee's typical getup is a great look for anyone hankering to be confused for a maître d'. Or a chauffeur. Or perhaps a casino croupier. And in essence, these men and women in dinner suits and white gloves do indeed belong to the world of the service industry.

Len Ganley was almost the exception, but the rule of thumb is that they'll never have star status. If a referee's performance ever stands out, chances are they've blundered or had the misfortune to be on the end of a barbed remark from a player or spectator; if they have an immaculate match, few if anybody will notice, never mind offer any acclaim.

A snooker referee is there to be a policing figure, subserviently picking balls out of pockets and ensuring propriety prevails. Their role is to make occasional judgement calls, tot up scores, remember every nuance of the rules, treat smart alec hecklers and sweet-wrapper rustlers with equal and utter disdain, and be as inconspicuous a third party as possible in a two-player game.

The pay packet tends to be modest, in keeping with the plaudits. Yet still they come through the ranks, year after year, new faces rolling on to the refereeing conveyor belt, each of them harbouring a familiar snooker dream; as with the players, to appear at the Crucible is the referee's Everest.

Referees have long been a curious bunch, with the workforce drawn from backgrounds as diverse as nursing, design, bus driving and the police force. Olivier Marteel in 2021 was treating Covid-19 patients one month and hushing Crucible crowds the next, Desislava Bozhilova is a computer graphic artist and landscape architect, Brendan Moore used to bounce buses around Sheffield's streets, and Leo Scullion moved on from policing and taxi-driving to become a globe-trotting constable of his beloved sport.

Len Ganley was dubbed a 'Jolly Green Giant' of the snooker tour, and this was because the former milkman, chimney sweep and bus conductor was built for such a caricature, being a) outwardly formidable but inwardly gentle and jovial; b) from the island of Ireland; and c) physically a heavyweight, who once claimed to have weighed 29 stone at his bulkiest.

The original Jolly Green Giant was a cartoon caveman designed by American marketing hotshot Leo Burnett to sell canned vegetables. Among other creations cooked up by Burnett's intrepid team were Marlboro Man and Frosties' Tony the Tiger, both originating in the 1950s but still going strong in the 1980s.

Ganley, who relocated from Lurgan to Burton upon Trent in his late twenties, stumbled on to the snooker tour, as many referees do. In his case, it came after encouragement from Ray Reardon.

Already a leading local player for Newhall Social Club, with century breaks to his name, Ganley had studied the rule book so diligently during his teenage years that he became the pick of the local Derbyshire referees too.

As such, he was handed the opportunity to referee a Reardon exhibition when the Welshman visited the Burton area in 1976, donning the white gloves before a 600-strong crowd.

The amateur official's expertise on that evening, efficiently hushing the crowd after the celebrity visitor reached a century, immediately turned the head of the then world champion.

Reardon reputedly asked whether Ganley had considered becoming a tour referee, and this was all the impetus that was needed. Within five years, Ganley was a familiar presence in the professional game, turning Reardon's hunch into a remarkable reality.

The Burton Daily Mail noted on January 22, 1981, that Ganley would be refereeing at that year's Yamaha Organs Trophy and the World Championship, with its dainty write-up stating: 'Mr Ganley does not have a job but is hoping that he will be able to make refereeing his profession – and these latest appointments must give him cause for optimism.'

Mike Ganley was in the fortunate position of being able to join his dad at the Crucible every year.

Looking back on his first visits to Sheffield, Mike says: 'For most of the eighties, there were only four referees at the Crucible, and they did the whole tournament: Alan Chamberlain, John Street, John Williams and Len Ganley.

'Generally they hogged it all and mucked in because at that time it really was all building up, and they helped out with the rigging and the like. They were all pretty good. I wouldn't say they all got on, because the characters were all different, from different backgrounds. Some worked in regular jobs, some didn't, and some took up refereeing as a profession. A lot of them ended up being professional referees because they could just about make a living out of it.

'Len made good money from the exhibitions, because for whatever reason he did have a profile, and an ego and a personality that went with it.'

Mike knew that if he headed to tournaments, he would surely see plenty of his dad.

There was fun to be had at a World Championship, too.

'I was lucky in that from the age of about 16 I went to most of them, so I've been around a lot,' Mike says. 'It was a completely different culture – a work-hard, play-hard culture – and that's what the eighties was in snooker. It wasn't as disciplined in some ways, and there was the drinking at the table and the smoking, and all those sorts of things, and Sheffield as a city was only just realising the potential of snooker.'

Len told the Observer in December 1983 he had not slept under his own roof since August of that year, so busy was he going from city to city on tour. His luggage included 26 shirts, five tuxedos and 36 pairs of white gloves, he explained.

This was close to peak earning time for Len, who appeared in a famous Carling Black Label beer advert. It depicted him crushing a cue ball in his gloved hands after John Spencer waywardly sent it jumping off the table, plum into Ganley's lower midriff.

The insinuation was that Spencer made a two-ball off-table plant at Ganley's painful expense. Sledgehammer subtlety.

Seeking retribution, Ganley appeared to pulverise the ball in his right fist, prompting Terry Griffiths to pipe up with the deadpan 'I bet he drinks Carling Black Label' catchphrase.

Ganley was said to be teetotal, albeit quite content to take the brewer's money. His newest nickname, 'Ball Crusher Ganley', was born with the commercial that was very much of its time.

When Ganley died in 2011, Steve Davis remarked: 'Len did a very good job of being a referee and a personality at the same time. A referee is supposed to be unseen, and he liked the limelight, but he still managed to do the job properly.'

Ganley refereed Davis' Crucible final triumphs in 1983 and

1987, before also overseeing two of Stephen Hendry's first three title matches, in 1990 and 1993.

With his growing clout, Ganley became a crusading fundraiser for muscular dystrophy and spina bifida charities, collaring anyone who crossed his path at the Crucible for a donation, seeking a £10 note usually, making it clear this was non-negotiable. Come the 1990s, Ganley had the gumption to successfully collar Sheffield boxing superstar 'Prince' Naseem Hamed for a tenner, confident there were plenty more where that came from.

'Len would carry it around in a plastic bag, all these tenners, and he was very abrasive. He had a lot of front to do that, but he was like that,' says David Hendon.

Ganley would later be appointed an MBE for his charity work and services to snooker.

He was also the referee when Ronnie O'Sullivan made a maximum break in five minutes and eight seconds at the 1997 World Championship.

'He really enjoyed being on the circuit, every aspect of that,' says Hendon. 'He was very gregarious and it's interesting Ronnie O'Sullivan was saying how good he thought he was on that five-minute maximum in '97, just allowing him to play at that speed.

'Len stepped back and wouldn't be walking around the table putting him off.

'He had a bit of a reputation for making mistakes, but if you comb through every match you'll find all referees make mistakes.

'In later life he was a diabetic and there was one match where there was a player, I think Graham Horne from Scotland, and to keep his energy up he had a little chocolate bar by his seat. Len was reffing him and Graham Horne was literally down on his shot and Len tapped him on the shoulder and said, "Can I have a bit of your chocolate?" because he was needing a rush.

'If that had been any other referee, they probably would have been suspended or something, but with Len you just accepted it because he was such a character, and it was an era of characters, with people warming to the people around the sport, and it was an eccentric band.

'It still is really, and it certainly was then. You had people who came from other walks of life, who'd had lives before snooker and just found their way into it somehow.'

In 1982, Ganley largely took a back seat in Sheffield but still made an impression, particularly leaving debutant Jim Donnelly with a fond memory, even if Donnelly's one and only World Championship experience was all too brief.

The Scot recalls: 'I'd never been to Sheffield before. One of the things I've always said is that you obviously look not so much at heroes, but at people you tend to go towards because they've got something special about them. And Ray Reardon, I looked at him as being the best, and I'd be watching him on television from the Crucible not knowing that the following year I was going to be professional and playing him in the first round.

'That's what I looked forward to when going to the Crucible as much as walking into the arena. It's something totally different. I remember hearing I'd got Ray and it gave me a bit of a gee-up, and about 15 or 20 minutes before the match I was in the dressing room, having a cup of tea and a cream bun.

'So I'm sitting, eating that, and Len Ganley came in, and he said to me, "You'll be ready in about 10 or 15 minutes?" and I said, "Yeah."

'"How are you feeling?" he said. And I said to him, "Oh, I'm looking forward to this."

'So he said, "Are you not nervous? It's Reardon you're playing."

'I told him, "Len, the Crucible holds 999 people, and there'll also be some players in the players' area, so there'll be over a thousand in there, because Higgins was on the next table. And also, because I'm the first professional player to get here from Scotland, there might be another million people in Scotland watching, and every one of them thinks that Reardon's going to win, and there's only one person that thinks he's not going to win. So that's me, and if anybody should be under pressure it's Ray Reardon, not me."

'So that was the laugh we had just before I went out. Len was a real character. He was as much of a character as the players were, as much a celebrity as they'd call it now. He was recognised as one of the top people in snooker, along with the players, as well known as any of them.'

Hendon agrees, saying: 'Len's personality came through, which is not easy when you're a referee, because they're usually just dressed smartly, in the background, doing their job. But he smiled and he just looked a bit different. He stood out and he became an unlikely celebrity. He was larger than life.'

**

Despite Higgins having a sideline in sideswipes, most leading referees in the early eighties were admirers of the Hurricane, even if grudgingly. Ganley and Williams went on record as putting him either at, or close to, the top of their list of favourites, no doubt all too conscious his shenanigans were putting snooker on the front and back pages of newspapers, and by extension heightening the sport's popularity and their own earning capacity.

It has been much the same today in the modern game with O'Sullivan. Although he might step out of line, or at least keep them on their toes, several referees have disclosed to me they relish taking charge of his matches, always with the potential for something extraordinary to happen.

One figure on the 1982 snooker tour staff was not to be messed with, by Higgins or anybody. Ann Yates worked on the press team from event to event and would later become tournament director. She was every player's backstop, fixing just about any and every problem.

It was Yates who sewed up heavyweight Bill Werbeniuk's trousers during a break in play after they split during a frame against David Taylor at the 1980 World Challenge Cup.

It was Yates who would call the shots in press conferences, too, demanding the players and the media toe the line.

Yates left home in County Cork in the early 1970s, an interior designer by trade, and soon found work on Embassy's press staff. Tobacco sponsorship was quite the catch and she worked on events as diverse as power-boating, show-jumping and golf.

No sport was booming quite as snooker was, however, and Yates, though not initially hooked, became a central figure behind the scenes.

From the press room through to the boardroom, Yates was as fundamental as many a player to the game's roaring prosperity during the eighties and early nineties.

Mike Ganley remembers her fondly.

'Ann was great, and she was my mentor later on,' Ganley says. 'I came through the press room, security and the media side. She was the Iron Lady of snooker and took no nonsense from anybody. And it didn't matter if it was written down or not, if Ann told you that you weren't doing it then you weren't doing it.

'If she said you needed a shave before you went out to play, you made sure you got a shave. They knew that if you stepped over the line, she'd nail you to the cross. When she got tournament director status, she was absolutely the one.'

Steve Davis would rarely cause Yates any consternation. It helped to have his ilk when so many others were pushing the boundaries.

'If ever there was a problem and you needed to sort something out, or if people needed to be pulled up for any reason, Ann Yates was the person who did it all,' Davis says.

'She was amazing when you think about it, how she was always there in charge. If ever there was a problem, you phoned her up. She was the person who once phoned up Fred Davis, when he was meant to be playing in the qualifiers, and all of a sudden she phoned him up out of concern because he hadn't turned up for his match in the summer.

'It was the qualifiers which were held at the Norbreck Castle in Blackpool, and she phoned him up and was like, "Fred, it's Ann Yates at the snooker, are you OK? You haven't turned up for your match." And Fred went, "Oh, is it July already?"

'You needed somebody in a position of authority that we all took notice of. She was good because even though she knew everybody, we all respected her, so nobody took the mickey. She probably had a few run-ins with Alex and she'd have given as good as she got, because she wouldn't have bowed away from Alex.'

26: 'It's still the greatest shot'

THE AIR INSIDE the Crucible was thick with a heady mix of tension, testosterone and tobacco on the evening of May 14, 1982, as Alex Higgins picked at his fingernails, scowled, and began to contemplate, possibly for the first time, the prospect of defeat.

When he trailed 20-year-old Jimmy White by 8-4 and then 11-8, Higgins knew there was plenty of time for a comeback. This was, after all, a three-day world semi-final, a best-of-31 battle, and a test of endurance and nerve. White was a novice at the long distances, Higgins a marathon veteran.

Yet the point at which Higgins was 15-14 behind was perilously grave, particularly when White built a 59-0 lead in the 30th frame too. The destiny Higgins had prescribed himself was drifting out of sight, the lucky charms his fan army had handed over at the stage door were turning from precious to spurious.

Higgins had a face on – as they say around Sheffield. He was waking from the fantastical dream he had sold himself, to be faced with a miserable, cold, rotten reality. And then White inexplicably missed, a sliding doors moment in snooker history.

Higgins had not risen at four o'clock on the third morning of the semi-final for the sheer contrariness of it all. Such an hour was previously considered more akin to bedtime for the Hurricane, but here there was business to attend to. White led 8-7, the match on a knife edge ahead of morning and evening sessions.

Entering the practice room soon after dawn, Higgins put in the hours to steel himself for whatever White might throw at him. And White duly threw plenty, until he threw his own hopes into the Sheffield night sky. Higgins had been gifted an opportunity, with the door almost closed on him, to gently lever it back open.

* *

As far as the audience could tell, White had been sprinting towards a maiden World Championship final. By playing a handsome screw shot off the blue with a heavy helping of right-hand side, navigating between green and brown and springing off the bottom and side cushions, White had teed up a slightly off-straight red with the rest. To his mind, though, it was as good as a gimme, so the young Londoner got down quickly to take aim. It was surely about to be 60-0; nobody expected anything else.

> DAVID TAYLOR: 'He was really special, Jimmy, wasn't he. He was very fast and just so natural. He was one of the most exciting and greatest players I've ever seen.'

A mere five seconds had elapsed from the cue ball rolling to a halt when White, having snatched the rest, jabbed at the pot on the red. This Whirlwind was whipping up – a phenomenal, glorious force of nature, in for the kill; red, colour, red was all he required now to leave Higgins needing snookers.

But this time the red rattled around the corner jaws and did not plummet into the pocket. White stared at the ball, affronted.

Both elbows dropped to the table, his head slumped. He had been almost over the line, but here was a sumptuous plot twist. Put snooker in a theatre and what do you expect?

Up went the gasps, the one-table set-up from the semi-finals onwards meaning White's fumbling of near-certain victory was witnessed by everyone inside the Crucible. What was done here could not be undone, as White immediately blanched.

The crowd, largely middle-aged men in fashions that flexed from Conservative Club brown to parish council sub-committee shades of grey, sucked in the stale, polluted air.

Jack Karnehm, commentating for the BBC, told viewers: 'So Alex breathes again... Still enough points on the table for Alex, if he can just take his opportunity.'

The reds were far from ideal, with two on the cushion, while the black was just short of the baulk line. Higgins, in an open-necked, electric-blue shirt, surveyed the table, checked the scoreboard, fiddled with his hair, and got on with the job.

Ahead of the meeting with White, Higgins had said in the Belfast Telegraph: 'I have only had about half a dozen wild shots in the championship this year, and I am certainly not going to take any chances against Jimmy.'

White was the coming man in snooker, an amateur world champion two years previously and now, aged 20, showing his prowess on the sport's most famous stage.

He had made a break of 69 in the seventh frame against Higgins that took a trifle under three minutes, a mini masterpiece that perfectly demonstrated the strength of this particular 'Wind.

Little did White realise during Thursday's play, as he rattled off seven consecutive frames from 4-1 behind, that Higgins would make a 69 break of his own when the match reached boiling point.

Higgins' dish of the day would be remembered as one of snooker's greatest clearances. Forty years later, they're writing books about it.

Surprised by White's slip-up and the sniff of a reprieve, Higgins made a flub of his first shot, sinking a red to a corner pocket but leaving the cue ball in no man's land between pink and blue.

Another look at the scoreboard, a ruffle of his fringe, and it was time to bring out those 'wild shots' the Northern Irishman knew would deliver either salvation or downfall.

Circumspection had left the building and a long green was the first punt for Higgins. In it went, and by swinging the cue ball around the angles, Higgins also moved the furthest red up the table off the side cushion. For narrative's sake, we'll assume that was the intention.

> MARK ALLEN: 'Any ball that he'd have missed in that break, that was the end of him. I actually just watched it again recently, the ball that Jimmy missed to let Alex in, and it was a bit of a careless shot. Maybe the writing was on the wall for Jimmy as well, for him not to win it.'

The other red that sat cosily by a cushion at the start of the break was more or less tight to the top rail; however, it could be potted given the right angle, and Higgins just about had that. From seven feet away, he clipped the red with immaculate precision but left the fate of the cue ball in the lap of the gods. It wound up around four inches shy of tight behind the yellow, with just enough space to hit the nearby black ball full in the face.

In went the black to the far left corner. A broad smile crossed the face of Higgins as he marched around to size up his next task.

He was warming to this death-or-glory mission.

NEIL ROBERTSON: 'If you dissect the break, it wasn't constructed very well in the sense of how you'd expect to clear up from that position. Every shot was like this miracle recovery shot, and at the point when he knocked in the long black he looked up to the crowd and to one of his friends on the balcony, and just laughed at how it was amazing the break was still going.'

The cue ball trickled down the table, Higgins now left with an awkward cut into the right middle pocket, taking on the red he had moved moments earlier.

PHIL YATES: 'The pockets then were definitely more generous than they are now, particularly the middles. There's one shot in the 69, the little dink back into the middle pocket, and if you speak to any player now, that shot would be impossible now, there wouldn't be enough pocket for that to go in.'

NIGEL BOND: 'They say the bags were bigger back then, but the balls still had to be potted. It was incredible really.'

Higgins sized up the red and was by now in no mind to elect for safety. A delicate clip, and the red rolled towards the pocket and down the hatch. Applause rang out, yet the cue ball trundled so far as to finish awkwardly between pink and blue, almost directly on the path between their respective spots.

By now Higgins had just 13 points on the board, meagre reward for having pulled off this initial sequence of audacious pots.

Toying with his options, studying the geography of the table and assessing his scoreboard prospects, Higgins fancied the daunting blue into the green pocket.

Here again was the match: miss, and Higgins would surely leave White in to finish him off.

Down Higgins got on the shot, leaning over the pink and remaining three reds, and shaped to deliver the masterstroke he had in mind.

Make this, and the frame stood to be at his mercy, providing he could find a way to bring the cue ball back towards those kindly split reds.

What followed was a shot for the ages.

Applying heavy screw and left-hand side, jerking violently as he made contact, Higgins not only sent the blue like a lightning bolt into the heart of the pocket, but a ferocious impact threw the cue ball off sharply to the left. It sprang back from the cushion eight inches baulk side of the middle pocket and jagged urgently back across the table, striking the opposite side a staggering three feet closer to the top cushion as that thudding cue action took effect. This time the applause was thunderous.

CLIFF THORBERTON: 'I never could manage what he did with that shot. It's still a shot from beyond; it's still the greatest shot. He played with a heavier type of cue and a spongy sort of tip, and that's how he could play that shot on the blue ball. You almost can't even play that shot now. There's two of the greatest shots: that one and the one Ronnie made on the last red in his 147 at the Welsh Open [in 2014] when he potted left-handed and came down and slid between the pink and black and finished perfectly on the black for the yellow. Alex was in a pretty good mood there playing Jimmy. I've got to look the other way.'

NEIL ROBERTSON: 'The blue was one of the greatest shots ever seen. A lot of players can play that particular shot now, but it's easier to do when you're 60 or 70 in front. That wasn't the case with Alex, so to do it knowing that if you miss, you lose and you're out of the final, it was just absolutely amazing, and it set the tone for many other players to play the flamboyant shots. Nobody really back then played those kinds of shots or had seen them before. It was a part of one of the most amazing breaks you'll ever see, particularly in the circumstances.'

Steve Davis had sobered up by now, but seeing Higgins strumming the greatest hits could easily have sent him scuttling back to the bottle. Ask Davis about the Higgins blue now, and he concedes it came from a place beyond his own repertoire.

STEVE DAVIS: 'You need great cue power to be able to do what he did with that shot, and not many people were blessed with the reflexes that Alex Higgins had. A lot of the time he threw himself at the shot. Players wouldn't do that these days – they'd have better technique. Alex still understood how to make the ball do what was required, even if it was maybe a little less sound of technique. We tried to reproduce that shot on the blue one year at the World Championship on the BBC, in a series of picking out some of the great shots and we all had to try them. I think Dennis Taylor, who had great cue power, did the best effort. But that was never my game, power shots, that was a struggle.'

DAVID TAYLOR: 'I've put a few of those shots up on the table and attempted them, but you just can't play them. But Alex found a way to play them. Fabulous, fabulous player.'

Modern Crucible patrons are forever on the lookout for players who might one day compare to Higgins and his maverick talent, those who might be roughneck one minute and radiant the next.

There are great shot-makers today, but potting balls was just one aspect of the whole Higgins shebang.

Crowds flocked to witness the sheer nonconformity of a Higgins performance.

NIGEL BOND: 'Alex was a bit like a Judd Trump nowadays. He just pulled out shots from nowhere that day. You can throw the coaching manual out of the window. He was up off the shot, he was feathering on the way in, everything completely unorthodox, but it worked for Alex. It was all over the shop and he kept rescuing the situation with unbelievable pots.'

JIM DONNELLY: 'The movement on the shots, the jumping up. Nobody, not even Ronnie O'Sullivan, could play shots and knock a break like that in the way Higgins did, with the same movement. There's nobody that could do it today. How he managed it, I have no idea. You'll never see any player from now until snooker finishes quite like Hurricane Higgins. Ronnie is far more talented than Alex was, but in a different way. He's got more control. But Higgins was getting these shots and getting control, and he was jumping and moving and the arm was twitching. How did he do it? A lot of players might try to play shots the way he did it, but they can't even pot the balls, let alone try to do what he has done. He was unique, absolutely unique.'

Higgins had pulled off the spectacular with his sinking of the blue, but he also bundled excessive power into the shot. Indeed, that blue would have been lost in the sands of time had Higgins missed the next ball and White reached the final.

While there was much to enjoy about the blue, Higgins had sent the cue ball past the reds to a resting point next to the black and he faced having to shoot towards the baulk end.

There was a red to the middle, but Higgins favoured a long-range alternative into the green pocket. He ripped that into the bag and this time secured perfect position on the black.

After reaching 19 points in bedazzling style, Higgins suddenly found himself on easy street. That can still be an unnerving place in Sheffield, any false move leaving a player vulnerable to being pickpocketed, but with the cue ball finally under control he sank the remaining two reds with not the slightest fuss.

'I'm feeling nervous for him, Jack,' said John Spencer, co-commentating with Karnehm. 'I think if he clears this, this would be the break of the tournament.'

The colours followed as Higgins briefly dialled down the drama, showing out-of-character clearheadedness.

Karnehm's declaration of 'Oh, marvellous!' as Higgins sank the black was a fittingly instinctive moment of commentary, the man behind the microphone rising to the occasion too.

A deciding frame beckoned. Higgins returned to his seat and lit up a cigarette, when a cigar might have been more fitting.

> STEVE DAVIS: 'That 69 break was the most surreal moment snooker's ever had because still to this day it must be up there with the top five clearances, if not the first.'

While Davis rates it in the context of table clearances, what about those who see it as the ultimate break, full stop?

> JUDD TRUMP: 'It's hard to tell if it's the greatest break. It's up to the individual. You can get perfect position and that can be your idea of a perfect break, or you can have these exhibition shots and that's what I'm attracted to. With Alex's blue, I love that kind of shot and not everyone can play that kind of shot. The crowd really enjoy it when you can, and it's important to always have a couple of players in snooker always being able to carry that sort of style on. Every shot in the whole break was a good shot. Alex and Jimmy are the players I base myself on when I get to the end of frames, just giving the crowd something to go home and practise themselves. It's always important to show that other side of the game.'

MARK ALLEN: 'I've watched it so many times, too many times. The thing about it is that it was the worst break you'll ever see because he got into position a few times and then the next shot he was back out of position, having to play a recovery shot. It was phenomenal.'

PATSY FAGAN: 'A lot of people call it the greatest break ever and all that. It's not really. It's nothing like it. But it's classic to watch because of the outrageousness; that's where the appeal is. It's an unbelievable break; that someone could be so far out of position so many times in the one break and clear up, and under that pressure as well. Miss and you're out, you're gone. It was sheer brilliance and one of the classic breaks to watch, but not a great, great break really. There was no real control of the white, but some of the shots were out of this world. He must have played three or four shots that were off the scale. They were more exhibition shots than the sort you'd play in a semi-final at the end of a World Championship. I'd tell players I'm coaching to avoid these shots if you possibly can unless you're 70 in front with three reds on the table.'

MARK WATTERSON: 'I was sat on the right-hand side in the press seats. I had Terry Griffiths sitting behind me. I remember I didn't want the match to finish, it was so good. I was thinking, "I don't want to go home yet." So when Jimmy went 59-0 up in that 30th frame I thought, "Oh no, I've got to go home now, it's finished." It had been such a great day, and then of course Higgins did what he did and it was fantastic.'

JASON FERGUSON: 'The clearance, and especially that blue, was just ridiculous, and he overcooked it as well, and it wasn't the only shot in that break he overcooked. But isn't this what makes great sporting moments from great sporting champions? It's those magical moments that are not textbook that make sport so special. My job nowadays is to create the platform for such special moments, and when they come along you cherish them. That moment from Alex will live forever. And it came at the moment when he was out! There was no way he was coming back from that, and he did. Incredible, really. It did wonders for snooker.'

The BBC's David Vine was not one for hysteria, but Vine was swept up in this commotion, acclaiming what millions had just witnessed as 'one of the most exciting frames of snooker ever'.

Little Lauren's prospects of being the daughter of a two-time world champion were improving as each ball was sunk.

In theory, Higgins and White were not finished yet. It was 15-all.

But the decider was a one-way street, Higgins making a 59 break to seize control before making sure of frame and match when it became clear White's tank was empty, his spirit sapped.

JASON FERGUSON: 'This is the moment you would always go back to. Winning and the trophy and the tears from Alex were one thing, but going back to that semi-final and you wonder, "Was that the one that Jimmy should have won?" People will always ask that. But it was magical.'

DAVID TAYLOR: 'Alex got the greatest clearance probably of all time that day, to help him reach the final. But Jimmy was brilliant and such a nice man. He's a darling, isn't he. He maybe can't remember those days, but he's a fabulous man.'

Karnehm delivered a pleasingly pithy sign-off, declaring that while White looked "rather sad", the fact he was just 20 years old meant the Tooting man would have many more chances in subsequent years.

It would doubtless have astonished Karnehm to learn that White remained pot-less at the World Championship some four decades later, and was still trying to put that right, year after year.

The theory is that the rushed red goes down as one of sport's great lost opportunities. Yet White told the Guardian in 2019 that to have won the 1982 world crown would have been the worst thing that could have happened to him. With cocaine entering his life, White feared drugs and alcohol may have killed him, as the new-found status could have magnified those problems.

Of course, beating Higgins would have been no guarantee of title glory itself, given Reardon was waiting in the final.

Two all-time greats saw White-Reardon as a tight match-up.

STEVE DAVIS: 'Obviously there is the possibility that if Jimmy beat Alex in that semi-final, that Ray Reardon would have won a seventh World Championship. Ray knew how to play, so that would have been an interesting game, for a young Jimmy White to play somebody who was still playing decent stuff then.'

CLIFF THORBURN: 'Jimmy and Ray... well, Ray might have beaten him. I understand why many people thought Jimmy would win though.'

White was on his way home this time, and Higgins was one step from glory. Only the gnarly Reardon could deny him now.

JASON FERGUSON: 'Higgins-White was massive for snooker. And then the final... in the history of our sport it was to be an unbelievable moment.'

27: 'Bloody hell, champion of the world!'

'Tremendous, top of the world. It's very nice at the moment. I think we'll celebrate a bit tonight.'

Terry Griffiths scooped the Crucible crown in 1979 and, despite being weary from the effort it took to fend off Dennis Taylor, there was a glint in the Welshman's eyes as he considered the prospect of the night that lay ahead.

Blowout celebrations are an ageless tradition at the World Championship. A post-final knees-up is a fitting way to end the marathon slog in Sheffield, for players, staff and media alike.

For any new sultan of snooker, the invitation-only gathering that runs deep into the night is a rite of passage, the last step on that long journey from rank and file to the very centre of the cueing cosmos. It is the night when the victor is roared into the room by those in the sport's inner circle, past champions on hand to welcome them to the pantheon.

Alex Higgins already had a World Championship to his name when his 1982 Crucible triumph arrived, thanks to that victory 10 years earlier in Birmingham.

However, the intervening decade had seen the fixtures and fittings of professional snooker dramatically upgraded, with the

World Championship's move to the Crucible as fundamental as the burgeoning interest from television executives.

Giving its showpiece a permanent stage, rather than operating as a travelling roadshow, demonstrated ambition and long-term vision.

From a handful of professionals when Higgins scored his 1972 success, a tour of players with fat wallets had emerged.

This was a strikingly different World Championship from the tournament he had won previously, barely recognisable, and by 1982 Higgins was itching to be crowned on this particular stage, particularly since his loss to Cliff Thorburn in the final two years previously, when he felt crowd-pleasing instincts were his downfall.

Success in Sheffield had become the Holy Grail for cue masters, and Higgins longed for the dopamine rush so many of his greatest rivals had already experienced.

* *

It is Monday, May 6, 2019, 7.35pm in Sheffield, and the BBC's Hazel Irvine has swapped the studio for the floor of the Crucible, where she is interviewing first-time world champion Judd Trump.

'Incredible. I can't put it into words,' says a beaming Trump. 'I've worked so hard for this and just for the people around me it's so special.'

He mentions the influence of brother Jack and dad Steve. Steve Trump balanced long-distance lorry driving with transporting the young Judd from one junior tournament to another, while Jack has been pushing Trump to new levels of dedication on the practice table.

At 7.41pm, Trump will get his hands on the trophy as ticker tape pours down from the rafters of the theatre, and he will spend the next five minutes posing for photographs next to the table: on his own, with family, and with his manager, Django Fung.

Come 7.59pm, the new champion is answering questions from reporters in the media room at his post-final press conference, with all concerned just about on their last legs.

And at 3.57am the next morning, Judd, Jack and Steve Trump and a gang of their friends are in a huddle on the dance floor at the after-final party, swaying and braying along euphorically as Queen's We Are The Champions brings the disco to a close.

In the eight hours between BBC Radio 5 Live's Jamie Broughton asking him the opening questions in the press conference, and the bash reaching its charmingly wholesome sing-song finale, Trump will let the giddy thrill of his achievements sink in and hope the memories stay with him.

Ronnie O'Sullivan, minutes after capturing his first World Championship in 2001, said he had 'never had an experience like it in my life'. It amounted to 'a dream come true and a big weight off my shoulders', O'Sullivan enthused.

Steve Davis was a first-time winner in 1981 and would be champion a further five times before the decade was out. He remembers that first Crucible championship rush being one of transient bliss, followed by a slow realisation.

'The adrenaline, the thrill of the match, has gone, and it's replaced by the euphoria of winning,' said Davis. 'And then there's the certain amount of stuff that you know's going to happen as a result of that. Which is things like press interviews, so it's all exciting, but the more interesting thing for me is a couple of days later when you wake up in the morning and you're on your own.

'I remember every now and again, thinking, "Bloody hell, champion of the world!"

'It was pinching yourself that maybe I'm the best player on the planet, the best player who's ever picked a cue up. That was the wow moment for me. For a while I totally got off on that, until somewhere down the line you realise there's tournaments coming up on the horizon.'

Those great moments that live forever on film still flash by in the moment.

Yet what happens in Sheffield does not stay in Sheffield. It travels with a champion, changes lives. That very instant when a player realises there is no way back for his opponent is the feeling that survives longest.

'It's just so much relief and excitement at the same time,' says Neil Robertson, a first-time winner in 2010 when he beat former champion Graeme Dott in a 12.54am finish. 'The relief puts you in a position where you just want to relax, but the excitement makes you want to jump out of your chair.

'It's an overwhelming satisfaction where you know that whatever else happens, being a champion at the Crucible is something no one can ever take away from you. It's like "mission complete" and you've done it and everything else you might achieve here is a bonus. You're just thinking, "I've done it!"'

Stuart Bingham, who defeated Dott, O'Sullivan, Trump and Shaun Murphy in his magnificent 2015 trophy run, experienced electrifying emotions as he crossed the winning line, like nothing the Basildon man had known before.

'It's an unbelievable feeling. I remember the shot I played, bridging over the blue with the extension on my cue and potting that red, and the crowd was deafening,' Bingham says.

'Everything goes through your mind. I was trying to concentrate on the next ball, but at the end of the break, when I shook Shaun's hand, that was when I was able to take all of it in. I remember coming here to the Crucible in 1993 and 1994, coming to watch Brian Morgan play and getting an autograph, being a snooker fan. I wore a Brian Morgan T-shirt as I sat in the crowd, just thinking how much I wanted to make it here as a player one day.

'Twenty years later to get my hands on the trophy, these events are every kid's dream. It's like winning the Masters or the Open in golf, winning the FA Cup or the World Cup, it's that same feeling.

'I was lucky to have family and friends there. My mum and dad had done a lot for me, my second coach Joe Lazarus was there, so little things like that, having all my friends there that night. I remember walking up the stairs, giving it the old Pat Cash moment, to see my manager who I'd been with since a year before I turned pro. It was just a priceless moment.

'My boy [Shae] was there and he was only four, and now I've got a daughter, and it makes it special when your family is there.

'I think this is the only tournament with the kudos. It's special. You've seen so many special world champions, great memories and it comes about because of this place, the Crucible, and Sheffield.'

Mark Selby enjoyed a purple patch in Sheffield, winning four titles in eight seasons from 2014 to 2021. On the night he won the second of those, May 2, 2016, his beloved Leicester City were also confirmed as Premier League champions for the first time. Only one of those feats had been a 5,000-1 shot at the start of the season.

This provided cause for a double celebration, with Selby in great spirits that night, all his Christmases having come at once. Yet the first title two years earlier remains the most significant.

'It's more relief than anything,' Selby says.

'It's mentally and physically draining, the 17 days that you spend here. Fatigue-wise, it takes a lot out of you. But at that moment it's relief and elation. As a child, playing snooker is all you've wanted to do, and what you want to become is a world champion.

'Until you actually get that trophy, you think that it might happen to you one day, but there's no guarantees, and it's a moment of elation. It just means that if you never do it again, nobody can take that moment away from you.

'For me, it was a monkey off my back because I'd won the Masters a couple of times, I'd won the UK, and everyone was always saying I was good enough to win the World Championship, but until you do it, it's all talk.

'Of course, you think of family and friends in that moment too. They're the people who've followed you around, and supported you, and when you've been down after big losses they're the people who've picked you up, so you owe them a massive thank-you.'

Vikki, Selby's wife, was proudly at his side after a staggering dismantling of O'Sullivan brought that first title in Sheffield.

'It's you out there doing the work, but there's a team behind you which includes family and friends which help you through it,' Selby says.

Murphy reflects on his own 2005 shock success and cringes when he recalls how he handled the moment after fending off Matthew Stevens. Just 22 at the time, Murphy was tentatively finding his way in the paid ranks when from almost out of nowhere he scooped the game's biggest prize, the first qualifier since Griffiths to go all the way.

He laughs now at how his younger self was so 'unconsciously incompetent' – a lovely Murphyism – when it came to soaking up the greatest feat of his snooker life.

'I remember that was my first professional win, so there were so many things going through my head, not least the fact that – bloody hell – it was the World Championship,' says Murphy.

'Obviously, I didn't know how to be when you won. I didn't know whether you should be jubilant, jumping around the room, or whether you should be courteous to your opponent, and I remember trying to be a bit of both.

'I've watched it back of course, once or twice, and I think, "Jesus, man, smile!" The penultimate red won me frame and match, and then I potted a blue and then a red down the cushion, and then I'm home and hosed. But you wouldn't know I'd won the World Championship. I was just like a rabbit in the headlights, and that's the overriding memory: that I had no concept of what I'd achieved. I was a 22-year-old boy who thought he knew everything, but I actually knew absolutely nothing. I was what we call unconsciously incompetent.

'I look back and think, "You had a long way to go there, son." But sometimes ignorance is bliss and I think sometimes that wouldn't it be great to go out there and play with that level of freedom again. I wasn't expected to be in that room, let alone in the final. As I got nearer the line, I remember when it reached 17-16 and I thought to myself, "I need to win this here and now, because I can't go 17-all, I won't be able to stand up for a deciding frame."

'This is going to sound silly, but it almost happened too soon for me. If I could go back in a time machine and choose my chronology, I would love to have won a few other ranking events first, and then, when I was ready, built up to the Worlds. Twenty-two years of age, ranked 48th in the world, that isn't when you win the World Championship, and because I was so clueless I didn't really get to enjoy what being world champion meant. It's changed my life, but I didn't really grasp that at the time.

249

'I can only look at it from the perspective of what it might feel if I won it again, as an established player and a proven winner. If I somehow reached the last day and lifted the trophy, that would be pretty special and the outpouring of emotion would be significant. Now I'd just have a bit more fun and be so much more informal about it. I'd be crying, having a laugh, and I'd just let my hair down.'

Joe Johnson's 1986 triumph was easily as much of a shock as Murphy's triumph, given he was facing Davis in the final.

'I honestly didn't think I could win until I potted the final yellow,' Johnson said. 'I went from being a nobody to a face everyone recognised. It was very weird, and I had to come to terms with it.'

For leading performers of the modern era, it is hard to comprehend how Higgins, whose accrual of vices suggested he was bent on self-annihilation, could piece together a title-winning run in Sheffield.

Although Higgins cut back on the binges during his title run, he had already put his body through so much during the season.

Clean-living Robertson says: 'In today's day and age you couldn't possibly get away with it. The standards are so high and everyone is so professional.

'The culture of snooker was different back then, when in an interval a player might have had a beer to relax, but now it just doesn't happen. The calibre of player is different, where I think back then you used to be able to play yourself into a tournament a little easier than how it is now.'

Bingham hints at a little envy as he considers the days when debauchery was rife.

'It would definitely have been fun to be part of it. It's a bit more professional in these days,' Bingham says. 'It was maybe a bit more relaxed then, with players having a drink and a smoke, but it's so professional these days that you have to be match fit.'

Rob Walker, the human dynamo who has become as familiar and popular a presence as many of the players, gives those stars great credit for pacing themselves during the Crucible marathon.

'The fact that the standard is so high now means they can't afford to go out between the first and second round and drink 12 pints and wake up the next day and still have a decent chance in the match,' Walker says.

'They're professionals and we've moved on from that era. Everyone likes to think of their hero as being the everyman in the pub who they can slap on the back and have a pint with, and these guys will do that, but there's a time and a place, and it's not in the middle of a World Championship.'

For Selby, money has focused minds in snooker. He is a case in point, with his poker-faced approach bringing regular six-figure rewards and putting the frighteners up opponents.

'It's a lot more serious now with the money at stake – there's a lot more – and the competitive side is probably harder than it's ever been,' Selby says. 'We've got lots of characters, but when they're out there on the table they probably don't show it as much as in the eighties. Back then, even though the standard was good, there were probably only five or six players you'd put your finger on as being contenders. Now you've got people outside the top 32 getting to finals and challenging for tournaments.'

Selby knows if he slackens off on the practice table, or becomes lax in his lifestyle choices, there will be someone better prepared to come along and dominate. The same goes for the likes of Trump and Robertson, who have profited from unrelenting dedication.

How did Higgins deliver such a famous success, then?

Robertson is at a loss. Higgins may have embraced moderation for the 17 days of his glory run, but moderation was still some way short of abstinence.

'You know that Alex was probably not going to go back to his room and think, "Right, I'm just going to chill out for a few hours,"' says Australian Robertson.

'It's incredible Alex was able to do what he did. If Alex was more in the Steve Davis mould, would he have gone on to win more tournaments? Maybe he would, but would he have been as popular with the general public and with all the fans all around the world? Maybe not. He probably would have regretted a few things and maybe could have done some things differently, but overall he lived an amazing life at the peak of snooker in the eighties.

'They were just like rock stars.'

28: Bring your daughter to the theatre

Nicko McBrain knows a great venue when he sees one.

As a globe-trotting rock musician, he's played most of them, so it's worth paying attention when McBrain portrays the Crucible as snooker's answer to Carnegie Hall, the legendary New York joint where The Beatles, Billie Holiday, Nina Simone and Duke Ellington have taken to the stage.

'It has that comparison to me in terms of the mystique and the mysticism of it,' says McBrain.

'Oh my sweet Lord, it really is powerful.'

There's the well-worn lost-tourist gag about the Seventh Avenue site.

Q. How do you get to Carnegie Hall?
A. Practise.

You could say the same for the Crucible.

London-born drummer McBrain, who joined Iron Maiden in 1982 and became a mainstay of the heavy metal behemoths, finds watching and playing snooker a soothing contrast to touring life.

He is drawn, instinctively, to the showmen, the mavericks, the great characters, which is why he has enjoyed dinner with Ronnie O'Sullivan and struck up a friendship with Ken Doherty.

McBrain's home for many years has been a plush villa in Boca Raton, Florida. This is where Mabel the Table also resides, a cherished 12ft x 6ft Star tournament table.

Alongside 'Mabel', and amid gold discs, drum paraphernalia and generally 'a lot of music stuff', there is a photograph of Alex Higgins celebrating in Sheffield.

'I've got sponsor boards from the Crucible, and a picture of Fred Davis – he was the ultimate champion of course – and a picture of Alex Higgins from '82 and a little shrine to some champions,' McBrain says.

The snooker room is McBrain's firm nod to his upbringing. He plays often, and invariably quite badly, by his own reckoning. When we last spoke, his highest break was 39. That's not bad.

'The thing is, the appeal is not only the game,' says McBrain.

He pauses, then adds: 'I first went to a snooker hall when I was seven or eight years old. My dad took me to the snooker hall in Turnpike Lane, Wood Green, in north London, right next door to the Wellington pub. I was hooked and now I practise twice a week. It's a stunning game, I love it.'

McBrain got his big break in life when getting the call from Maiden. When McBrain convinced the band's tour manager to create a window in the band's 2017 globetrotting tour, allowing him to pay Sheffield a visit for the World Championship final, it was a pilgrimage that took him back to the days of watching Higgins on the small screen. McBrain had visited the Crucible in 2014 and 2015, too. The place draws you back.

'I felt that sense of awe when the lights went down and the players came down the steps and past the press area where we were,' he says. 'Even a whisper sounds like you're shouting.'

From sitting next to McBrain in those press seats, I can confirm his whispering did indeed at times sound like shouting. He was a kid in a sweet shop, bowled over by the experience, charmingly so. Banging the drum for this latest thrill in his life.

For McBrain, snooker in his youth was a father and son experience.

For Higgins it became part of an immortal father and daughter bond. And on the weekend of May 15-16, 1982, it was a case of bring your daughter to the theatre. The final had arrived.

* *

Higgins had begun the 1982 championships as a 25-1 title shot, an outsider that few sober observers thought stood any hope. He went into the final against Ray Reardon as a 2-5 hot favourite. From being a distant outsider, he had become the player everyone wanted to back, however short the odds.

Higgins' mother, Elizabeth, told the Belfast Telegraph from her Abingdon Street home she would not be watching her 'Sandy' in action. 'When he comes on, I just get well away from the television,' she said.

It was not specifically Elizabeth that Higgins was playing for this time, however, but the other significant women in his life: Lynn and, particularly, Lauren.

'I would love to do it for my little girl,' Higgins told the BBC. 'I don't think I've changed much over the years; I get into all sorts of controversial scrapes and what have you, but deep down I do like to please people.

'I do appreciate other people playing good snooker against me, and I love to actually see the furtherance of snooker, no matter what anyone says, and it'd be nice to be the People's Champion again.'

Higgins would take a lap of honour weeks after his Crucible

campaign, with Jimmy White joining him on a famously rambunctious tour of Northern Ireland. The way Higgins told it in his autobiography, My Story, the trip involved both men going from town to town in a primitive motorhome, with the tour promoter doing a bunk with a bundle of appearance cash four days in, prompting the players' driver to hold both men's cues and the World Championship trophy as ransom until he was paid, action which is said to have drawn interest from police and a passing army patrol. Higgins, so the story goes, coughed up £250 to get the driver back behind the wheel and the show on the road. That telling of the adventure has the ring of slapstick about it, but perhaps it was absolutely accurate. Somewhere along the line, White and Higgins ran into Def Leppard and Thin Lizzy on that trip, too. A quiet one, then. Snooker players were becoming well paid, but there was still a whiff of artless amateurism that only bolstered the sport's everyman appeal.

You could hardly imagine Reardon becoming entangled in such brouhaha, and it was the striking difference in character between the 1982 finalists that meant the spectator in the theatre and the viewer at home would naturally find one more of a kindred spirit than the other, and side with him.

The 19-year-old Phil Yates, a future correspondent for the Times, was firmly behind Higgins.

'When I was at university, I was quite progressive and liberal, left wing, in my politics – and I still am to this day. Back then, if you were at Bradford University in 1982, you stuck out like a sore thumb if you weren't, and Higgins was the ultimate anti-establishment character, wasn't he,' says Yates.

'They say never meet your heroes, and when I started working on snooker in 1988 I soon realised that he wasn't a very nice person, and he was very hard to get on with, destructive, and he could be very cruel, that sort of stuff, but of course back in 1982 I didn't realise any of this and he was my big hero. People associate Ray Reardon with being a miner, but he was also a policeman, so he was the establishment. It was the perfect kind of moment.'

Such clashes of character still exist in the game, some players don't get along, but you would struggle to conjure any contrast of personality to come close to Higgins versus Reardon.

Higgins said he was suffused with a case of 'the 10-year itch' on the eve of the final. Reardon, meanwhile, might have been quietly relieved it was not London fireball White awaiting him.

Like every World Championship final, there was a lot resting on the outcome. The Higgins life story would have been incomplete without his victory and the famous scenes afterwards, while the impact of a seventh Reardon win might have been felt for years to come.

'If Ray had been a seven-times champion, only two of those would have been at the Crucible but maybe that's the record that Stephen Hendry would have been chasing,' says Michael McMullan.

'Stephen, when he reached seven, was overtaking Steve Davis' Crucible record of six, but also there was the fact that the modern era record was six, shared by Davis and Reardon, even though most of Reardon's had been won in the pre-Crucible era.

'But had Reardon got to seven, then Hendry – and now Ronnie – would probably have been more motivated to keep on going and get to eight. If Ray had won in 1982, snooker history might have been very different.'

Reardon considered Higgins to have an 'evil' streak.

The Northern Irishman certainly had a light-fingered approach to other people's property, as Thorburn remembers.

'Higgins was innovative, a good safety player too, and I used to watch him go into billiards clubs and take the best tips off the cues. He'd go in on the sneak,' says Thorburn.

It is the small details that make up the big picture. Higgins the cue tip bandit: something only those who cast a careful eye on the Hurricane's antics would ever know. Just another of those many Higgins eccentricities, which in today's world might be seen more as failings.

'I know a lot of people who dealt with him and he could be very difficult,' says David Hendon. 'If he was around now, there's more awareness of mental health issues and I think maybe he could get help for some of his issues, but he didn't seem to want help really. Everything was on his own terms.

'He was not looking for respectability or acceptance and his attitude was, "I'll do what I want to do."

'That was what he was, and a lot of people really warmed to that, because in their own lives maybe perhaps they couldn't do that. I remember when I was growing up that if he was playing I'd always try to watch, because he was an exciting player, but also there was the sense that something might kick off.

'That makes it exciting. With Steve Davis, you're not going to get that. You're just going to get a display of excellence, which in itself is great, but with Alex you would get the sense of danger and the unexpected. I think we're lucky that he came along, definitely. People remember '82 clearly, and a lot of things have happened since then that we've forgotten.'

There is the irony of Higgins being abstemious, just about, during the 1982 World Championship, and the strait-laced Davis being soused in Sheffield day after day, drinking to numb the pain of his first-round humiliation, not ready to go home.

'I assume that during that event he was pretty much on the wagon,' says Davis. 'It was a good effort.'

On the table, Higgins twirled around an early 5-2 deficit to lead 10-7 after the first day of the final, with Reardon losing each of the closing four frames in the evening.

'I thought Reardon would have tied him up more, but you tend to forget that Higgins' tactical game was superb,' says Jim Donnelly. 'His tactical brain was as natural as his ability.'

One day after the 1982 final, Davis was named winner of the Pye Television Personality of the Year award. He had barely been off the small screen, whether in the day job or as an in-demand guest.

Davis would allow himself to be lampooned on the Morecambe & Wise Christmas show, a plaything in a Cannon and Ball snooker skit, and he joined Adam Ant and Kevin Keegan as a guest on Saturday morning kids' show Multi-Coloured Swap Shop.

He was a bystander on the biggest day of the snooker year, though: day two of the World Championship final.

Sunday Grandstand, presented by Des Lynam, began at 1.55pm on BBC Two, after Open University programmes took care of the morning and early afternoon schedule. Snooker was the chief offering, after a touch of golf action from the Martini International at nearby Worksop, barely 20 miles down the road from the Crucible.

The snooker coverage was the climax to the BBC's commitment to what had become a flagship tournament, with 103 hours of action on the schedules, a gargantuan commitment by the standards of the era.

'Alex and I were both a product of the fact the BBC decided if they showed the World Championship in its entirety, that actually it would work,' says Davis.

'Whoever bit the bullet and decided it was not a risk made an amazing choice. Then overnight the players got so much recognition, exponentially it exploded once they started showing it like that, so by 1982 we'd had three years of blanket coverage and everyone at home was becoming addicted to watching it.'

It was clear there would be high anticipation for the second day of the final. Sundays in the UK were different beasts in the 1980s from what they would become, with shops largely closed and pub opening hours restricted in most parts.

Church. Lunch. Snooker. In that order. For many, this was the model for an ideal Sunday.

Following a rare fumbled handover from Lynam, Clive Everton in the commentary booth teed up day two with a touch of class, rolling out his immortal epithet on the biggest day of the snooker year.

'Thank you, Desmond,' said Everton, introducing the pictures being watched by millions at home. 'The protagonists in the arena for the last lap of this 17-day marathon of the mind.'

29: HIGGINS LIFTS WEIGHT AT JIM SESSION

THE MAN ALEX Higgins beat in round one of the 1982 World Championship was the same man whose words had breathed life into the flatlining confidence of the Hurricane just weeks earlier.

Higgins was never in trouble against Jim Meadowcroft, winning through 10-5 against the 35-year-old Lancastrian, an assured first step. Higgins and Meadowcroft had been close acquaintances since 1969, when they and Dennis Taylor forged a north-west clan, initially based at the Benarth club in Blackburn, then at the Elite in Accrington.

In Meadowcroft's 1986 book, titled Higgins, Taylor and Me, he recalled being summoned by Lynn Higgins to gee up her 'terribly depressed' husband just weeks before the trip over the Pennines to Sheffield, with the Hurricane having been downgraded to a light breeze by a series of stinging defeats at the hands of Steve Davis.

'We sat and talked for ages. Alex was desperate for a boost, anything to lift his sagging confidence,' Meadowcroft wrote. 'He needed someone in whom he could confide and it had to be someone he trusted. I told him: "Alex you're a brilliant player and you're just going through a bad patch. It happens to all top players at one time in their careers. But you've got to drag yourself up from the floor and shake it off because it's your future, your life, your family's future."'

It has been revealed Higgins spent time in a Rochdale 'nursing home' during this 1981-82 season, to dry out, deal with negative thoughts and prepare himself for what was on the horizon. His former manager Harvey Lisberg recounted the story in his 2023 book I'm Into Something Good, with Higgins said to have accorded to this attempt to clean up his act.

Having Lisberg in the driver's seat – the guidance of a man who also managed hugely successful rock bands and their irregular, ego-driven foibles – was to be a brief blessing for Higgins. The alliance between Higgins and this famed chaperone of showmen was supremely short-lived but no doubt helpful, yet perhaps not as vital as the timely heart-to-heart with Meadowcroft.

The one occasion when I spoke to Meadowcroft came in early 2015, the year he died. He had been a modest player but recalled with great fondness his later career in the commentary box.

We might reasonably rank his 1982 buddy-buddy session with Higgins as Meadowcroft's most impactful impact on snooker.

Without that timely call from Lynn, without the words of persuasion from Meadowcroft, Higgins was heading for the Crucible dumper.

* *

As day two of the World Championship final arrived, there was work to do against Reardon, but Higgins was buoyant.

He had his great friend, Newmarket-based jockey Peter Madden, by his side throughout the semi-final against White and for much of the final too, sitting in the nearest available seat. On the first day of the joust against Reardon, Madden dashed off to ride at Beverley, winning the 4.45 on Lady Justice, before hotfooting it back to Sheffield.

It was reported that Higgins had slapped £250 each way on Madden coming good in the saddle at 7-1 odds, learning about the result at the end of the Saturday afternoon session. With a pep in his step, Higgins left Reardon stewing in his chair for much of the evening.

When Reardon snipped the deficit from 10-7 to 10-9 early on Sunday afternoon, commentator Clive Everton told viewers: 'We're seeing definite signs of tension from Higgins now.'

This Reardon rearguard effort came as no surprise to Patsy Fagan.

'It was amazing, Ray's run that year. But Ray was always a great player and his all-round game, his safety plan, meant he was never going to be easy for anybody to beat,' Fagan said. 'Ray wouldn't have won it six times if he hadn't got a great game.'

Higgins nudged away again to 12-10, and early in the next frame referee John Smyth had to tell the audience to 'keep those sweet bags quiet please', with every crackling noise, every yawn, wheeze or sneeze from spectators liable to irritate the players or even distract the referee.

Reardon closed the gap to one again, and it was Smyth whose mind wandered at the beginning of the next frame. As Reardon cued up to break, Smyth said: 'Thank you ladies and gentlemen, the 24th frame, Ray Reardon to break. Alex Higgins leads by 12 frames to seven... to 11.'

Reardon wasn't going away; old Dracula had sunk his teeth into this match. Perhaps the words of Meadowcroft were whirring around Higgins' mind at this point, particularly his 'your family's future' message.

Now was the time to fight, to talk the brain away from self-sabotage and the instinct to freestyle. Players many years later, led by Ronnie O'Sullivan, would consult with psychiatrists and psychologists to cultivate resilience to mental fragility, but here Higgins had no mind guru, just a little help from his friends.

Understated in a grey silk shirt for the afternoon action, Higgins had a safety game to rival the great tacticians whenever he deployed it, but it was hardly his hallmark. However, he had won deciding frames against Doug Mountjoy and Jimmy White on this particular journey and fended off the dangerous Willie Thorne in another tight match sandwiched between those nerve-janglers.

Never one to undersell the scale of his fan club, Higgins said after his 13-12 win against Mountjoy: 'The gods answered my prayers. I was preparing myself to lose.'

His feats might be romanticised as swashbuckling, but Higgins had needed to summon plenty of pluck to come so far, and there was no turning back now.

'I always think everyone knows about the magic. He was a maverick and could be half-mad, we know that,' says Nick Metcalfe. 'But I think he had some real battling, grafting abilities on the table, matchplay abilities, that are somewhat undersold.

'I remember that 1983 UK final with Steve. You can't be 7-0 down to Steve and come back to win 16-15 and not be a scrapper to some extent. And I reminded myself of that Crucible run, because obviously I know all about Jimmy in the semi. But I'd forgotten he beat Doug Mountjoy 13-12, Willie 13-10, and of course Jimmy 16-15 on the way to the final. That's just staggering, mind-blowing.'

Showboating from Higgins had knocked him off track in the 1980 final against Thorburn. Reardon's best hope, perhaps, was that the same would happen again.

Higgins found a cross-double red to secure a 13-11 lead after

Reardon bungled an attempt at a snooker behind the green, guaranteeing a lead to take into the evening.

It would be a slender 13-12 cushion, though, with Reardon taking the last frame of the afternoon.

Mike Ganley was watching on in Sheffield.

'For him to keep himself composed – I say composed but I don't think there could ever be a composed Alex Higgins – was amazing,' Ganley says. 'It was one of those occasions when you knew it would go down in history and you were glad to be there, because with Alex you never knew if he'd do it again.'

* *

There remains a strong Irish appetite for the World Championship, with Antrim's Mark Allen having been the player whose shoulders have carried much of the burden of expectation since Ken Doherty's gradual decline began in the mid-2000s.

Hang around long enough in a Sheffield hotel bar during World Championship time and you might catch a boozy choir of snooker visitors mauling Danny Boy or Fields of Athenry, Whiskey In The Jar or The Irish Rover.

Having champions in the shape of Higgins, Dennis Taylor and Doherty, plus challengers in Allen and Joe Swail, has meant there has always been a large Irish following on the ground in Sheffield.

Broadcaster and snooker writer Michael McMullan has been making the pilgrimage across the Irish Sea in a professional capacity for a quarter of a century.

While McMullan feels Higgins irrevocably tarnished his legacy later in life, he regards the Hurricane's victories in 1972 and 1982 as priceless moments, especially considering hostilities back in Northern Ireland. The 1972 final was contested just weeks after the events of Bloody Sunday, the deadly shooting of unarmed civilians by soldiers for which it took the UK government almost four decades to offer an apology.

No sporting success will ever resolve conflict on the streets or be any more than a sticking plaster for the deepest pain, but it might spark a flash of common focus.

'I wouldn't have said I was a Higgins fan. I recognised his unique style of play and his unique manner around the table, there was no denying that. And I understood his significance to the game and the role he played. The one thing was that he was from Northern Ireland, like me,' says McMullan.

'It obviously is a big thing in this country, both Northern Ireland and the Republic, that we get behind people, our own, in any sport.

'Particularly with Northern Ireland, it was an unspeakably bleak time, so for someone to provide a bit of cheer, you were on their side in that regard.

'As time went on, more and more he brought the game into disrepute, but nobody can deny he was great to watch and certainly at a very bleak time for Northern Ireland.

'That's the case with both of his world titles. In 1972, things were literally at the worst they ever were, pretty much in the very week he won the championship the first time around.'

Professional sport is one of life's great distractions: a frivolity to some, a fundament of our existence to many others. As much as Higgins had his own reasons for wanting to beat Reardon, there were many back home who desired the same outcome just as badly, for the sake of rare glad tidings.

30: MAKE IT A NIGHT TO REMEMBER

DES LYNAM served as one of television's great big-moment wordsmiths. A lightness of touch – quips in all the right places – meant Lynam connected with those who sensed triviality at play. This same gift meant staunch sporting disciples adored him too.

Lynam's famous 'Shouldn't you be at work?' line, when introducing a Monday afternoon England game during the 1998 World Cup, was masterful broadcasting, a marvellous tease.

That was nothing new to seasoned Lynam watchers, though. He'd been at it for years.

As Alex Higgins and Ray Reardon reached the end of the Sunday afternoon session, ahead of the climactic tranche of the 1982 World Championship, the baton was passed from Sheffield to Lynam in the Grandstand studio.

'Well, I guess I know what many of us will be doing this evening,' he said, grinning away below that thick moustache. 'We'll be following the fortunes of those two guys all over again.'

As a final session, it was the easiest of sells: the enigmatic Higgins versus the pragmatic Reardon, the man on a mission versus the man who'd seen it all before, rivals locked as tightly as they possibly could be after the opening 25 frames.

Then, as the big night in Sheffield went live to the nation at 7.15pm, David Vine set the scene for BBC Two viewers.

'For 17 days and 16 nights, this now famous sporting theatre has commanded and received the country's attention,' Vine began. 'And now, on this final night, we join the 968 ticket holders, waiting to watch the last stage of the best professional snooker championship of the world ever staged.'

Vine spoke of witnessing 'shocks and surprises, matches full of tension and frames of snooker that have had even those who claim to have seen it all before gasping with admiration'.

Bringing Higgins and Reardon to the audience's attention, he declared the finalists offered 'a contrast in play and in person that a scriptwriter would be proud to invent'.

Between them, Nick Hunter and Vine had decided how the night should ideally begin and end, and it was therefore a case of seeing what happened in the between hours, the unscriptable element of a live sport outside broadcast.

Vine doorstepped the players as they emerged from their dressing rooms, attempting to put both men at ease while at the same time hoping they might cough up a gem of a soundbite.

Higgins, in a green shirt this time with red cuffs and collar, told Vine his back pocket contained a host of lucky charms, so many they were weighing him down.

'Peter Madden rode one at nine and six the other day,' Higgins said. 'I think I'm carrying overweight in this particular race. But apart from that I think for the public it's been a good match so far, 13-12, and we always have a good tussle, us two.'

Higgins strode into the arena, lapped up the adulation, and gave Madden a brotherly hug, before a dapper Reardon followed him in, bowing to all corners, all smiles and off-mic repartee as the players posed with the trophy. Bonhomie briefly abounded.

Moments later, the grins fell from the faces of the contenders and the crowd buttoned up, spellbound by possibility. Higgins convincingly took the opening frame of the night, helped by a 48 break, before pinching the nervy next too to pull 15-12 clear.

Chain-smoking between visits to the table, swigging from his glass of Coke, Higgins was still on edge. Three frames away from the Arcadian scenes already painted in his mind, this was an inopportune time to be snookered by the jitters.

Reardon, who was dug out of danger at the Florence Colliery all those years earlier, had to do the shovelling and clambering by himself this time, but shovel and clamber he would.

Gallantly, back he came to 15-15, winning two frames before the interval and then the next having needed a snooker. In the BBC commentary box, John Spencer and Jack Karnehm made way for Ted Lowe and Rex Williams for the closing stages.

It was granite snooker, sporting hardball. A Crucible classic.

Reardon lit a cigarette, pulled a goofy face, and just when he looked to have all the upwards momentum, so the snooker gods turned on the Welshman. He began to miss and Higgins needed no second invitation, keeping Reardon off the scoreboard in the next frame to lead again, with Spencer in the BBC studio telling Vine: 'It's become a match of courage now.'

This was all occurring just a year after Higgins declared his mind seemed 'to be rejecting the game'. Here, he was blissfully back in business, a run of 73 in frame 32 taking him to glory's doorstep.

'Such talent,' Lowe growled. Higgins' time had come again. A mesmerising 135 led him across the winning line, Reardon having lit up a smoke as the flame went out on his trophy hopes.

Lowe's verdict – 'Fantastic!' – spoke for the millions watching at home.

Meanwhile, in West Yorkshire...

'There was a personal connection with my time at Bradford University and that Higgins final,' remembers Phil Yates. 'I watched it on a little black and white TV in a little attic room that I had, and the reception was terrible and I had to keep messing about with this flimsy aerial to get a picture, but luckily it held for the final few frames.

'I was a massive Higgins fan at the time and when he cleared up to win – that 135 for me is one of the greatest breaks of all time – I jumped in the air, whacked my head off this low beam in this attic. I really did whack it, and it didn't leave me sparko but my goodness it hurt, and as I came down I knocked the aerial and the picture went completely, so I never saw him get the trophy.'

Cecil Mason and Madden observed the trophy lift from close quarters and were the first to celebrate with Higgins.

Despite the recent spat with Higgins in Derby, David Taylor stood in admiration of his old mate's finest hour.

'Did I think Alex could win the title when the tournament began? No, not at all,' Taylor said. 'He'd played terrible that season and I didn't think he stood any chance at all. But now the pressure was off. The only pressure was from within himself, wanting to win for Lauren, and he suddenly realised, "I can win this championship."

'In the end, he played fabulously. I was delighted that he won. There was nothing false about him. When he won, it was so genuine.'

In the moment, it was impossible to accurately quantify what wider impact Higgins' Crucible consummation might have on the sport. Even today, we might ask what would snooker have been like without Higgins, or how would the sport have shaped up if Steve Davis had not come along.

'It's very hard to say. Alex and Steve Davis were different sides of the coin,' says David Hendon.

'The 1972 championship definitely brought people to the game and Higgins was an intoxicating figure and he brought along a working-class audience.

'Steve brought a certain middle-class audience, and they merged together and the sport went along from there. I think Higgins is a very significant figure. He was often on the front pages of newspapers and kept the sport in the public consciousness. A lot of people didn't like him.

'Nans always liked Steve Davis and didn't like Alex Higgins because he was badly behaved, but I guess kids liked him because he was badly behaved. You need the two. It's like having a villain in a soap opera; you need a Ken Barlow as well. Those two were the key figures of the era, in terms of making snooker popular, which Alex did, and respectable, which Steve Davis did.

'That brought in sponsors and it's why TV wanted a piece of it. I don't think Higgins decided one day to make snooker big. He's a figure that will be remembered forever because he was a very unique character.'

Mark Allen will never tire of watching TV re-runs of the Hurricane's greatest triumph, being particularly drawn to how Higgins held himself together.

'The '82 World Championship is one of those great moments, without a doubt,' says Allen.

'It just shows how remarkable he was. Alex was a troubled mind, to say the least, but it shows how talented he was on the table that even with those distractions away from the table he was still able to go on and win the World Championship.'

31: TIME FOR PAY DAY

AS SOON AS the final ball is potted in a World Championship final, bedlam is unleashed. The crowd noise lurches from cathedral silence to a football stadium roar and then into a celebratory rolling rumble, the champion is ecstatic but possibly also tearful, and while the runner-up fights to remain stoic, a bubbling wave of people spills on to the stage floor.

The wave feels unruly, before you observe this is organised bedlam, with TV camera operators shuffling into pre-planned positions, photographers being shepherded forward for the trophy shots, VIPs wriggling into their places amid the throng, and the winning player's entourage stepping closer to the scene of victory.

This incoming tide may have been carefully choreographed, yet it still manages to bear a striking resemblance to utter chaos.

It was usually David Vine's job to walk down the steps and into the arena with a microphone in hand, to announce 'pay day' for the runner-up and the champion.

This was not so in 1982, however, when Mike Watterson, along with two executives from Embassy, came forward to hand over the trophy and microphone to Higgins.

272

Stepping into an arena that has gone from calm to cacophony in barely a couple of minutes is quite an experience.

Hazel Irvine knows exactly how Watterson and co. would have felt as they crossed the floor, with camera lights flashing, shutters clicking, wires everywhere, and a rapscallion of a world champion waiting.

On television, people look to glide into their allocated places, but sometimes, despite the best-laid plans, it's not quite that straightforward.

'You come from the cool of backstage and you hit this heat that comes at you,' Irvine says. 'You walk down the stairs at the side and there's a melee in front of you. There's a scrum of people and your floor manager wrestles you through that. There's an incredible surge of adrenaline that you get.'

Then comes the interview moment with the players. For all the best planning, this delicate moment can be thrown off course by the raw reaction from the champion and runner-up.

'You have to be alive to every possibility and sometimes it goes well and sometimes it doesn't. You can't predict what's going to happen,' says Irvine. 'You're armed with what you feel is going to be appropriate, but clearly you're having to react to what the guys are saying, to try to be there to help them sometimes if it becomes too much, or help them to express themselves fully.

'You don't really know what you're going to get, so that's the terror of it, but also the great thrill of it too.

'The Crucible audience has been very, very respectful, because they want to hear what these guys say at the end of it all. It becomes much more difficult if it's a total melee, but if you feel people are paying attention and the guys are with you and you can ask them stuff and you're going to get good replies, it's brilliant.

'There are moments that stay with you. There've been a few dodgy ones as well, believe me, but in the main it's been a privilege. It gets the heart thumping because you're down on that stage, where they've basically poured their heart out and put their heart into every shot for two days of that final, and you walk on and it's quite visceral.

'You can feel that atmosphere, it's a physical hit that you get from that. And with a packed house, it gives you just a little taste of what they go through for 17 days.

'You get a hint in those final moments of just how powerful the Crucible theatre is, and what it's given us over the past years and days, and then you try to get out of it, you try to take the programme off air, and you go and lie in a darkened room for a few days.'

32: HERE FOR THE HAPPY ENDING?

BY THE TIME Alex Higgins was handed the microphone amid the Crucible hubbub, BBC Two had switched from shots of baby in white to The Woman In White.

Nick Hunter had secured just enough added time to show the Lauren moment, but there the flexibility ended.

There was a drama series finale to be broadcast and the snooker had massively over-run its slot. The final whistle had blown.

Higgins' post-victory waterworks, and his stirring family man performance, had got their airing though. The show of unity, delivering on the pledge to win for Lauren, meant everything to Alex in the moment, too.

With Lauren in the champion's arms, Lynn was left holding the trophy in those final seconds of television coverage.

'There it is, that's the picture,' said David Vine, with the clock ticking. 'And would you ever see an emotional scene like that.'

Moments later, turning to a momentarily bestilled crowd, Higgins reflected on the turbulent journey he had travelled and said: 'This kid from nowhere, I've actually done something, I was so surprised myself.

'I'd like to give my kindest regards and warmhearted feelings to Ray because he really made me fight.

'I'm just a very, very happy man. I probably will die happy, and thank youse all very, very much indeed, cheers.'

Once he left the arena, shuffling through to a press conference, Higgins kept running with the theory that blessed days lay ahead for him.

Ronnie Harper, writing in the next day's Belfast Telegraph, observed the physical change in Higgins between his 1972 victory and this success, pointing out how 'the lifestyle he leads has added a few wrinkles to his 33-year-old countenance'.

Harper remarked on how Higgins looked to have previously been 'washed up', but this time he 'studied his position carefully and with cold, clinical skill moved in for the kill'.

The next couple of days' newspapers had Higgins predicting the victory would bring 'financial security for life', promising 'to be very good in the future', and even suggesting he might cut his golf handicap from 18 to 12 due to the blessings of great wealth.

Two weeks of vitamin pills, milk and modest helpings of Sheffield's own Mackeson milk stout had seemingly served Higgins well. He asked the world to believe he could be a changed man, just wait and see. And so the world waited.

One man, more than most, wasn't buying it. As Clive Everton wrote in his Snooker Scene editorial the following month, the sensible conclusion was that 'no one should assume that this is a happy ending to the Higgins story'.

Everton agreed it was a win worth savouring but warned of 'pressures and problems which success tends to redouble rather than reduce'.

This was cool-headed prescience and hard-headed scepticism, Everton unwilling to be duped by a fortnight-long flipping of the narrative, after bearing close witness to a decade of Higgins rarely being good to his word.

Insurrection followed by resurrection, repeated often enough, could only lead one way: to career deceleration.

It would still have been easy to be carried along by the whimsy of it all, the idea of Higgins reinventing himself as a winner with a charmed life, writing himself a new story.

For reporters up against deadlines, the instinctive and only realistic option may have been to parrot the Higgins bombast and not seriously question the content or context.

But years of evidence showed Higgins was unreliable, his own worst enemy, and prone to going off the rails in the blink of an eye. This concept of dying happy was dying to be disproved.

As much as he labelled himself the People's Champion, Higgins was often not even sufficient of a champion for his nearest and dearest.

By the end of the following year, Higgins would become a father again, to Jordan, a son with Lynn. But that marriage would be hanging by a thread. He would have survived a reckless overdose of pills amid a row with Lynn in Majorca, checked himself into and out of rehab, and perhaps most surprisingly of all, after everything preceded it, he would round off 1983 by beating Steve Davis 16-15 in the final of the UK Championship, revenge for being skittled 16-5 in the Crucible semi-finals that year.

Goodness knows how that golf handicap was coming along.

Alex and Lynn were in an 'on' stage of their on-off relationship towards the end of that UK Championship, after a separation, and there was another big trophy presentation moment, albeit this time a happy couple picture, without Lauren or Jordan.

Just as Lynn gave Higgins more chances than he perhaps deserved, so snooker has been remarkably forgiving of his many sins. WPBSA chairman Jason Ferguson gets emotional when 1982 is mentioned, saying: 'That moment of him winning the title, there wasn't a dry eye in the house, both in the Crucible and any house around the country.

'It was magical, the moment of bringing Lauren down. So many people wanted to see Alex win. He had a huge following of people and it was fantastic really.'

Neil Robertson would hardly endorse the Higgins lifestyle; but how could the man from Melbourne, who knows what strength it takes to scale the sport's Everest, not be moved by the sight of another player reaching the summit via the craggiest of paths – especially a player that few foresaw getting far from base camp.

'The important thing, after beating Jimmy, was he went on to win the tournament and we had the amazing scenes with his daughter. It's still inspiring watching it now,' Robertson said.

Mark Allen headed to the Crucible in 2023 for a 17th tilt at winning a first World Championship title.

Allen has come through strained times in his own life, picking up a Masters and UK Championship title along with a recent bankruptcy and a divorce. Thankfully, the off-table tumult has not reached Higgins proportions, with Allen an amiable whizz of a player who in a bountiful 2022-23 season enjoyed the fruits of persisting throughout his darkest days, culminating in a semi-final run in Sheffield. At the time of writing, matching Higgins at the Worlds still eludes him.

Allen will persist, ever eager to follow in the footsteps of a man whose mention draws a mix of emotions.

'I had a couple of meetings with Alex which were not so good, maybe got him on a bad day, but I'll never speak badly of Alex because he's done wonders for the sport and he's been a real Northern Irish sporting hero. That's the way I want to remember him,' Allen said. 'He was before my time, but it was probably watching Alex that got my dad interested, and that led to my dad taking me to the club, so there's the knock-on effect. I only see him on videos, but you hear all the stories from some of the players back home, from the amateur ranks, of how Alex was, and it would have been great to have been around him then.

'I got a small taste of that when I won the Masters. The reception I got for that was beyond anything I'd had before and I imagine if I won the Worlds it would be on an entirely other level, so it's up to me to try and do it. We'd have open-top buses – I'd hire one myself.

'Northern Ireland's such a small country, and we punch well above our weight, not just in snooker but in lots of sports. To win two world titles 10 years apart is no mean feat, and there's the way he did it too, the charismatic way he achieved what he did.

'I know Davis was winning everything, but it was Alex and Jimmy who changed the way the game was seen. We wouldn't be here playing for the money we are today if it wasn't for those two.

'Winning in Sheffield just shows how remarkable Alex was.'

Later in life, stories abounded of Higgins rolling up to pubs and snooker clubs in Belfast and playing all-comers for pin money, a tenner here or there that would go straight on a horse.

Oh, how he loved the horses. Especially the slow ones.

* *

Higgins checked himself out of Belfast City Hospital in April 2010 and headed for the Crucible, having been invited to take part in a Snooker Legends show, a week before the World Championship.

Still wearing a hospital wristband, Higgins came face to face with Thorburn again, the long-time enemies going head to head some three decades on from the 1980 final.

While Thorburn presented a picture of health, Higgins looked far from well. He was three months from death, and while some of the old sparkle remained on the baize, Thorburn knew this was the end of the road for their rivalry.

'And of course I felt terrible for him,' Thorburn said, finishing off his coffee. 'I played him twice when he was dying and he still wanted to beat me, and that was him and that's very admirable.

'I wanted to give him a hug by that stage and not play him. I felt terrible for him, didn't want to be there, and it was so sad to see him the way he was.

'I felt terrible about Alex's death, terrible that no member of the press tried to get hold of me after he passed away. I wanted to say something nice.'

The punch, though, Cliff. This was a guy you once wanted to pummel after all the sniping. Who'd have expected a kind word?

'I felt terrible about doing that with him,' Thorburn said.

Yet the thought of Higgins at his insufferable worst crosses Thorburn's mind, and he remembers why he threw the punch. A man can take only so much bombardment without returning fire. 'It just seemed to go on and on, it was non-stop. It was relentless.'

Higgins and Thorburn had also gone head to head in Glenrothes in the autumn of 2009, and while these seniors events were clearly lining the pockets of both men, Thorburn's shock at seeing his old foe at his most pinched and pallid sticks with him. All these years later, he continues to be moved by the memory.

Others were affected, too, by the sight of Higgins on his way out.

'It was horrible really,' said David Hendon. 'They hated each other for years, but in the end Cliff put his arm around him as if to say, "After all these years, we're just a couple of old snooker players, let's forget everything else."'

There is no fairy tale ending to this story, we know that. But once upon a time, there was a boy from Belfast with a gift for potting balls, who climbed to the pinnacle of the sport he loved, and then conquered the summit again.

This boy became trouble: a drunk, a snake, a bully.

This boy became legendary: a magician, a charmer, a faithful friend.

You could know both sides to the character and still only want the best for him. You could know both and be utterly repulsed.

Was he a black heart then? Many credible voices would counter the notion, but of those who entered his orbit, it's clear only a handful got genuinely close to Higgins. That's what comes from it being prudent to keep a safe distance from danger. That's also what comes from him pushing many away before they could eyeball his volatile yet fragile self at close quarters.

Some suggest a dialled-in psychologist would have had a field day with Higgins and could have helped him build on that 1982 triumph, avoiding the crash and burn that came in its aftermath. That fanciful notion is built on the unlikely premise of Higgins permitting such a stabilising figure to ever enter his life.

The impression I get is of a man afraid of himself, all too aware of deep character flaws and his addictions, conscious of how he might find help but too deep into being Alex Higgins and playing the vulgarian that there was no way back. To change his ways and straighten out would have meant killing off the Hurricane avatar, waving goodbye to the delinquent edges that made him this so-called People's Champion. Like with so much in his life, it appears Higgins became easily addicted: in this case the drug being the public's acclaim that gave him validation. Alex, 'Hurricane Higgins' and the 'People's Champion' would win together, revel together and hit the rocks together.

Ken Doherty stuck by Higgins, from fandom to friendship and to a final farewell on August 2, 2010. The boy who marvelled at the 1982 triumph never really grew out of being Higgins' biggest supporter. The admiration in this case was even a two-way street.

Doherty was a sorrowful but proud pallbearer for Higgins, along with a pair of breakout stars from the greatest World Championship of them all: Jimmy White and Tony Knowles.

'Alex was a character. He was brilliant,' says Doherty.

**

Doherty has built up a memory bank of stirring snooker stories. Among them are moments of personal kindness from Higgins.

'So I won the World Championship in '97 and I was playing John Higgins in the final the following year, and Alex sends me a telegram because I didn't have a mobile telephone then,' he says.

'He sends me this telegram to the Crucible, and it says, "Alex Higgins here, babes, best of luck today, go and be the second man from Ireland to win two World Championships."

'I didn't keep it, but I should have, even though I lost that final. And then there was another time when I fell out of the top 16 and was trying to get back to the Crucible. We were qualifying in the English Institute of Sport, and I managed to get back to the Crucible, so when I picked up my phone I listened to my messages, and there was Alex Higgins, the very first message, and he goes, "Congratulations babes, great to see you back where you belong, at the Crucible, keep it going."

'I had a tear in my eye while I was listening to it, you know,' says Doherty. 'It was a lovely, lovely touch. I knew he was a rogue, a Jekyll and Hyde character, but to me I loved him.

'He never did me any wrong, never did me a bad turn, and I was honoured to be a friend of his.

'I had some great times with him; great, great fun.'

EPILOGUE

THE DOOMSDAY CLOCK struck midnight for Alex Higgins long ago, but here in Sheffield the evening is just getting going.

Another Crucible campaign is tiptoeing towards its climax.

Is snooker the talk of the town as the sun fades from view on day one of the 2023 final? Honestly, it would be disingenuous to say so. The lager lovelies on Division Street and Carver Street probably aren't discussing Si Jiahui's long-term prospects after the 20-year-old's shock semi-final run, but Tudor Square by the Crucible is attentive enough, drinkers keeping beady eyes on the outdoor big screen as balls are potted inside the adjacent theatre.

It's 9.54pm on April 30 and Mark Selby is sinking the pink and nervelessly adding the black to complete the first 147 in a World Championship final.

Tonight, I'm on the outside of the Crucible bubble, at a low ebb, questioning whether there's a way back into that inner sanctum.

You see, I'm being laid off, along with a dozen or so eminent journalist colleagues, by my latest employer. Perhaps the offices pumping out the written word are going the same way as those old Sheffield steelworks and South Yorkshire pits, great homes to venerable skills dumping their unwanted baggage on the streets.

It's all ChatGPT and AI this and TikTok that, and death to the sub-editor, or at least that's how the doomsayers see the media industry going. Computers crowding out the craftsmen.

I've a fortnight or so left before gardening leave kicks in.

So, I've not embarrassed World Snooker Tour by requesting a press pass this year, and I'm perching on a stone block of street furniture instead of a ringside seat inside the arena. Here, it hardly matters if you cough, or rustle your bag of sweets, or spill your drink, or have a self-pitying sob. In a sense, it's liberating. In a more acute and pressing sense, it's a little cold.

When Selby completes that magnificent maximum, his feat is not merely cheered to the rafters inside the arena but also rapturously appreciated by the hundred or so freeloaders outside.

What few will notice is what happens next. Barely five minutes later, out through the front door of the Crucible come Selby's wife Vikki and daughter Sofia.

The excitement inside the arena had perhaps become overwhelming, with eight-year-old Sofia now turning cartwheels next to the theatre doors. They stay near the entrance, taking a moment in the fresh night air to reset, Vikki quietly catching her breath and gathering her thoughts and Sofia performing some more playground gymnastics.

They soon head back inside, in time to see Selby trim Luca Brecel's overnight lead to one frame, heading into the decisive Monday finale.

This won't be Selby's year, as it happens, with Brecel carrying off the trophy as mainland Europe gets its first world snooker champion, but Sunday night's perfect clearance from the Leicester man was another goosebumps moment in his family's poignant relationship with this great venue.

Vikki was pregnant when Selby first won in Sheffield, in 2014; then she and toddler Sofia joined in the 2016 title celebrations.

At that moment, how could one not think of Higgins beckoning down Lynn and Lauren to the theatre floor all those years earlier?

How different life would have been for Higgins if he had but a fraction of Selby's steely focus and dutifulness, on and away from the table, rather than the narcissism that tarred his journey from cradle to grave.

At 9-8 to Brecel, with Sunday's play over, I head to the nearby Graduate pub for an Alkoholfrei Erdinger.

It would have been a Guinness or eight after the snooker ended five years ago. Tonight, after my wisest move for many years, I'm confident I won't topple on to my tush in front of Jimmy White.

Tomorrow I'll head home and watch the conclusion of the final from an armchair. At that point the Crucible press room will be at its most broiling, every seat at every desk taken, with reports being rushed to newspapers, blogs, websites and agencies across the world.

There'll be tension in the air here, adrenaline levels will be soaring. You get the gist.

I'll miss it, but it turns out I won't miss out entirely.

I've been in the Graduate barely five minutes and in walk many of the press crew. There's the Racing Post's Adrian Humphries, there's David Hendon and Michael McMullan, the BBC's Steve Sutcliffe, World Snooker Tour's Roddy Bisset and agency man Shane McDermott, and they're enquiring how the book's going, whether I'll be in the press room tomorrow, why an employer would possibly let me go.

I feel the warmth of friendship and the kindness, and we chat deep into the night. About snooker, about life, about turning points and starting again. About Higgins, about the day's football, about the usual pub bunkum.

Chris Downer, a super chap and snooker obsessive who produces the much-mythologised Crucible Almanac each year, wanders over to say a quick hello. Familiar faces everywhere.

Eventually, at 2am or so, the press gang splinters and we each go our separate ways, to hotels spread across Sheffield's sprawl.

Walking to Sheffield station on Monday morning, I briefly encounter and share a few friendly words with Rob Walker, a long-time press room pal and a man with such abundant vitality, even at this late stage of the tournament, they should plug him permanently into the National Grid and solve the nation's energy crisis at a stroke. Much like last night, this chance meeting is pure sunshine on a rainy day.

See, this is the thing with the snooker 'family', which extends to the players, the staff, and the many fans, too, whose faces, names and life stories you come to know over the years: any son or daughter might go missing in action, but there is always a warm welcome back to the fold. The friendships endure and enrich us.

There's a cruel world out there, but this short trip to Sheffield has been pure balm. Of course I'll soon be back on my feet, but it helps to be told so.

Alex Higgins forsook such kinship and chose darkness, but at least he left behind the gift of 1982 and all that. And in a way this collection of stories connected to that championship – his championship – has become 'my baby'.

I've lost count of how often the book's kept me up at night, how many wrinkles and grey hairs it's brought out, how I've worried about it going out into the world on its own.

There's been considerable catastrophising, and the odd minor catastrophe, but what's the worst that could happen?

I hope you've enjoyed the book.

If that's the case, please tell your friends.

If not, consider that clarion call from the Hurricane.

'Keep your traps shut.'

With thanks to...

Much of what you have read has come from first-hand recollections, and I thank those below who have kindly given up their time to speak with me:

Steve Acteson, John Airey, Mark Allen, Carol Bear, Stuart Bingham, Nigel Bond, Steve Davis, Ken Doherty, Jim Donnelly, Patsy Fagan, Jason Ferguson, Silvino Francisco, Mike Ganley, Barry Hearn, David Hendon, Nick Hunter, Hazel Irvine, Tony Knowles, Arder Lavery, Cecil Mason, Nicko McBrain, Michael McMullan, Nick Metcalfe, Brendan Moore, Shaun Murphy, Neil Robertson, Mark Selby, Joe Swail, David Taylor, Cliff Thorburn, Judd Trump, Rob Walker, Mark Watterson, Gary Wilkinson, Phil Yates.

Thank you to Jon Fisher for his editing support.

Many thanks also to the small army who helped this book come together, directly or in any small way, including: Ivan Hirschowitz, Roddy Bisset, Jason Francis, Hector Nunns, Neil Goulding, Shane McDermott, Michael Hunter, Jamie Broughton, Ashley Broadley, Laura Stevenson, Simon Lovell, Mike Watterson, Will Skilbeck, Stewart Skilbeck and Helen Skilbeck.

Lesia T. Bear's documentary about her father, Jimmy Bear, is in production and a trailer can be seen at jimmythebear.com

Sincere apologies and gratitude to anyone I've missed.

Reading and research sources

Snooker Scene magazine, Jan-Dec 1982

Bill Borrows – The Hurricane (Atlantic Books)
Steve Davis – Interesting (Ebury Press)
Chris Downer – Crucible Almanac
John Hennessy – Eye of the Hurricane, The Alex Higgins Story
(Mainstream Publishing)
Alex Higgins – My Story, From the Eye of the Hurricane (Headline)
Alex Higgins with Tony Francis – Alex Through The Looking Glass, The
Autobiography of Alex Higgins (Pelham Books)
Alistair Lofthouse – Shiny Sheff (ALD Design & Print)
Jim Meadowcroft – Higgins, Taylor and Me (Arthur Barker)
Hector Nunns – The Crucible's Greatest Matches (Pitch Publishing)
Jean Rafferty – The Cruel Game, The Inside Story of Snooker (Elm Tree
Books)
Ray Reardon with Peter Buxton – Ray Reardon (David & Charles)
Willie Thorne – Taking a Punt on my Life (VSP)
John Virgo – Let Me Tell You About Alex (John Blake)

Contemporary newspaper reporting, via:
Britishnewspaperarchive.co.uk
Newspapers.com
Sheffield Library

Websites (to name but a few)
Youtube.com – for its incredible archive of snooker footage
World Snooker Tour: wst.tv
Alan McManus' blog: alanangles19.wordpress.com
Cuetracker.net
Sheffieldguide.blog
Sheffieldhistory.co.uk
Belfastforum.co.uk

About the author

John Skilbeck was four years old when Alex Higgins won the greatest World Championship of them all. At the time, he was watching Morph rather than Mountjoy, Rainbow instead of Reardon. He first watched snooker after a Sunday roast dinner at his granny's bungalow, while those around him were nodding off, and before long he was potting balls off the lampshades on his 4ft x 2ft table.

He achieved a long-held ambition to work in sports journalism and is immensely grateful to have spent a decade reporting on snooker for the Press Association news agency, also working on women's football and tennis, before covering Champions League football and a host of sports in a stint at Stats Perform.

A Yorkshireman, who has gone on to join BBC Sport but still dreams of writing for the Melody Maker, this is his first book.